WITHDRAWN

KINSEY

A BIOGRAPHY

Color photo: Tripp & Dellenback

KINSEY

A BIOGRAPHY

Cornelia V. Christenson

Indiana University Press

BLOOMINGTON / LONDON

Published in Canada by Fitzhenry & Whiteside Limited, Don Mills, Ontario

Library of Congress catalog card number: 72-154897

ISBN: 0-253-14625-9

Manufactured in the United States of America

CONTENTS

FROM THE KINSEY PAPERS

Photographs following pages 52 and 116

FOREWORD

Viewed from the perspective of contemporary public morality and mores, the research begun by Dr. Alfred C. Kinsey in the late 1930's may seem neither extraordinary in its conception nor courageous in its undertaking. It was, in fact, both. American society and a large part of the academic world were unready then to accept research into sexual practice.

Except for his early interest in and commitment to discovering the ways of Nature, the shy, studious and musically talented young man who was recruited by Indiana University's noted ichthyologist, Dr. Carl Eigenmann, to join the faculty of the Department of Zoology would have appeared to be a very unlikely candidate for the role of scholar-tilter against this longstanding taboo.

In portraying the development of Alfred Kinsey from a young boy, inspired by a biology teacher to devote his life to research, to the university professor who pried open a door shutting out an area of knowledge, Mrs. Christenson has not only recorded the steps in the unfolding of a scientist's career but the drama of an instant in man's long combat with the forces which would deny him enlightenment.

As Dr. Kinsey's research into human sexual behavior was conducted while I was President of Indiana University, I have often been asked how it was that the University lent its support to the Kinsey research project. The answer is simple: a member of the faculty with proven competence and judgment in research wished to undertake it. In the process of implementing his research, Dr. Kinsey gained the backing of two respected scientific bodies: the Medical Division of the Rockefeller Foundation voted him funding and the National Research Council's Medical Division, through its Committee for Research on Problems of Sex, cooperated by agreeing to administer the funds.

A second question has usually been posed to me, for research into a subject so guarded from mention and revelation as sexual practice did, indeed, embroil the University in a contest to preserve the principle of free scholarly inquiry against numerous and diverse attacks. The question, however phrased, usually called for an assessment of the long-term effect on Indiana University of protecting Kinsey's research. I have said and I believe that it has been beneficial in every way. Throughout history, attempts to keep people in ignorance of human nature and of the world with which they must cope have invariably proved misguided. Moreover, nothing presents so clearly to the public the creative role of the scholar as his penetration through assumptions and traditional beliefs to fact. In the long run, the University's willingness to battle for freedom of inquiry in this controversial area and to sustain criticism when the results were published has been a source of great pride, even among those who disagreed with Dr. Kinsey on one aspect or another of his research. Events proved that a university can win out on the issue of academic freedom if the university community stands together. The backing of the University's Trustees was critical in maintaining a unified front and they deserve considerable credit for their stalwart stand in the face of public criticism.

For his part, Dr. Kinsey was always ready to cooperate with me by accepting the various administrative decisions which were made for the protection of his research. I found Dr. Kinsey a stimulating and valuable colleague.

At the dinner celebrating the 50th Anniversary of the Rockefeller Foundation, Dr. Robert S. Morison, then head of its Medical Division, told me that the Kinsey research had profoundly affected at least one branch of medicine, gynecology, and that time had proved the wisdom of the Division's initial support.

The Institute for Sex Research is now firmly established. It carries on its work with no more notice than other institutes on the campus receive, and its projects attract the grants which Dr. Kinsey sought in vain during the final years of his life. These developments are a tribute in part to the vision, courage, energy, and persistence of the Institute's founder and to the soundness of the research program he initiated.

Dr. Alfred C. Kinsey has a secure place in the annals of pioneering American scientists. Mrs. Christenson, by assembling and presenting data that illuminate the character of this remarkable man, has furnished us with a valuable addition to the history of sex research and a needed supplement to the published work of the biologist, A. C. Kinsey.

Herman B Wells
Chancellor of Indiana University

PREFACE

This biography had its origins in 1961, five years after the death of Dr. Alfred C. Kinsey. At that time the Institute for Sex Research was in a fallow period, with no new investigations under way. My proposal was that we take this opportunity to collect biographical material on Kinsey from his friends and former associates without any definite plans as to when it would be used. Subsequently we wrote to nearly a hundred persons asking for an account of their associations with Kinsey and his research. Eventually almost half of them sent contributions to the project. It is well that it was done in those years as several of those who responded are now deceased. New research projects at the Institute soon pushed the "Kinseyana" folders to the back of my file drawer. There they remained for eight years, a potential source for a biographical study.

In 1970 Indiana University's sesquicentennial celebration in honor of its 150th year provided an opportunity to utilize this rich material. The Sesquicentennial Committee under the chairmanship of Claude Rich approved our suggestion to push ahead with the Kinsey biography, and the Indiana University Foundation generously provided the financial support necessary. It was to stand as another witness to the many great achievements of the University during its century and a half of existence. Since by then I had retired from active duty at the Institute, I was asked to turn my full attention to writing the biography. Supplementing the earlier material with further letters and personal interviews, and drawing upon my own years of service at the Institute, I have completed this small volume.

Dr. Alfred C. Kinsey and his wife Clara McMillen Kinsey were familiar to me as campus figures at Indiana University from the early 1920's. I faced her when we both played soccer on Dunn Meadow as undergraduate coeds. My father, Dr. Bert J. Vos, an older faculty colleague, spoke at home in complimentary terms of the young biology professor. They were serving together on the hard-working curriculum revision committee at the time. My mother added iris roots from the Kinsey collection to her garden. As a graduate student I remember seeing Clara on a fine autumn day pulling her three children in a gay red express wagon down a campus walk near Biology Hall on her way to meet her husband at the close of his afternoon's work. By 1932 I had become a faculty wife myself, and during the summer of 1938 I attended the lectures of the first Kinsey-directed Marriage Course. Ten years later, when it became known that more women were needed for interviews for the second book, *Sexual Behavior in the Human Female*, I became a subject, and my sex history was added to the ever growing accumulation of such records in the files of the Institute for Sex Research.

My professional involvement with the Kinsey project, however, started when I went to work there in April, 1950. For the next six years I worked directly under Dr. Kinsey's supervision as one of his several research associates. My tasks included key punching of data cards; bibliographical research; editing; and some writing, more particularly of extensive footnotes for the volume on the female. Following Dr. Kinsey's death in 1956 I continued my work at the Institute until my retirement eleven years later in June, 1967. It is from this vantage point that I am relating the story of Alfred Kinsey's life, both the uneventful years and the poignantly dramatic ones.

Dr. Paul Gebhard and Blaine Johnson of the Institute staff have been of great help to me and have furnished the encouragement I needed. More than half of the illustrations are taken from William Dellenback's incomparable documentary photographic file of Institute history. My editorial assistant, Gertrude W. Lindesmith, provided me with her indispensable expertise. Miriam S. Farley of the Indiana University Press skillfully guided me past many pitfalls during the editorial process. Bettie Silverstein did a typing job that neared perfection. I thank all of these.

I am even more indebted, however, to the scores of informants who furnished firsthand information by letter, over the telephone, and in personal interviews. Mrs. Clara Kinsey, Mr. Robert Kinsey, Dr. Robert L. Kroc, Dr. Fernandus Payne, Dr. Theodore W. Torrey, and Dr. Frank N. Young have been especially helpful in answering my questions and in supplying information to fill in the many gaps I found in the story.

As I explored the Institute files and read the Kinsey letters, notes, papers, and memos, the tremendous spirit of the man came through in a way I had never comprehended it during my years of association with him and his work. Thus it is really to Alfred Kinsey himself, his virtues and his faults shining bright, that I owe the largest debt of gratitude for making this book possible.

CORNELIA V. CHRISTENSON

December, 1970

INDIVIDUALS

Individuals

BY ALFRED C. KINSEY

THIS BRIEF STATEMENT, written when he had spent twenty years studying gall wasps and was just embarking on the study of sex, epitomizes the philosophy that underlay all of Kinsey's work. As a taxonomist he was impressed by the limitless variety of living creatures, whether gall wasps or human beings, and by the scientific and social import of recognizing their differences.

This address to fifteen newly elected members of Phi Beta Kappa was delivered at 9:15 A.M., preceding the Commencement program, on Monday, June 5, 1939. Dr. Kinsey was then president of the Indiana University chapter.

WITH INDIVIDUAL VARIATION AS A BIOLOGIC phenomenon I have been concerned during some twenty years of field exploration and laboratory research. In the intensive and extensive measurement of tens of thousands of small insects which you have probably never seen, and about which you certainly cannot care, I have made some attempt to secure the specific data and the quantity of data on which scientific scholarship must be based. During the past two years, as a result of a convergence of circumstances, I have found myself confronted with material on variation in certain types of human behavior. Consequently I may attempt to correlate the broader generalizations with affairs which have a more everyday, human interest.

The fact of individual variation is one of the fundamentals of biologic reasoning. In its universality it is practically unique among biologic principles. The phenomenon is startling in its magnitude. A conventional estimate allows for something like five or six million plant and animal species now existent on the face of this globe. Our generalizations apply to the variability of the individuals in each and every one of these millions of species. Pearl's recently published figures seem to warrant an estimate of 2,104 millions of individuals in the single animal species which is called human. Wheeler estimated that a single mound nest of some of the ant species might contain as many as 100,000 individuals; an old field may have a hundred such nests; and the species may extend from Maine to Louisiana, and from the Atlantic to the mountains of Colorado. You may be interested in trying the arithmetic which will give you an idea of the numbers of individuals in a single such species of ant. I have flippantly experimented with an estimation of the total number of individuals of all kinds of plants and animals in the world; suffice it to say that the resultant has some twenty to fifty zeros after the initial figure. It is a number of such proportions as would seem Utopian even to a New Dealer, though it startles a mere biologist. While philosophically the possibility still remains that someone, sometime, will find two individuals among these many kinds of plants and animals which will appear identical, the burden is on the agnostic and not on the scientist. We have measured enough of these individuals under our microscopes to allow us to conclude, in our crude scientific way, that the phenomenon of variability is universal in the living world.

The characters which have been involved in our studies of

4

variation include everything from gross to minute anatomical structures, every detail of specific physiology, and such generalized activities as are described as the creature's behavior. The insects which I am studying average smaller than a small ant; on each individual I am measuring 28 characters in which the variation is readily discernible with a low-powered microscope. There are nearer a hundred structural characters which would be measurable under a higher-powered lens. Similarly, in the single circumscribed field of human behavior which I am studying I am recording variations in something more than 250 items for each individual who figures in the records. Endless recombinations of these characters in different individuals swell the possibilities to something which is, for all essential purposes, infinity, even in such genetically and environmentally limited systems as living organisms.

The failure to recognize this unlimited nonidentity has, even in biology, vitiated much of our scientific work. The morphotic sciences and taxonomy have filled thousands of printed pages with descriptions of what are supposed to be species, genera, and higher categories. In actuality they are too often descriptions of unique individuals and structures of particular individuals that are not quite like anything that any other investigator will ever find. In physiology, I find that four out of five of the research papers represent experiments on one or two, or at most on ten or twenty individuals of a single species, although the conclusions are usually so drawn as to appear applicable to all individuals of a whole species. Psychologists are particularly careless in this respect. A mouse in a maze, today, is taken as a sample of all individuals, of all species of mice under all sorts of conditions, yesterday, today, and tomorrow. A half dozen dogs, pedigrees unknown and breeds unnamed, are reported upon as "dogs"—meaning all kinds of dogs—if, indeed, the conclusions are not explicitly or at least implicitly applied to you, to your cousins, and to all other kinds and descriptions of humans. The medical profession is prone to treat you according to charts and standards which were worked out for somebody, but not for you. The science of endocrinology started with the assumption that hormones were nonspecific—the assumption that thyroid was thyroid, whether it came from sheep, or from rats, or from humans; that laboratory experiments with chickens injected with rat hormones could be the bases for the clinical control of endocrine disturbances in the human. And if the dose works in the first few cases which are reported, the failures in the next cases are usually ascribed to the inadequacy of the clinician's technique, or to the impurity of the supply of the hormones—while the unique nature of the contrary patient is quite forgotten by all concerned.

To emphasize my point with further instances: I recall an English scientist, an authority on blood physiology, who addressed the American Association for the Advancement of Science on the differences between the blood of caterpillars and the blood of cats. In the course of the address he never told us which of the twenty or thirty thousand known species of caterpillars were used in his experiments, or allowed for the variations which you and I know exist among the cats even in a single neighborhood. A noted American colloid chemist startles the country with the announcement of a new cure for drug addicts; and it is not until other laboratories report failures to obtain similar results that we learn that the original experiments were based on a half dozen individuals. Economic entomologists develop formulae for poisons which will kill codling moths at their particular experiment stations. The formulae are not as effective when applied to what is supposedly the same species of insect in the next locality. Strange to say, some years are spent in looking for errors in the experimental work before anyone suggests that the moths at one point may be, in reality, not quite like the moths at other points where experimental laboratories are located. What is one caterpillar's poison may be the next worm's meat, quite as meat and poison are relative terms when introduced into the affairs of the human.

If biologists so often forget the most nearly universal of all biologic principles, it is not surprising that men and women in general expect their fellows to think and behave according to patterns which may fit the lawmaker, or the imaginary ideals for which the legislation was fashioned, but which are ill-shaped for all real individuals who try to live under them. Social forms, legal restrictions, and moral codes may be, as the

6

social scientist would contend, the codification of human experience; but like all other averages, they are of little significance when applied to particular individuals. I am sceptical as to the worth of all biologic formulae, whether they govern the feeding of infants, the hygiene of adolescents, or the social relations of older men and women. Prescriptions are merely public confessions of prescriptionists. Argumentation *ad hominem* is bad argument, however moral the purpose of its advocate, because it is based on unique, unduplicable experience. What is right for one individual may be wrong for the next; and what is sin and abomination to one may be a worthwhile part of the next individual's life.

The range of individual variation, in any particular case, is usually much greater than is generally understood. Some of the structural characters in my insects vary as much as twelve hundred per cent. This means that populations from a single locality may contain individuals with wings 15 units in length, and other individuals with wings 175 units in length. In some of the morphologic and physiologic characteristics which are basic to the human behavior which I am studying, the variation is a good twelve thousand per cent. And yet social forms and moral codes are prescribed as though all individuals were identical; and we pass judgments, make awards, and heap penalties without regard to the diverse difficulties involved when such different people face uniform demands.

The origins of these differences between individuals are both genetic and acquired, the outcome of the hereditary equipment with which the individual came into the world, and the product of all the environmental circumstances to which that hereditary gift has been subjected. As far as it is genetic, variation is hardly the fault of the individual concerned; and one's environment is more often a happenstance than community gossip and the courts care to acknowledge.

The distribution of the various kinds of individuals within any given population is either dichotomous or continuous. In the simple case, dichotomy, the population breaks into two groups between which there are no intermediate types. In heredity this is the simple Mendelian case, controlled by a single pair of allelomorphic genes. Outwardly all individuals which are so conditioned represent one or the other of two possible types. Black guinea pigs and white guinea pigs are the contrasting products of a single pair of hereditary units. White corn and yellow corn may represent the variants in another instance. In a part (not all) of the human population blue eyes and brown eyes suggest a similar dichotomy. Once upon a time biologists thought dichotomous variation was the rule among plants and animals; but we now know that the control of most characters does not lie in a single pair of genes. Multiple pairs of factors more often operate upon each of the individual characters. As a final outcome of the multiplicity of factors which both heredity and environment bring to bear upon a given character, we get a multiplicity of types which range continuously from one to the other extreme within the population. Men are not all tall or short; they show every gradation among intermediate heights. Hair color, nose shape, skin color, finger length, baldness, blood chemistry, sensory capacities, thyroid metabolism—in fact every known character in the highest animals, and nearly all of the hereditary characters of lower organisms—show graded rather than contrasted differences within any large population. Dichotomous variation is the exception and continuous variation is the rule, among men as well as among insects.

There is, however, something in human thinking which leads us to attempt dichotomous classifications even where continuity exists. In primitive societies essentially all activities are classified as acceptable or as taboo. Under the laws of our own society, the decision between an acquittal and a ten-year sentence too often depends upon the theory that there are two classes and only two classes of people: acceptable citizens and lawbreakers. In ethical evaluations we commonly recognize right and wrong, without allowance for the endlessly varied types of behavior that are possible between the extreme right and the extreme wrong. Psychologists and physicians continue to think in terms of normal and abnormal, even though all studies of human behavior show continuous gradation between the limits of variation. Our conceptions of right and wrong, normal and abnormal, are seriously challenged by the variation studies.

Biologically I can see only two bases for the recognition

of abnormality. If a particular type of variation is rare in a given population, it, perhaps, may be called abnormal. The rarity of adult humans who measure under three feet or over eight in total height is, perhaps, some reason for calling such extremes abnormal. I should prefer to call them "rare."

The second biologic test of abnormality is the physiologic malfunction which it may produce. In that sense cancers and tumors may be called abnormal. But popular judgments of normality more often represent measures of departure from the standards of the individual who is passing judgment—an admission that "only thee and me are normal, and thee, I fear, is a bit queer." The psychologist's more presumptuous labeling of the abnormal is, too often, merely an attempt to justify the mores, a reassertion of society's concept of what is acceptable in individual behavior with no objective attempt to find out, by actual observation, what the incidence of the phenomenon may be, or the extent of the real maladjustment that the behavior will introduce. Scholarly thinking as well as the laymen's evaluation still needs to be tempered with the realization that individual variations shape into a continuous curve on which there are no sharp divisions between normal and abnormal, between right and wrong.

These individual differences are the materials out of which nature achieves progress, evolution in the organic world. Standardized, unchangeable genes in the primordial bit of protoplasm would have covered the earth with nothing but primordial bits of protoplasm. From the changeability of genes, from the recombinations of genes, and from the segregation of diverse genes in local populations, we have derived the world's diversity of plants and animals, and the endlessly different kinds of men in it. In the differences between men lie the hopes of a changing society.

I trust that our University has not put any standard imprint on you who have gone through it. In fact, from what I know of some of you who are the newly elected members of Phi Beta Kappa, you are a strange assortment of queer individuals; and that is why I respect you, and believe in your future.

KINSEY

A BIOGRAPHY

I.

Profiles of Youth

IN HIS MID-FIFTIES, ALFRED C. KINSEY WAS SUD-denly catapulted into world-wide fame and notoriety by the publication of his sensational findings on sexual behavior. The social and scientific impact of his two controversial volumes, *Sexual Behavior in the Human Male* (1948) and *Sexual Behavior in the Human Female* (1953), may never be fully measured or documented. That they had a profound effect on the life of our time is certain. To measure the influence of his work and to attempt to disentangle it from the other important currents of change contemporary with it would be a social historian's nightmare. I tend to share the view that the sexual revolution which has brought us franker, more realistic attitudes toward sex and a greater tolerance of variant behavior was inevitable and that Kinsey's work only helped to hasten these inevitable changes.

What kind of man was Kinsey, and what impelled him to enter on, and persevere in, a course of research that entailed so many obstacles and frustrations? I have tried here to sketch an unbiased portrait of a notable man of our time, building it on a groundwork of sound biographical fact. Beyond that I would hope to set in more correct focus some widely held misconceptions and also to highlight the principal contributions of Alfred Kinsey's pioneering research in the field of human sexual behavior.

After the appearance of *Sexual Behavior in the Human Male*, a number of people who shared his surname wrote to Dr. Kinsey asking about the possibility of a family relationship. He courteously answered each such inquiry personally with a detailed explanation of his own origins. To Mrs. Sarah Kinsey of Seattle, Washington, he wrote:

> All the Kinseys that I know in the United States were descended from three brothers who were Quakers who came over from England to Philadelphia with William Penn. They settled originally in the Philadelphia area and near eastern Pennsylvania. A main branch spread eastward toward New York and my father, Alfred Seguine Kinsey, was a descendant of that branch. His father was Benjamin Kinsey, born in Mendham, N.J. My mother was Sarah Ann Charles, born in Salt Lake City.

Elsewhere "eastern Pennsylvania" was identified more specifically as near Bethlehem. "For generations," Kinsey wrote, "the family lived near Denville, which is near Morristown, New Jersey." In answer to an Indiana inquirer, Kinsey noted:

> There is a big Indiana and Ohio branch [of the family] and there is a San Francisco branch with many of those now spread hither and yon over the whole country.

Alfred Kinsey senior was a self-made man who had finished only the eighth grade at Cooper Union night school. He was not one to easily tolerate differing points of view. His strong drive and his determination to accomplish what he set out to do were clearly mirrored in his first-born, Alfred Charles Kinsey. There was an inevitable clash of wills between the two as the son grew toward adulthood.

Kinsey's mother, Sarah Ann Charles, a carpenter's daughter, had only four years of schooling. This minimal education betrayed itself only in her letter writing, not in her manner of speaking, Clara Kinsey, her daughter-in-law, recalls. Clara calls her mother-in-law "the sweetest person I have ever known." With this disposition it is no wonder that she submitted readily to the domination of her disciplinarian husband.

A vivid glimpse of Alfred's early boyhood years is given in a letter he wrote in 1949.

> I was born in Hoboken on June 23, 1894. My Father was an instructor at that time in the Stevens Institute of Technology. He had entered in his early teens as a shop boy, and ultimately became head of the department of mechanical arts. We lived in Hoboken only until 1903, when we moved to South Orange, where I got most of my grade school and all of my high school work.
>
> I attended Grade School #2 in Hoboken from kindergarten through third grade only. Since I left that city when I was 10 years of age, my memories of the city are only those of a young boy. The first solid paved streets came into the city at that period. Since we lived on Garden Street, we had good opportunity as children to see the first automobiles, most of which broke down before they had gone many blocks. Garden Street, the park at Fourth Street, the fireworks held in holiday celebrations in the west end of the City, the May Day parties held at Weehawken, and similar things are part of the memories.

The ten years there gave him, he added, "some comprehension of what growing up in a densely populated city area might mean to a child. This has been of some use in the work we have done in city areas in connection with the research we are doing on human sexual behavior."[1] A childhood playmate[2] of Kinsey's, recalling these early days, points out that while Hoboken at this time was largely populated by families of German extraction, the Italian section in the west side was the source of the "holy days" fireworks. "The Church Square Park at Fourth Street is still there, as well as Kinsey's grade school Number 2 on Garden Street between 9th and 10th," he adds, but the Kinsey family lived on Bloomfield street, rather than on Garden Street, as he remembers it. The neighborhood had tree-lined sidewalks with two- or three-story red brick houses side by side, and the May Day celebrations Kinsey mentions were at King's Woods in Weehawken.

A second autobiographical note on this early period in Hoboken is contained in the only article that Kinsey wrote on a nonbiologic topic, "Living with Music: Music and Love as Arts" (42).* He described his first experience with a "talking machine" thus:

> It was just before the turn of the century when I first heard a talking machine. We had to cross the Hackensack and Passaic meadows on the Jersey plank road (in a day when it was actually made of planks) and visit the house of a cousin in the city of Newark, in order to hear this marvelous invention. Uncle Josh spoke from the surfaces of the cylinders that revolved in the machine. He and most of the other cylinder notables of that day ended their performances by announcing that we had listened to "an Edison Rec-cord." Even after all these years I can still hear the intonation and the exact rhythm of that phrase, "an Edison Rec-cord."

Much later, during the first World War, the army draft passed young Kinsey by because of his physical condition, a double curvature of the spine and a possibly defective heart. The former was probably caused by a case of rickets in his childhood. He also suffered from bouts with rheumatic fever as a youngster, and a severe case of typhoid was thought to have cured this ailment. Plagued by these childhood illnesses, he was kept out of school and in bed for long periods of time. It was after he recovered from typhoid at age ten that he moved with the family from Hoboken to South Orange. He often spoke with distaste of his Hoboken childhood, as his memories of those early days were unpleasant. In spite of his tremendous attachment for plants and almost all growing things, he admitted a strong dislike for certain flowers apparently associated with this early period, namely marigolds, zinnias, and wisteria. He would never allow them in his garden.

In South Orange the family lived in a modest two-story white frame house on the corner of Roland Avenue and Academy Street, where Alfred spent his next eleven years. His bedroom was a converted storeroom on the third floor adjoining the attic space.

---

*Numbers in parentheses refer to the Kinsey bibliography; see below, p. 231.

Both of his parents were deeply religious during Kinsey's youth, and the family were members of a nearby Methodist church. Sunday observance was so strict that father Kinsey forbade his family to ride to church on Sunday, even with the minister. Nor was the milkman permitted to make Sunday deliveries. A neighborhood boy remembers that all the family was permitted to do on Sunday was "to go to church and eat." The head of the house also taught in the Sunday school and set an example by taking his family to triple Sabbath services —Sunday school, church, and evening prayer meeting. Later Kinsey also taught a Sunday school class at the behest of his father. It is not difficult to believe Kinsey's boyhood story of his young aunt being put out of the house for playing selections from *Cavalleria Rusticana* on the piano on a Sunday afternoon.

Young Alfred was on occasion used as a decoy by his strait-laced father, who sent him, as a minor, to buy forbidden cigarettes. Once the transaction was completed, the authorities were promptly notified, and the law pounced down on the surprised shopkeeper. It is hard to believe that this device worked more than a few times at the various local shops, but it must have made a strong impression on the young informer, who later looked back upon it with clear distaste.

When the Kinsey family first moved to South Orange the community was still a rural village to which the nearby city dwellers were just starting to move. The local Orange boys resented these Johnny-come-latelies. At first there were fights and bloody noses. Kinsey was frail and not by nature or experience a toughie. At first his life was made fairly miserable, but later things changed. Learning from their parents that Alfred "had heart trouble" and should not be "picked on," two of the leaders of the local boys, Girard (Jiggy) Oberrender and Don Salisbury, took him under their wing. Even though he wasn't interested in the same things they were, they protected him against the more aggressive bullies and the three of them gradually became good friends.

The sequel came several years later. Ever since Alfred had been in the seventh grade, he had ranged the countryside on Saturdays to collect botanical specimens. This hobby continued all through high school. His friends, preferring their ball games and other sports on weekends, had steadily refused to go with him. Finally they accepted his invitation and joined him on a hike. Each carrying nearly twenty-pound packs, they set out. Young Kinsey walked their legs off and could easily outstrip them on the hills and steep cliffs where they were looking for specimens. They covered nearly twenty miles and his companions arrived home exhausted. Young Oberrender, recounting the day's experience, observed to his father that Alfred couldn't possibly have heart trouble. The father, puzzled, went to Kinsey senior, who explained that their family doctor had given them this diagnosis following Kinsey's early boyhood illnesses. Oberrender's father then arranged for Alfred to be examined by a specialist. The verdict was a clean bill of health. It was clear that his family had been unduly concerned about protecting him for many years.

Alfred had played the piano from early childhood and took lessons later when he was in high school. Industrious practice combined with his natural musical ability resulted in his developing from an eager student into a competent pianist during these years at home. As soon as he was far enough along, he in turn started giving music lessons to neighborhood children to help pay the cost of his own instruction. There were even little recitals held in his home at which he would play. At school he shared with two classmates, Anna Geiger and Sophie Pauline Gibling, the responsibility of playing for the school assemblies.

Sophie Pauline, now Mrs. Schindler, remembers well the scene at Columbia High School in South Orange and furnishes this description:

> There were about 200 students in the whole school. First thing in the morning, we all gathered in the main study hall, each at his own desk; the boys and girls, of course, separated, the nine or ten faculty members seated solemnly on the platform.
>
> "Page 81," Mr. Freeman, the principal, would announce as the clock hands came to 8:25 exactly. Whereupon one of us— Alfred, or Anna Geiger, or I—would march up to the grand piano in front, and all would rise to sing the national anthem. Then followed a reading from the Bible, and another song, nonreligious.

A discussion she and Alfred had on the Darwinian theory of evolution is another memory of her high school associate. It ended in their deciding they believed in it and feeling rather daring in taking such a "radical stance at that time." Mrs. Schindler concludes:

> Alfred was, of course, a youth of utmost gentleness and principle. Biblical and ethical concepts were part of the general atmosphere of that period. Sophistication was absent. . . . At that time such a word as "sex" was totally unmentionable.

While in high school Kinsey wrote poetry and this, plus his musical ability and good grades, earned him the respect of his classmates. One of these, Elliot C. Bergen, has supplied these personal memories of Kinsey as a high school youth:

> I can see him walking along Academy Street, preoccupied and serene, hatless as he usually was, winter and summer. He and I often lunched together in study hall, out of our collapsible metal boxes. He was naturally looked upon as the wisest among us, one to turn to for counsel. When I was on a debating team he helped me organize my material. One of my vivid memories is of his playing Beethoven's Moonlight Sonata in the school auditorium. Another is of his valedictory address, from which these words have always stuck in my mind—"It is only through partings that goals are reached."

Another acquaintance, Alford B. Tunis, recalls him as "always smiling, blond curly hair, fast walking with big strides, and a nice looking young man." By preference he often walked in the street, and he wore his scout uniform more or less regularly.

He did not date or show any interest in girls. In fact, in his senior year the South Orange High School year book placed under his picture a quotation from *Hamlet:* "Man delights not me; no, nor woman neither." A classmate recalls that he was "the shyest guy around girls you could think of." Kinsey senior did not approve of dating in any case, so socializing on young Alfred's part would have undoubtedly led to increased friction at home.

Mildred Kinsey, Alfred's sister, two years his junior, was a shy, quiet girl. She attended a local business college and later worked as a secretary. Her special gift lay in sewing, especially millinery work. At one time she owned a share in a tearoom in South Orange. Mildred married late in life but had no children. After an illness of many months, she died in 1955. Kinsey's only brother, Robert, who operates his own park planning service in Livingston, New Jersey, was younger by fourteen years. It was doubtless his older brother who interested Bob in nature, and he had the engineering bent which Alfred lacked. In the summertime the children looked forward eagerly to the treat of visiting at Aunt Lizzie's in Broadway, New Jersey, a village in the western part of the state. This was an idyllic spot. Faded photographs show cows in the field, chickens and geese being fed, a rowboat on a small stream that passed in front of the house, and timid girls in gingham dresses on makeshift rafts, with swimmers splashing nearby.

Alfred's family life might be described as unduly restrictive during his boyhood and adolescent years, but he was already reaching outside of his home into the beginnings of his lifelong romance with nature and the out-of-doors. This developing interest was strongly encouraged by Natalie Roeth, a young, enthusiastic biology teacher at South Orange High School. These excerpts from a sprinkling of letters written to her over a span of more than thirty-five years are clear evidence of the lasting impression which this early field and classroom training in science etched on the mind of her young student. In January, 1921, he wrote to Miss Roeth:

> If you care for it I should like to send you other [reprints] as they come out, for I feel that they are in large part yours, having come as a fruit of the lot you did for me, now some years ago. . . . And I hope that if the opportunity ever arrives that I can in some way repay you for the start you gave me, you will let me have that privilege.

One month later he wrote:

> I well recall the club we had in the South Orange school, and know how important it was in adding to the interest in the biology work. . . . In regard to the trips you ask if I remember: I can recall every single spot, I think, and each object we found on all those trips. The Dutchman's breeches we photographed,

the meadowlarks we chased over the fields, the periwinkle I brought for you to identify! That sort of memory for the utmost detail is one of the things that I find I have for the out-of-doors things that I do not have for anything else; and therein lies one of the greatest charms of biology work, I think.

Miss Roeth, now Mrs. Natalie Hirschfeld, in turn describes these events thus in a recent letter to the writer:

While attending H.S. we spent considerable time tramping about the country-side in search of specimens and enjoying the scenery. We were both interested in native ferns and Alfred planted many in his garden. A discovery of Dutchman's breeches in a shady nook was quite a triumph when he took me there. Alfred was a sincere and faithful student.

A letter to her from her former student in 1924 includes this tribute:

Don't forget that you gave several of us a whole lot of inspiration—even more important than the specific knowledge, I think—when we had you in South Orange a long time ago! I know you shall never know how much you have done with the hosts of people that have gone out from you, but in your imaginings don't stop at too small an estimate!

A gift copy of his first book, a high school biology text published in 1926, was accompanied by this note of appreciation:

Perhaps you will not care to assume too much credit for this book, but nevertheless I must repeat that you had a great deal to do with starting my interest in both plants and animals, and I have never been able to disassociate the two in my mind since then.

More than twenty years later, after the publication of *Sexual Behavior in the Human Male*, he wrote once more:

I shall always consider that you did more than anyone else at the very crucial age to turn me to science. That is saying a good deal. . . . You did an exceedingly good job in giving individual attention to science students at South Orange High School, and you must know that a good many more than I are indebted to you for it.

Excerpts from "Living with Music" provide a vignette of his earnest pursuit of his musical interests during his late adolescence:

In my high school years I began accumulating the first of the three record collections which I have made. The family finances did not allow me to hope to make a collection of the sort that my older and wealthier acquaintances were accumulating; but I did manage to persuade some of my relatives and friends to give me records as birthday and Christmas gifts, and I even essayed to give piano lessons in order to obtain the wherewithal to buy more records.

Although these first records provided only fragments of great compositions, to them he attributed his lifelong passion for record playing. He told it thus:

The acoustically recorded, pre-electric disks of the first two decades of this century presented bits of great music which had been lifted out of symphonies, operas, sonatas, and chamber music suites. They gave us only portions, and rarely more, of the original compositions. Often as not these were arrangements of the original score—Casals playing a theme from a Bach organ composition, sentimental tunes of Kreisler-made imitations of old masters, single arias, or arrangements from some opera. Recent hearings of these pre-electric disks show how badly they were made, but they did bring us great performances by Kreisler, Paderewski, Cortot, Mischa Elman, Schumann-Heink, Caruso, and others of the world's great. For the first time in history great music had become accessible to those of us who were not princes or great musicians in our own right. It is to these records that I am first of all indebted for the fact that I have spent such a large proportion of the last half century in listening to music.

Alfred joined the Boy Scouts soon after their founding in 1910 and, with his strong bent for nature craft and the outdoors, worked energetically and persistently on the many tests and badges. He progressed through the necessary qualifications and became an Eagle Scout, one of the earliest in the country to gain this rank. During this time he also took over the full responsibility for the South Orange Troop of about fifty younger boys, although the Rev. D. D. Burell, minister of the sponsoring Presbyterian Church, was the official scout-master for the group. He remained an active scout leader through his late teens. During his early years of scouting he had his first experience of camp life. He went probably first as a camper and later as a counselor to Kamp Kiamesha in the Kittatinny Mountains in western New Jersey, sponsored by the local Y.M.C.A. This early experience paid off handsomely in the many summer camp jobs he held during his college and graduate years, and even after his marriage.

Alfred's father was determined that his son should be trained as a mechanical engineer, which led to increasing conflict between them. This was an economical program, since he could live at home and go to Stevens Institute without paying regular tuition. After graduating from high school, he did attend the Institute from 1912 through 1914, including some summer periods. There he was enrolled in courses in German, mathematics, physics, chemistry, and mechanical drawing. Years later he ruefully recounted his painstaking and laborious efforts to complete a detailed drawing of a steam engine in the mechanical drawing course. At one point he was close to failing in physics, but a compromise was reached with the professor, who agreed to pass him if he would not attempt any advanced work in the field! By this time it was apparently clear to him that he had given it a fair try but that his gifts were not in the field of engineering.

Robert Kinsey, Alfred's brother, remembers clearly a dramatic family scene he witnessed one evening as a child of six or seven. It took place after the family had returned to their home in South Orange from a graduation program at Stevens Institute in nearby Hoboken. Alfred, who was now twenty years old, took this occasion at the close of the school year to announce formally to his parents that he was making a drastic change in plans. Up to now, he said, he had done what his father had wanted him to do, and from now on he was going to do what he wanted to do. His career in engineering was certainly cut short at this point, probably not without some harsh words between a determined father and an even more determined son. The confrontation between the two may have been softened somewhat by the mediation of Miss Roeth. Always a welcome visitor in the Kinsey home, she recalls that she helped to convince Alfred's father that the reluctant engineering student was "better fitted to work in his chosen field—biology."

In the fall of 1914 Alfred Kinsey enrolled as a junior in Bowdoin College, Brunswick, Maine, headed for study in biology. He had chosen Bowdoin because of the high reputation of two of the professors, Manton Copeland and Alfred O. Gross, under whom he wanted to study. Following this change of career plans, the young student was thrown largely upon his own financial resources. He was given some subsidy for his college expenses by Mrs. Mayhew, an elderly widow whose husband had been president of the South Orange Town Board. His father, however, did not propose to aid him further in his education, since its course was counter to his own expectations for his son. According to Kinsey's account, a single suit of clothes costing $25.00 was the only help he received from home from this point on.

2.

Student Years

Kinsey's two years at Bowdoin (1914-1916) were busy but not eventful. He came to the campus as an upper classman, obtaining junior status as the result of his two previous years at Stevens Institute. He was able to enroll at once in the biology courses he had looked forward to, and his record shows sixteen hours of zoology during his first year of residence, plus a general biology course of four hours. Sociology and psychology courses rounded out the year's work. There was, however, also time for extracurricular interests, including the "Y," the *Quill* Board, Biology Club, and the varsity debating team. His public speaking talents were recognized by the award of second place in the Bradbury Prize Debate. As a senior he was to win the H. L. Fairbanks Prize for debating, a top honor.

That this serious young student with his career already set before him did not fit easily into the "rah-rah" college life is not surprising. The fact that he entered in his junior year, when friendships and cliques had already been formed, de-

nied him the intimate associations which his classmates and
fraternity brothers had already developed during their first
two years at Bowdoin. His personality was also in considerable contrast to that of the average member of his class and
fraternity. One of his classmates, Paul K. Niven, wrote:

> At that period, the majority of Bowdoin undergraduates were
> from State of Maine homes, with relatively limited knowledge of
> the "outside world" and, for the most part, the average carefree,
> irresponsible, purposeless college lads of those years. By contrast,
> Al was somewhat more mature, and certainly more studious, and
> he knew what field he wanted to enter following graduation in
> 1916.
>
> For those reasons he had little in common with the rest of us.
> He spent hours on end, days and evenings, in the laboratories and
> in soaking up the knowledge of professors Copeland and Gross.
> In the college-boy antics of his college and fraternity associates,
> Al took little interest; for example, a pre-football game student
> rally with its cheers, bonfires, etc. was simply not his dish! Nei-
> ther were college dances, fraternity houseparties and other social
> occasions.
>
> Because of the depth of his college work, it was far beyond the
> comprehension of most of his friends. Perhaps Al may have
> wanted to discuss his courses with us, but most of us were not
> up to it. In that area, then, he pretty much went his own way.

Nevertheless Kinsey joined the Zeta Psi fraternity and
hence became a member of the so-called "Zeta Junior Delegation." This group took their meals together at one table for
two years until they graduated, and most of them lived in the
chapter house.

At that time, at Bowdoin, any student interested in joining
a fraternity had a chance to do so, and only a few chose not
to. Young Kinsey liked especially certain aspects of fraternity
life—the pie for breakfast, the access to good records, and a
piano he could use. Several of his fraternity brothers remember his playing with pleasure. The yearbook, the *Bugle*, called
him a "professional at the piano," and mentioned specifically
his playing of the Moonlight Sonata. The image of his "striking figure at the piano, with his curly blond hair, cleancut
face, swaying slightly as he felt the rhythm of his music in the

deserted living room of the chapter house," is recalled by one classmate. Another wrote:

Clear in my memory is the picture of Al at the piano in our fraternity house. Following dinner each evening, it was customary for the fraternity members to gather around the piano and sing. But the pianist was what we would call a "ragtime" player and the selections were the popular songs of the day or songs of college or fraternity. In such sessions Al just plain preferred not to join.

However, in midevening and sometimes in midday, when no one else was in the large living room of the fraternity house, Al would sit down at the piano and play classical music. To the rest of us there was little interest in such "stuff," but quite frequently we would gather around him in sheer admiration. There was indeed an aura about him as he played. His eyes mirrored the deep enjoyment he got from the selections he was playing. With his shock of wavy, blond hair, his soulful expressions, and his artistry at the piano, he was indeed a magnificent figure.

Kinsey evidently enjoyed solitary playing as well, for we have this description of the young musician from the vantage point of a dormitory window:

During my senior year I lived in South Maine Hall and the window of my room looked directly out on the side of the Chapel and the entrance to the Music Department, which was in a rear section of the Chapel. There was a grand piano in the Music Department, and Kinsey had been given a key to the entrance and permission to use the piano whenever he wished. I saw him frequently letting himself into the building, usually late in the afternoon. Then, for an hour or more, I would hear him play the piano. He was an excellent musician and played classical music for the most part. The main thing that impressed me was that he often played tempestuously, and I was quite sure that this was the way he took of relieving the tensions which must have been built up in him by the long hours he spent on laboratory work in his courses. I doubt, however, that many students thought of him as a tense person, for he had as an undergraduate the same ready warm smile which was characteristic of him in later life.

Most of his days and many of his evenings were spent in the college laboratories and classrooms, withdrawn from the social affairs of campus life. He was generally considered shy and scholarly and somewhat of a "loner." The thumbnail sketch in the yearbook terms him "dignified and noncommittal, with little to say to anyone" and ends: "If you loosen up a bit more, Al, you will make quite a man." Yet one of his college friends has commented:

> Al was by no means unsocial. Far from it. He had an excellent sense of humor and even wit. We all enjoyed bantering with him and we believed that he did too. He'd take part in the "bull sessions" of that day and displayed a wealth of general information.

During his senior year he added fifteen hours more zoology to his record and served as an assistant to Dr. Manton Copeland in the department. During this time he worked on the college collections of insects and designed and built a mount for exhibition purposes which showed representatives of the many orders of insects. Dr. Copeland reported that he used it on his lecture table for many years.

While still an undergraduate, Kinsey twice made trips to the northern Maine woods with classmates to trap specimens of live animals for the Bowdoin Museum. On one of these camping expeditions, which took place during a wintry Thanksgiving recess, Alfred had the bad luck on an especially bitterly cold day to sink through the too-thin ice into a beaver pond. His clothing was frozen stiff on his body, and in an attempt to dry it out at the campfire he singed the bottoms off his long underwear. Drying the sodden shoes was the most difficult problem; but the winter campers accomplished it by pouring in their precious dry oatmeal to absorb the dampness, removing it to dry out over the fire, and refilling the shoes with it. Whether the oatmeal was later cooked or not has not been recorded! During the same trip the young campers agreed to stop their watches so that they could feel that they were really living on nature's own time cycle. This wish to be close to nature is a recurring leitmotif throughout Kinsey's life.

His biological interests were versatile. Birds, flowers, and particularly snakes fascinated him. The college yearbook remarked that "on entering his room one never knows whether

Mr. Kinsey or a large, able-bodied snake is going to greet him!" At one time, according to Dr. Alfred O. Gross, his Bowdoin zoology professor, Kinsey had more than twenty of the reptiles in assorted species and sizes. Dr. Gross described an experiment in hibernation which was conducted by the aspiring biologist in the professor's yard. In autumn the snakes were buried four feet deep. The following spring Kinsey was delighted to find them dormant but all alive. Detailed notes on the experiment were recorded, Dr. Gross recalled. Kinsey made use of this incident ten years later in the opening chapter of his high school biology textbook.

A mutual interest in ornithology led to a first invitation to go on an early morning bird hike with Dr. Gross, who tells it thus:

> He knew his birds thoroughly and exhibited great enthusiasm for every bird seen. This initiated regular week-end trips in quest of bird lore. Many times he would arrive at our home before we were up and we would be pleasantly awakened by beautiful classical music he played on our piano down stairs. In those days our house was never locked and was open for students who never needed to knock or ring the door bell. Needless to say the many bird trips were of mutual interest.

Alfred's early enthusiasm for leadership in scouting was carried over into his work with the Y.M.C.A. youth program during his time at Bowdoin. Later in his even busier years of graduate work at Harvard he again found time to be a boys' club leader. A group of yellowed snapshots of cheerfully grinning youngsters on the trail, self-consciously posing in a group or around the campfire eating lunch, testify to those halcyon days. A second volunteer activity while he was a student in Brunswick was teaching English classes for local French-Canadians.

Kinsey was graduated *magna cum laude* from Bowdoin in June of 1916 with a B.S. degree. His commencement address was consistent with his ever-growing biological interests. It also reflected ideas he had probably absorbed from the art history course taken from "Frenchy" Johnson during his senior year. Describing a grey squirrel that he fed and made friends with on the campus, he developed the theme that art had found "beauty and worth" in the animal by individualizing it. Science in concerning itself with the animal's form and function had also made it worthy by individualizing it in another way. Kinsey recommended a combination of these approaches, but warned against sentimentality in art. The greatest danger, he believed, was that the scientist might shut out the appreciation of art and hence lose his comprehension of the balance of life. A quotation from Darwin was used tellingly at this point:

> My mind [said Darwin] has changed during the last twenty or thirty years. Now for many years I cannot endure to read a line of poetry. I have also almost lost my taste for pictures or music. My mind seems to have become a kind of machine for grinding general laws out of large collections of facts. If I had to live my life again, I would make a rule to read some poetry and listen to some music at least once a week. The loss of these is a loss of happiness.

Kinsey's later life-style suggests that he took these words to heart.

After his graduation Kinsey's only visit back to the campus was in August, 1932. He was on a summer motor trip east with his own family, including the three children. They stopped to have a look at the college, found that Professor Copeland was away, and visited with the Grosses at their cottage on the shore. To alumni appeals for funds he responded regularly with small checks. At the height of his career Kinsey was recommended for an honorary degree at Bowdoin but he was turned down by the College Boards because of "imagined possible ridicule of the nature of his research."

The summer following graduation he spent working in summer camps, by now a well-established pattern for his summer vacations. With the closing of camp he set his face toward Harvard University, which had awarded him a scholarship, and in the fall of 1916 he started his postgraduate studies at the Bussey Institution on the campus there. Bussey was a small but distinguished graduate school for research in applied biology, which was then operating in a more or less autonomous fashion. Later it was to be amalgamated with

Harvard's graduate group in biology. Kinsey's period of graduate studies spanned the war years, and the shrunken enrollment severely limited his contacts with fellow graduate students. Dr. Edgar Anderson, who had been one of the very first to return to campus after the war, described Kinsey as practically alone during this formative period. "I am almost the only friend that he made in his own profession during his graduate years," he declared. In fact, he became one of Kinsey's closest friends, an association that held fast until Kinsey's death in 1956. Anderson described the "offhanded" and "strange" ways of the school he and Kinsey were enrolled in:

> In an old-fashioned, high-ceilinged building, a few fortunate students studied in an informal way with an equally small group of first class scholars, William Morton Wheeler, W. E. Castle, E. M. East, Irving W. Bailey, Oakes Ames, and C. T. Brues. There were no required courses and each student was treated as an individual. Dr. Castle's colonies of rats, mice, and rabbits filled the basement and part of the first floor; Oakes Ames' growing collection of economic plants and their products and a library without a librarian took up several rooms. There were experimental plots, a good small greenhouse, and the living collections of the Arnold Arboretum joined the property on two sides.

Both Anderson and Kinsey had a strong bent toward natural history, and within a few weeks they were spending hours together afield. The details of a daylong excursion to Nobscot Hill in Sudbury were later recounted by Anderson:

> We planned our trip on topographical field maps, started off in the early morning on the rickety interconnecting streetcar system of greater Boston, hiked some fifteen or twenty miles, and returned late in the evening via the electric interurban which then ran from Worcester to Boston. At noontime he deftly built the smallest cooking fire I had ever seen, heated tomato soup in its own can, mixing it with evaporated milk, and there was tomato bisque to go with our sandwiches. The few remaining coals were extinguished to the last spark, the cans were flattened and tucked away under a rock, our sandwich papers were collected and folded up. In less time than it takes to be served in a restaurant, we had had a pleasant meal and no scar was left on the landscape.

Kinsey at this time, Anderson noted, was already out-standing in more ways than one. His active outdoor life more than compensated for his physical disability, the spine curvature which had kept him out of the army. He is recalled as "a lithe, slender, almost athletic young man more often in field khaki than in tweeds, with an engaging smile, a twinkle in the eye, and an enthusiastic earnestness about his research."

His interest had already been drawn to the study of gall wasps, more particularly, the American Cynipidae. These are insects about the size of a small ant which produce an abnormal growth or gall on a plant, most commonly on oaks, by laying their eggs deep inside the plant tissue. The egg usually lies dormant for several months before it hatches into a larva. At this point the gall begins to form and the growing insect uses it as a source of food. The larvae live inside the galls until they mature, which may require from a month to three years. They then become pupae and later develop into winged adults, at which stage they work their way out of the galls. As free insects they mate soon after they have emerged and then lay their eggs in the host plant again. Thus within a few days or weeks, sometimes within even a few hours, the insect has fulfilled all of its functions and dies.

The steps leading to Kinsey's selection of this particular insect, which he studied so intensively during the next twenty years, can be traced. At Harvard in graduate school, with entomology under Dr. Wheeler as his chosen field, he began to cast about for a group of insects to study intensively. He first picked a certain variety of beetle, did a little work on them, but dissatisfied, decided to look further. While investigating gall wasps as a possibility, Kinsey found that while there was a considerable body of scientific literature on the European varieties, only a limited amount of research had been done in this country on the typically American species. Their curious life history sometimes includes alternating generations, a rather rare biological phenomenon, in which offspring do not resemble their parents. One generation may be agamic—that is, able to reproduce without sexual union. This had misled scientists into failing to classify them correctly at times. Galls made by different kinds of gall wasps vary widely in appearance, size, and structure. The correlation between the galls and the insects interested him as a reflection of physiological characteristics which could not be studied otherwise.

Kinsey's youthful enthusiasm for his studies is reflected in his letter to Miss Roeth, his faithful correspondent, during his second year of graduate work at Bussey:

> If you care to know of my "stunts" I shall tell you. Work is perfectly enjoyable this year because I am doing research only. I managed to finish up all the required courses last year. My problem is in determining the extent of alternation of generations among the American Cynipidae—Gall wasps. Adler, you will recall, proved the existence of an alternation among many (not all) of the European gall wasps—an alternation so remarkable that the different generations occur on different plants or parts of the plant, produce galls utterly dissimilar, often one generation is agamic, and always so different in structure that it had been placed in a separate *genus!* We assumed that a similar thing occurred among our greater number of species, but thus far no one has experimented on the problem. That is my task.
>
> It involves the gathering of the galls by the thousands and tens of thousands, and breeding the adults out and putting them on the trees to form the next generation of galls. You can appreciate that it means a great deal of field work, and detailed observation of the tiny things—a job that is much more to my liking than the laboratory work which would be required if the problem were concerned solely with histology or anatomy.

Although well started on his research and serving as assistant in the laboratories of Radcliffe for the Zoology I courses (1917–18) and in those of Harvard for the Botany I courses (1918–19), he still found time for another project not associated with work toward his degree. This involved compiling a book on edible wild plants under the direction of Professor Merritt Lyndon Fernald at the Gray Herbarium. He gave this description of the work:

> It is a piece of work which is of interest to the camper and surburban dweller possibly more than to the strict scientist, but of course needs a good deal of scientific work to make it a safe product. Searching thru a great quantity of old literature, gathering the plants and testing out their various edible qualities, photography to illustrate the book, and now the final writing—these are the jobs. I appreciate it, not only for the out-door fun it

involves but also for the chance it offers for a training under Prof. Fernald, and publishing with him.

This definitive work, *Edible Wild Plants of Eastern North America* (37), was not actually published until 1943, when the conditions of World War II developed the concept of survival training, which led to sudden interest in how man could live off the countryside. Kinsey had planned to use his fine photographs as illustrations, and it was in part the prohibitive cost of reproducing them that delayed publication. Line drawings were substituted for many of them later. The volume's high merit was recognized by the Trustees of the Massachusetts Horticultural Society, who voted it the most important and valuable horticultural book of that year. That Kinsey was adept at cookery from native wild plants was proved when he was scheduled to talk on the subject to a New England botanical society monthly dinner meeting in Boston. He confidently told them that they could dispense with the caterer, and with some help he supplied an entire meal based on the recipes in the handbook. Bread made from acorn meal was one of the features.

Kinsey's entomological research was not only pleasing him; it was equally pleasing to the eminent professors under whom he was working. Anderson recalled:

> I was working in Dr. East's laboratory one morning when Dean Wheeler [with whom Kinsey had been studying] came in with Kinsey's thesis in his hands. "It's a remarkably fine piece of work," he said to Dr. East. "He is really of very high calibre." All of the Bussey professors left the students pretty much to their own devices but Wheeler as a matter of principle carried this policy to greater lengths than any of the others. He really had seen so little of Kinsey that he had not sized him up until the graduate years were practically over.

During these years in graduate school he continued to supplement his income from his scholarship by his work in boys' and girls' summer camps as an expert in camping and woodcraft. One former camper was moved to write to Kinsey by the newspaper accounts of *Sexual Behavior in the Human Male*, in 1948. He recalled the interesting instruction in nature study he had received from Kinsey at Pine Island Camp, Belgrade Lakes, Maine, thirty years earlier. Even though only a boy of six or seven years at the time, he remembered clearly an experiment that he did under Kinsey's direction as well as a "remarkable dinner served entirely from wild growing herbs and vegetables." Later, when the Girl Scout movement was in its formative years, Kinsey was one of those specially versed in camping who helped set up their program. Anderson contributed these comments on Kinsey's philosophy of camping:

> For one of the national training schools for camp leaders he worked out his definition of real camping, "living out-of-doors comfortably." It was not camping, said he, unless the whole phrase applied. One must be really living out-of-doors, cooking, eating, sleeping, not just tarrying there for a short time. It must be out-of-doors and not in elaborate permanent buildings. Furthermore, it must be more than just a sketchy getting by; one must have learned to make oneself comfortable under wilderness conditions, and in camping he practiced what he preached.

Because of its convenience to Bussey and Arnold Arboretum, Kinsey had chosen to live in Roslindale, which was at that time a modest suburb on the southern fringe of Boston. He was fortunate in being taken into the household of Miss Elizabeth Weld as a resident student. Miss Weld, who was related to the eminent entomologist, L. H. Weld, traditionally chose a Bussey Institution student to work in her home in exchange for room and board. Edgar Anderson followed Kinsey in the Weld household. Kinsey helped the housekeeper with the dishes, polished silver, washed windows, and did the Saturday work in the yard and garden of the fine home in return for his room and meals.

A major extra activity during his three years of postgraduate studies was the Bethany Boys' Club at the local Bethany Methodist Episcopal Church. Saturday hikes and weekend overnight camping trips with Kinsey as a leader took them through the Blue Hills of Milton and then beyond to Ponkapoag Pond in the Blue Hills Reservation. An enthusiastic member of the group wrote this nostalgic account of one of these expeditions:

I can remember clearly planning for these trips because food supplies came out of the family pantry. Our larders provided the necessary potatoes, canned vegetables, fruits, cakes and sweets. I also recall my boyish pride in a khaki knapsack and my feeling of achievement when I learned to pack a blanket roll wrapped in a poncho; and how to make a sleeping sack out of blankets. A few pots, a fry pan, a scout knife and we were ready for the challenge of the great out-of-doors!

To me, however, Mr. Kinsey was the enthusiastic leader of our Boys' Club. I remember the thrill of hiking over woodland trails and the joy of looking out over the valleys after we had climbed each of the Blue Hills in Milton. I remember the comradeship of the campfires on these trips. I remember that we used to sing to the accompaniment of Mr. Burke's zither or to the melody of a harmonica. All of these experiences were wonderful to a boy of thirteen. . . .

The highlight of Mr. Kinsey's year with the Bethany Boys' Club was a hike through the Berkshires in western Massachusetts. This, of course, was a big venture for us. Mr. Kinsey persuaded three members of the church to drive us to Greenfield, Massachusetts—in 1918 a full day's trip from Boston.

We boys having been trained in hiking and in camping were to hike over the Mohawk Trail—our objective the top of Mount Greylock. Mr. Kinsey planned the trip to take about one week. We were to return to Boston by train.

Only the highlights of this trip remain with me. I do remember that I was the first boy to report for First Aid. I had been exposed to sun and wind for eight hours in an open sedan while en route to Greenfield and the inflammation in my eyes caused me great pain. Mr. Kinsey treated me at a roadside brook by putting cold compresses over my eyes. After a night's rest I knew I could continue on the trip and not handicap the rest of the party.

Each night we would choose a campsite near a brook or a spring, first requesting permission from the farmer, if property lines were clearly marked. We would make camp in open fields protected only by our blankets and ponchos. Our meals were carefully planned and cooked over open fires by Mr. Kinsey and by Mr. Burke.

We boys—there were about ten or twelve of us—had our tasks

assigned and we did the chores—gathering wood, carrying water, preparing vegetables, and scrubbing pots and pans.

Only one night were we driven indoors—this by a thunder storm and a drenching rain. That night, at the foot of Mount Greylock, we were camped on the edge of a golf course. During the middle of the night Mr. Kinsey located the greens keeper and persuaded him to let us spend the rest of the night in the club house.

The next day we climbed Mt. Greylock. It was foggy and overcast as we made our way to the top and I am sure we made a sorry sight as we reached the observation tower, tired after a sleepless night and damp from moisture-laden clouds. I recollect no details of the train trip back to Boston. I just know that for boys of our age the Mohawk Trail Trip, a hike of thirty-five miles in three days and the climb up Mt. Greylock, was a great adventure.[1]

In those days Kinsey's tremendous drive was pretty well hidden, according to his long-time friend, Dr. Anderson. He gives this picture of him:

He walked rapidly but without hurrying, his gait quietly relaxed. He had gentle manners and considerable charm; only when he was aroused by something about which he felt very deeply were there strident overtones in his mellifluous speech. His desire to do something and do it superlatively well had made out of him a pianist of almost professional ability and he knew the flora of New England better than many botanists; yet as seen from day to day he was characteristically relaxed and at ease, only very occasionally did the steel within show through the surface. It was almost impossible to open a door for him, he always opened it for you. Complete relaxation, however, was something I never knew him to achieve. Late one summer he went on a yachting trip with some college friends in quite a large sailboat. Long lazy hours in the bright sunshine with the sails flapping idly overhead did not appeal to him. He tried to break his boredom by reading the only available book, Conrad's *Youth*, and it left a bad taste in his mouth. Only on moonlit nights when everyone lay on deck and sang together was there for him any magic in the sea. He frequently referred to this fortnight as time which might have been much better spent in climbing mountains or collecting insects.

Later Kinsey was to talk often to his own students of his graduate days at Harvard. They heard a great deal about both Wheeler and Fernald. He made it clear that he had learned his general approach to biology from Wheeler and his taxonomy from Fernald. These two men, both giants in their own right even though they feuded with each other, were clearly the major influences in Kinsey's own graduate training, and he in turn tried to inculcate their principles and attitudes into those studying under him.

After the completion of his graduate work he spent the better part of a year traveling to the South and to the West Coast and back on a Sheldon Travelling Fellowship, collecting gall wasps and getting a better understanding of the continent in which he lived and the kinds of people in it. He went on foot with a rucksack, using trains and buses to get from one collecting spot to another, sending his collections back to Harvard by mail and express. These galls he sent back evidently hatched out unexpectedly in at least one instance. Twenty years later Kinsey was told by a friend that a biologist who had been a student at Harvard just after Kinsey "vividly recalled the stew that Brues got into when the Cynipids you sent from the west coast emerged and filled the buildings!"

Many days were spent on foot, and he often camped comfortably all alone for a week or so at a time in the deserts and forests of the West. He noted many things besides insects, and was immensely curious about how people spent their lives and what they did and why. Shortly after his return from this *Wanderjahr* in the West, he told his friend Anderson about a tramp he had met on a refuse dump in the outskirts of Butte, Montana. The man was living there quite happily in a hut put together from odds and ends of salvage. He had begun the conversation by saying in a cultured voice, "Ah, I perceive that you are an entomologist. What kind of insects might you be searching for here?" So Kinsey sat down and spent the afternoon trading technical information about the Cynipidae for an inside view of life as a penniless squatter on city dumps. Adequate shelter was not difficult. Food was something more of a problem. But it was the maintenance of an adequate supply of alcohol in spite of prohibition that provided a real challenge.

Kinsey's own exuberant account of this ten-month interlude of travel, during which he collected 300,000 specimens
for later study, is revealing. The following winter he wrote
this report of it to Miss Roeth:

> I had obtained my travelling fellowship from the University,
> so for the next ten months I spent the time wandering over the
> country, collecting insects, especially the gall wasps on which I
> have been working. In all, counting the summer time that I spent
> at either end of the trip, I got fifteen solid months out-of-doors!
> Think of that for a life! I am more and more satisfied that no other
> occupation in the world could give me the pleasure that this job
> of bug hunting is giving. I shall never cease to thank you for
> leading me into it! I got into thirty-six of the states of this Union!
> And not as a tourist, hurrying thru, getting a glimpse of the
> civilized part of the world. But as a biologist, wearing khaki,
> living with my all on my back in my pack, getting off into the
> wildest parts of the country, often into regions where few people
> ever get. Inasmuch as oaks, on which the gall wasps occur espe-
> cially, are found only in the highest mountains of most of the
> country, I got into practically every one of the mountain ranges
> except those of the far north. In one range in Arizona, for in-
> stance, I got off where for four whole days I didn't see a solitary
> man; I was about fifty miles from the nearest town, living on my
> own camping wit. I spent most of the time on the trip in Florida,
> Texas, Arizona, and California, tho many of the other states were
> not slighted. In all I covered about 18,000 miles, of which 2,500
> were on foot.
>
> After a month spent in packing up my material, and a couple
> of months spent as usual teaching elementary biology in camp,
> I came out here to Indiana to teach.

With his move to Bloomington, a small college town in the
heart of the Middle West, the scene changes. Kinsey was fast
to become engulfed by the activities of the next segment of his
life: teaching, marriage, a family, and the authorship of textbooks and scholarly treatises on gall wasps.

3.

The First Year at Indiana

K<small>INSEY'S FIRST IMPRESSION OF INDIANA CLI-</small>
mate was a negative one gained from a short stay at the Culver
Military Academy summer camp near Plymouth, Indiana,
where he served as woodcraft instructor. He found the sticky
August heat very unpleasant and in sharp contrast to the
invigorating weather he was accustomed to in New England
camps.

Thus, when he was invited by Dr. Carl H. Eigenmann,
Chairman of the Zoology Department, to come to Bloomington in April, 1920, to be interviewed for a teaching job at
Indiana University, he was unenthusiastic about the prospect
of taking his first job in a spot where he felt the summer
months would be so unpleasant. At the time he was visiting
the department at the Ohio State University and still on his
appointment as a Sheldon Travelling Fellow. After being
assured by the men at Ohio that the terrain around Bloomington was hilly, in contrast to the flat country around Culver,
he decided, in spite of his doubts, to make the trip to southern

Indiana to be looked over and to see the Bloomington campus. On one of the first evenings of his visit Dr. Fernandus Payne invited the young job candidate to attend a Sigma Xi lecture as his guest. It was here, in the entrance to the lecture room and just before the program, that Kinsey was first introduced to Clara Bracken McMillen, later to be his wife. The result of his trip was that he accepted a position as Assistant Professor of Zoology to start the following fall.

News items from the *Indiana Daily Student* during this period provide a backdrop against which Kinsey's first year at Indiana University can be set. The University was celebrating its Centennial year. The campus fall enrollment was 2,296, with only 37 students coming from out of state, and 50 enrolled in graduate studies. Three meals a day could be had for $5.50 a week at an eating club, one block from the campus on Sixth Street, and $45.00 a month was the average cost for room and board.

The motor car had only started to make its impact on the community. Each bent fender or encounter with a horse and buggy made news. In one accident a student was grazed by an auto at the corner of Indiana and Kirkwood, fainted dead away, was carried into a nearby house, and revived to discover she was uninjured! Both she and the driver of the car admitted that their attention had been diverted to the sight of an auto truck which was being crowded to the middle of Indiana Avenue by a buggy.

Campus lecturers included Carl Sandburg, Vachel Lindsay, Hamlin Garland, Ida Tarbell, and Lorado Taft. The Garrick Club staged Shaw's *Androcles and the Lion.* Campus highbrows attended meetings of the Browning Society under the sponsorship of Dr. Will Hale, and campus lowbrows published the *Crimson Bull* with a sprinkling of off-color jokes.

Hoagland Carmichael, freshman, was pledged to Kappa Sigma, Charles M. Halleck, junior, was running for a class office, and next fall Ernest Pyle was to be city editor of the *Daily Student.* The Dean of Women, Agnes Wells, provided cards to be given out to offenders on the dance floor at the Student Building who failed to cooperate in the campus ban on "cheek dancing" and "camel walking." She denied, however, that any fraternities had been blacklisted as a punitive measure. Even though the terms "moonshine," "white mule," and "home-brew" are found here and there on these news pages, it was evident that the "roaring twenties" had as yet scarcely touched Bloomington.

Dr. Theodore W. Torrey, long-time chairman of the Indiana University Zoology Department, has traced the department's growth:

> From its very beginning in the days of Jordan, the Department of Zoology at Indiana University has maintained a strong research program. The spirit of original investigation has always prevailed and that was never more true than it is today. In large measure that reflects the views and attitudes of the three distinguished men—Jordan, Eigenmann, and Payne—who have headed the Department. It is to their everlasting honor that Indiana zoologists have always received the encouragement and opportunity to conduct research and as a result the Department throughout its history has been a leader in the advancement of zoological knowledge.[1]

Thus it was with a department with a high reputation for scholarship and research, but with a comparatively small faculty—Eigenmann, Payne, and Scott—that Kinsey cast his lot in 1920. He brought with him the prestige of his Harvard degree, and this, plus his inquiring mind, driving ambition, and unrelenting hard work, brought him rapid academic advancement. He came as an assistant professor, was given the associate professor rank in 1923—three years after his arrival —and was promoted to full professorship in 1929. In one of his very early letters from the campus to a close friend he wrote with youthful optimism of the possibility of some day becoming chairman of a separate department:

> The opportunity is rather unusual, for there are only two men ahead of me in the zoology department, and better than that is the plan to make the Entomology a separate department some day if I can build it up to that degree. So it all depends on what I do.

It was certainly a very different kind of campus from those at Bowdoin and Harvard, but the evidence is that he was highly pleased with it. He had found a comfortable room in a faculty home on East Third Street facing the heavily wooded area. "Folks are very congenial here, and I've found a great many friends already," he wrote after four months of life in Bloomington. In November he was elected to Sigma Xi, the elite honorary fraternity for scientists. In January he wrote:

> One of the best things about this position here is the opportunity to get out into the open country. Unlike the rest of the middle west, this part of Indiana is rather hilly, forested, and wild. I have been able to conduct a large part of my work in the field, wearing khaki, sleeves rolled up, collar open. Think of that for a University job! Nothing but biology could offer that! This next semester I shall have one whole day each week with my class out-of-doors. In addition I find a great group of people here who are interested in hiking; we hold zoology faculty meetings about the camp fire after a *real* supper, and in all I'm having the best bit of play that work can ever become.

In the same letter he wrote this spirited description of his teaching:

> I enjoy the teaching very much. . . . I do not expect that it is ever going to be necessary for me to grow old, if I can keep up the sport that I find in field work in biology, and keep in touch with the continually young student body. It is great fun doping out new methods of teaching; trying plans, to have them fail, and to have them suggest new plans. I hope that I will never reach the point where I will not be able to want to do things in some different way than I have done them before.

He was clearly equally well pleased with the opportunities available for working on his previously collected specimens:

> I find a rather unusual amount of time for research. I have about three hundred thousand specimens from my last year's collecting. They contain practically all of the described gall wasps (about four hundred), about a hundred new species; and a host of important data on the biology of that remarkable group of insects. So I shall have work enough for a life time with those bugs!

When Kinsey joined the staff the Zoology Department was located in the newest classroom building on campus, Biology Hall. Since the departments of Zoology and Botany were frequently at odds, it was well that the former was on the third floor and the latter on the first, while the English Department on the second floor furnished neutral ground between them.

It is generally agreed that Alfred Kinsey was an excellent teacher and lecturer, and he enjoyed the expository discourse of undergraduate teaching. With years of summer camp work behind him, he was far more experienced in instructional techniques than most young teachers fresh from graduate studies. Mrs. Saul Rosenzweig, a former pupil, has graphically described his classroom appearance and manner in a general biology course she took in 1926:

> ... On the dot of the hour he entered the classroom ... with a long, measured, rather brisk step. He was a tall man; his blond hair was closely cut in pompadour; his shoulders somewhat stooped. He had large eyes with lids that dropped slightly over them and wore horn-rimmed spectacles. His suit was dark, his shirt white, and he wore a black bow tie. He walked to the front of the room, looking neither to right nor to left, went immediately to the blackboard where he wrote, in printlike letters, an outline of the important topics, with subheadings, to be covered in the day's lecture. When he turned and began speaking, he had a precise manner of enunciation, richly modulated, as though he enjoyed using the English language. For most of the hour he stood in one spot except when he occasionally referred to the outline on the blackboard. His restrained manner seemed both aloof and shy. As he lectured, his enthusiasm for the subject-matter warmed the rather awesome atmosphere of the room.[2]

At intervals Kinsey took his general biology classes out of doors to study at first hand the principles he lectured about in class. The shorter field trips might be simply to the neighboring small ravine just back of Biology Hall on the wooded campus, or to an outlying meadow near enough to be included in the two-hour class period. On special occasions it was an all-day Saturday trip to hilly Brown County or to the Mitchell area with its virgin woods and caves. It was on an early fall field trip to the former place that Clara and Kinsey met a second time. A friend of hers who was a member of the class making the trip requested permission to bring Clara along with her.

The First Year at Indiana

Later in the fall of 1920 Clara McMillen and Alfred Kinsey met for the third time. The occasion was a Zoology Department picnic to Mitchell, about thirty-five miles south of Bloomington. The nearby caves were still owned by the University and had been one of the sites of Dr. Eigenmann's experiments with blind fish. Later, Spring Mill State Park was established there. Clara, who was a chemistry major, had taken a course in ornithology from Dr. Will Scott, and was invited by him to go on the picnic. The young instructor Kinsey was still in his first semester on the staff. The circumstances of this incident fit perfectly into the life style of both of them. The group set up their picnic lunch area and the faculty leader built a campfire, primarily for warmth and fellowship, but also probably to make coffee. But Kinsey, who had brought along food to cook for his lunch, was not satisfied with it, and chose to build his own separate fire in his own style. Clara, approving of its functionality, decided to share it with him in preference to the group fire. The ice was now broken and the friendship began.

On their first date they went on a picnic with friends to nearby Brown County. This was in December, and the snapshots taken show bare trees, warm clothing, and a cosy campfire. Among other topics discussed, Alfred described in detail his church work with the Bethany Boys' Club while he was at Harvard. Clara, a free-thinking young coed, made a mental note that the young instructor was probably "too churchy" for her. But the romance developed rapidly. By the second semester, in Clara's words, "they were practically engaged." This growing relationship prevented her from signing up for a second semester course in entomology which she planned to take. "I didn't think it would be right for me to take a course from the man I was going to marry," she explains. When Clara's boarding house on Atwater Avenue, run by the Wyman sisters, closed down for a while, she was pleased that she and Alfred now could meet often for meals at the university cafeteria in the basement of the Student Building.

Most of the young couple's six months of courting was within the framework of their second love, outdoor life. On Sundays Alfred felt free to take the day off, and he and Clara would hike out to a nearby scenic area, sometimes with other couples, taking along a campfire lunch. A short train ride would often be utilized to get them closer to a choice spot such as Cataract Falls or McCormick's Creek. Once a group of them took the morning Illinois Central passenger train east to Trevlac and then set off to walk the twenty or so miles back to Bloomington with another couple. Charles Snow, a young English professor who attempted the same feat on that day, finally gave up and called a taxi to transport his "lady friend" and himself back to Bloomington. Alfred, Clara, and the rest of their group made it back on foot, but only long after dark, as she remembers. On one occasion they were given a lift by Dean Pat Edmundson in his old Model T Ford to the spectacular Cedar Bluffs, eleven miles south of town. Later in the day he returned with others for a joint picnic.

The intimacy of the Bloomington college community in the 1920's is reflected in a story Kinsey told about his faculty landlady during his bachelor year on campus. Mrs. Foley asked him during Christmas vacation if he wanted to continue to rent his room for the second semester. Rather surprised, he replied that he certainly did and asked her why she inquired. Her reply was that she had thought he might be getting married. Since he and Clara had been dating for only a month or so, it was clear that the grapevine was in good working order. It is even possible that Mrs. Foley first put the thought into his head with that question!

In April Alfred wrote to his loyal South Orange friend, Miss Roeth, the exciting news that he was planning to be married.

> Did I tell you that I am to be married early in June? . . . The girl is a graduate student working in chemistry at Indiana University. She is a very brilliant scholar; is one of the best athletes in the place. She knows the birds better than I do, knows the flowers and trees, etc., is a capable hiker and camper, a champion swimmer. We are to spend the major part of June hiking in the wildest country in the White Mountains.
>
> So you see I am even more certainly headed into a life with the open!
>
> I shall hope to have the great pleasure of introducing you to Mac someday!

"Mac" she was then called by her fiancé, and this became her lifelong nickname. Its basis was, of course, her family name. In turn, "Prok" was the nickname which Kinsey's campers had given him early in life, and which followed him to Bloomington. Clara and all his close friends used it. It was formed from a contraction of the first syllable for "professor" and the "k" from his last name.

Clara Bracken McMillen had come to the campus from Fort Wayne and the small town of Brookville, a quiet canal town on the winding Whitewater River, where her maternal grandparents lived. Clara's mother, Josephine Bracken McMillen, was musically talented and taught grade school as a young lady in Brookville in order to earn money to go to the College of Music in Cincinnati, where she was graduated with a major in piano. After her marriage she taught in an "Opportunity Room" for slow learners at Fort Wayne. Clara's father, William Lincoln McMillen, was the son of a country doctor in West Lebanon, Ohio, who, after teaching in country schools and in Indianapolis, came to Indiana University to teach and to finish his degree. There he taught English for three years, and later joined the faculty at Fort Wayne High School.

Clara made an outstanding scholastic record in her four years at the University. She majored in chemistry, graduated with high distinction, and was elected to Phi Beta Kappa. During her junior year she had won first place in a national contest sponsored by Alpha Chi Sigma, the honorary chemistry fraternity. A single local candidate was chosen by the chairman of the chemistry department to compete on a two-day written examination. Clara was selected by Dr. Robert Lyons as the most promising undergraduate chemistry student and wrote her paper in his office. She kept on into the night and, when the University power plant doused the lights at 10:00 P.M. because of the coal shortage, he offered to let her continue by gaslight. She preferred to return the next morning, however, as she had written all afternoon and evening. When her paper won the top national honors she received a medal, and the local Alpha Chi Sigma chapter sent her a dozen red roses. As a result of this she was elected to Sigma Xi, science honorary, the following fall. This was a real mark of distinction as at that time undergraduate members were rare. She was also active in intramural sports and was awarded her I.U. sweater by the Women's Athletic Association.

The Kinseys were married on June 3, 1921, at the home of Clara's grandparents in Brookville. The ceremony was in the parlor with only relatives and a few close friends present. Clara's mother made all the arrangements for the occasion as the bride was, according to her own accounts, "not interested in the details." She missed her own commencement exercises to go on their honeymoon. The prediction by her friends that she'd live to regret this omission has not yet come true, she now smilingly says almost fifty years later.

For their honeymoon the couple took a private car to Cincinnati and then the Pullman car east, stopping en route to see Niagara Falls. A brief visit with Alfred's family in South Orange followed, which gave Clara an opportunity to meet his mother, younger brother Robert, and sister Mildred for the first time. During these few days they carefully carried out previously laid plans for their honeymoon hiking trip in the White Mountains. Clara had thoughtfully been given a pair of Bass hiking shoes, a knife, and a compass by Alfred the previous Christmas, before they were engaged. Food was bought for the two weeks on the trail, every item having been carefully planned. Prunes were even pitted to lessen their weight; packages were wrapped and mailed to themselves in care of resort hotels.

The Fall River Boat Line furnished ready transportation to Boston, where the new bride was an honored luncheon guest of Miss Weld, in whose home Kinsey had lived during his Harvard graduate days. Then the couple took a second overnight boat trip to Portland, Maine, as the plan was to approach the border mountains of New Hampshire from the northeast. Bethel, Newry, and North Newry led into Mt. Moriah, the Presidential and the Franconia Range. Train, electric cars, or rented autos provided transportation between points. The honeymoon hikers usually packed four days' food to carry and then picked up a new supply from packages awaiting them at the still-closed resort hotels. At Berlin and Gorham they met civilization again and purchased more supplies. When necessary they built a lean-to for shelter from the wind and rain. The evening routine was to take off their boots and belts and to put on clean socks, plus all the extra clothing available, before climbing into their blankets. It can be very cold in June in these areas, and this June of 1921 is recalled by Mrs. Kinsey as a perfect example. They climbed Mount Washington in a blizzard. Since Clara had never seen a mountain before, this was a real initiation into rugged climbing and all-weather camping. On the first stiff ascent Alfred selected a firewarden's trail, which is the shortest feasible route and, in Clara's words, "straight up." Alfred, in good trim, led the way, with his new bride lagging somewhat behind. When he gained too much lead on her he would rest and wait for her to appear. As soon as she caught up, he strode on to climb ahead again, according to her somewhat rueful description. It was clearly a test of her mettle, and she was equal to it.

Clara tells how she was taught to pick up and handle a snake on her honeymoon camping trip. It was a harmless grass snake, and she soon learned to share a naturalist's interest in reptiles with her new husband. This experience often served her well in her later years of camp and scout activities.

During the rest of the first summer of their marriage, the young couple both worked at Camp Aloha on Lake Morey near Fairlee, Vermont, not far from the New Hampshire border. Alfred served as head of nature study and camp-craft for the girls, and Clara assisted in both of these programs. Bird hikes before breakfast, insect trips, outdoor cooking, camping, and path finding were among the activities that Alfred and Clara supervised. This work was not new to Kinsey, of course, as he had worked in summer camps before. The camp tuition was $350, a large sum at that time.

Kinsey wrote the following account of his summer to Miss Roeth:

> We had a big and busy summer of it, with eight counselors giving their time to our end of the work, and with the difficulties of introducing a new sort of work to the camp. . . . At the start they were a bit scary of the notion that a girl could take care of herself on a long hiking trip, that men did not have to do all of the woodchopping, that they could carry their blankets into the wildest country, there to find things of a sort that were beyond

49

ordinary reach. But by the end of the summer we had them all in fine swing, and their interest was fine. We got into the mountains over ten times, guiding over a hundred and fifty girls into them. The biological interest of the White Mountains, especially above tree level, was an endless source of good times.

4.

The New Household,

Teaching, and Writing

THE KINSEYS' FIRST HOUSE IN BLOOMINGTON was at 620 South Fess, which they rented for the school year. Kinsey's newsy note to Miss Roeth a few months later draws a vivid picture of their beginning in householding:

> We have started our home here in Bloomington, and it has been great fun doing it. We are having painted furniture, doing the dyeing of our curtains, and such things which take considerable time, but it pays, for we get just what we want, and feel the further interest in it. Mrs. Kinsey is continuing her work in chemistry, and I am most particularly busy getting out some of the results from the Cynipid material I collected over the country over a year ago.

At a stopover in Fort Wayne Clara and Alfred had bought their first modest household goods, almost all of which are still in use after fifty years. The chief purchase was a set of marked-down summer porch furniture consisting of a settee, rocker, and straight chairs with woven splint seats and sturdy rustic frames. There was also a massive library table which has stood for years in the southwest corner of the living room. Next to the rustic furniture the most striking feature of their furnishings has long been the braided rugs covering the living room floor. These are well over an inch thick and extremely sturdy, for they have stood up under the wear of many years of steady use. Kinsey made them himself, developing his own technique. He used a hard, twisted braid which he borrowed from his skill as a rope maker—an art he had learned from one of his professors at Harvard. The rug-making venture originated about the time they moved into their newly built house in the late 1920's. The chance incentive was a too-bright pink braided rug from Aunt Lizzie. She had sent them one earlier that they liked very much, but this second one was not to their taste. Neither of them liked the garish color, and Alfred started to rework it to tone down the pink. He fast developed his skill. Soon he was ordering yards of unbleached muslin which were dyed suitable colors at the local laundry, and stuffing the fat strands going into the finished braid with either wool or cotton scraps. His daughter Anne has a clear childhood picture of her father sitting cross-legged on the floor working on the braids while he listened to music from his classical record collection.

Clara's plans for furthering her graduate work were dropped during the first semester; she lost interest in the research project she had signed up for. Soon she found she was pregnant, with the baby expected in July. In June the expectant parents moved to a frame bungalow on the corner of Park and University, a block away. They lived here until 1927, when they built their permanent home on East First Street.

The Kinsey children were born in fairly rapid succession. Donald came in mid-1922, Anne followed on January 1, 1924, Joan was born on October 16, 1925, and the fourth child, Bruce, the only one not born while they lived in the house on Park Street, in November of 1928. The pleased father wrote to Miss Roeth early in 1924:

> Our home is great fun. Wish you might stop in it sometime! The second baby, a girl, came the first of January. The boy is now running all about, getting into everything, and rapidly learning

Vacation Spot—Aunt Lizzie's

Alfred with Bob, Mildred, and parents. South Orange, 1917   Grandmother Buxton (insert)

With Sunday school class

Eagle Scout—1913

Boys' Club leader

Counselor at Camp Wyanoke

Engaged

Brookville wedding. June, 1921

Camp counselors, Vermont, 1921

Prok and Mac on back porch, 1940

Brown County Picnic, 1934. Bruce on friend's shoulders, Kinsey, Anne, Joan, and Clara

The family grown up: L-R: Bruce, Joan, Anne, Mac, Bob Reid, and Prok

MEXICAN TRIP, 1935

Loading the truck when roads failed, Cordoba

Candy hand-out

A conference on road conditions

Asking directions

Kinsey, galls, and gall wasps

to talk. So between them it is a merry house. Often it keeps several people jumping for them, but they are lots of fun.

Many of the early snapshots of the children were taken out-of-doors at this Park Street house. They show a pleasant, light-colored frame bungalow with a well-cared for yard and garden.

Music was already playing an important role in the new household. The Kinseys have always had a piano in their home. Kinsey played regularly for the children while they were growing up and gave his two daughters, Anne and Joan, piano lessons. When he played informally for the family, Chopin and Beethoven were his favorites. He never practiced, but could sight read fairly readily, and Clara often gave him sheet music as a Christmas gift. He played classical music by preference, partly, he admitted, because it was easier than the more modern compositions. It was clear, however, that he never had any illusions as to his musical potential. He remarked more than once to his wife: "It's a good thing I didn't go on with the piano. I would not have been successful."

The Kinseys regularly attended the special concerts scheduled by the University in Assembly Hall. This old frame building had been used at one time for gym classes, basketball games, and assemblies. Now it served for informal dances and "mixers," and, with wooden slatted folding chairs set up, for Wednesday morning convocation programs, Garrick Club plays, and concerts. When the building, which was just east of Owen Hall, was torn down, the area became a parking lot. An *Indiana Daily Student* editorial pointed to the shameful lack of interest in the "highbrow" concerts and described the handful of people that turned out for a concert by Alberto Salvi, a famous harpist.[1] Musicians who gave concerts in the Assembly Hall in the 1920's included the Gordon String Quartet, the London String Quartet, the Flonzaley Quartet, Albert Spalding, violinist, pianists Harold Bauer and Walter Gieseking, and the Minneapolis and Cleveland Symphony Orchestras. Professor and Mrs. Kinsey attended many of these programs.

Even though his regular summers of camp counseling were now well behind him and his family and an academic career had set his adult life pattern, Kinsey again took time the summer of 1923 to lead a final camp training program. He served as director at a Camp Director's Association Campcraft Conference at Camp Lanikila at Fairlee, Vermont, and filled in the rest of the summer at Camp Aloha, where he and Clara both worked on the nature and campcraft program. At the close of the season they took a trip to have a second look at a camp site near Milan, New Hampshire, with a view to establishing a boys' camp of their own. They had first seen it two years before, the summer of their marriage, and had then considered buying it and developing a camp there. Nothing came of these plans, however. The following summer Kinsey spent a month at Camp Winona in Maine, alone this time, since Clara now had two children, Donald and the new baby, Anne, under her wing.

One interesting sideline resulting from Kinsey's camp work was the design of a lightweight pack advertised as the "Kinsey Pack" in the camp equipment catalogues of Von Lengerke and Detmold, a firm that sold out later to Abercrombie and Fitch. It was a bag type rig, small enough so that a junior camper could carry it with what trip equipment he needed. It could also be used by an adult for a load up to thirty pounds. Originally custom-made for Camp Lanikila, it was later included, with a flap added, in a 1928 Sears Roebuck camp outfitting catalogue.[2]

From early records one can reconstruct the exact course of Kinsey's teaching program during the more than twenty years that he met regular classes on the campus. One of his first assignments was the "General Biology" course which he developed along the lines of his own thinking. He had hoped to gain the approval and understanding of the botany department for his "unified approach," and had prepared an outline for the course before he started teaching it his first fall in residence. In keeping with the feuding between zoology and botany which was generally typical of this period, the chairman of the Department of Botany refused to look at the outline when it was submitted to him. He informed Kinsey that no one knew enough to teach both botany and zoology.

This course, intended primarily for nonmajors, was based on his conviction that every educated person should know

something of the life sciences. In most years he offered seminars in entomology and insect taxonomy, and also directed
research in these two fields. New staff members were added
with the intention that they would share the growing load of
the general biology course, but this did not work out as
planned. In collaboration with the School of Education, Kinsey developed a course in teaching methods for high school
biology teachers in 1933, and introduced a summer school field
course for elementary teachers in 1941. These later courses
were peripheral to his main interests, however. The really
new departure in his teaching was the offering of Zoology 233,
"Evolution," in the fall of 1936, following his second Mexican
trip. This proved to be one of his favorite courses and was the
only one he taught from 1941 to 1945, his final years of teaching.

Many younger faculty members at the University followed the practice of teaching regularly during the summer
sessions to eke out their rather meager salaries, which at this
time ranged from $1,500 to $2,500 for the nine-month regular
academic year. But for many years the only summer courses
in biology were taught at the Biological Station at Winona
Lake, near Warsaw in northern Indiana. Kinsey was not willing to take advantage of this possible additional income as he
felt he could not leave his precious gall wasp collections for
the summer months. Only once, in 1927, did he teach a two-
week teacher training summer course at Winona.

Whether Kinsey was teaching his popular undergraduate
general biology course in a lecture room filled to capacity, or
a small graduate group in an entomology course, or substitut-
ing for the "bird man" by leading the early morning bird
hikes—as he did for a semester in 1939—there is general agree-
ment that he was a superb teacher. On occasion he may have
been impatient and sometimes opinionated, but he was always dynamic and stimulating, according to the reports of
those who studied with him.

During the four years from 1925 to 1929 Kinsey was supported in his research by a Waterman part-time appointment.
This meant that $400 of his annual salary came from this
fund, which was outside the teaching budget. To justify this
support he submitted to the President or to the Trustees a

resumé of both his work accomplished and his future research plans each year. These documents sound somewhat grandiose, and one feels in reading them that no human being, no matter how hard he labored, could possibly accomplish the tasks Kinsey lists for himself. He set his sights high, and perhaps to a young energetic scientist in his early thirties the goals may not have seemed excessive. Numbers always had a magic for him: the 4,200 miles clocked in field work in twelve months; the 80,000 specimens collected each year; the forty-two states explored; the twenty-seven cases of mutation found; and the eleven cases of alternation of generations. These, plus the countless pages of manuscript produced, all were clear-cut and to him satisfying evidence of his industry, his application to his work and, hopefully, of his progress as a research scholar.

In January of 1930, when his first major work was in press, he was thirty-five years old. In his report, as he lists the fourteen "Major Research Problems" ahead of him, he has inserted a matching column of figures in the right-hand margin headed "Years." The total adds up to thirty. He then added in the figure "36," the age that he would be the following June, when he expected to start this program. The grand total of years then becomes sixty-six. A proposed life plan of work is charted in these numbers!

By the Christmas vacation period of 1921, the first year of his marriage, Kinsey had started to draw together material for a high school introductory biology textbook intended for the ninth and tenth grades. Clara recalls that he took along his notes to work on during their visit at Fort Wayne to spend the holiday with her parents. He was aiming at an age group he had worked with successfully in his many summers of camp experience. As counselor he had responded warmly to the enthusiasms of youth and established rapport with them easily. Their unspoiled eyes saw the near-miracles of the natural world as he wished them to. Tutoring youngsters in nature's exciting, intricate lessons was one of his real pleasures.

He worked intensively on this manuscript during his spare time and over holiday vacations for the next few years. He had it with him in 1925 during the weeks spent in Rochester, Minnesota, at the Mayo Clinic while awaiting the diagnosis and treatment of Donald, the ailing son.

Lippincott published the first edition of *An Introduction to Biology* in October of 1926, providing strong promotion and advertising. Most reviews were enthusiastic, even in British journals, and adoptions began to flow in. One of the book's chief merits was that it insisted that fancy equipment was not needed to teach biology and that a thoughtful teacher could demonstrate some of the most fundamental problems on almost any vacant lot in the city or the suburbs. It was directed not to the rare high school student who would seek biology for a profession, but to the average future citizen. Its purpose was to awaken his interest in the living world and to equip him with the scientific method for interpreting that world. The following year an accompanying *Field and Laboratory Manual in Biology* was published.

Kinsey once wrote to a friend that he considered his textbook writing "in some ways a side issue," and it is true that he constantly directed his larger energies toward his gall wasp research. But his biology text furthered a concept always close to his heart—that of "unit biology" rather than a combination of the separate units on botany and zoology. This led naturally to an exploration of the problems of ecology, the then newly-emerging science of the complex and delicate adjustments necessary between plants, animals, and man in the world.

In a talk to high school teachers of biology in 1929 Kinsey vigorously defended his point of view, saying:

My second specification is for a biology course that is a unit, a synthesized program which is neither botany nor zoology, nor half of one and half of the other, but a course dealing with phenomena and emphasizing the principles which are common to both worlds. I think to the boyhood day when I roamed the fields and hills in fine ignorance of the sharp distinction "they" would have had me make between botany and zoology. Between the plant and the bug that fed on it. Between the flower and the bee that came to it. Between the plant tumor and the insect that caused it. Between the immigrant weed and the immigrant worm. Between the green of the clover and the nitrogen factories on its roots and the beef of the cow in the pasture. As my studies have progressed, they have served to emphasize the similarities rather than the differences between plants and animals, and I still fail to see why the average boy, wandering the hills of this world, should be asked to be interested during this semester in nothing but the plants of the way, and to transfer his interests to the animals of that same path only after the school calendar has sufficiently revolved.

He also resented the extraneous subject matter that was often included in biology courses and castigated it in these sharp words:

Again, I object to the use of our limited time in biology for disseminating propaganda on every conceivable fad and fashion that can be construed to concern human happiness. . . . In current texts and current curricula, I find extended exhortations on wasting foods in kitchens, on coffee, tea, cocaine, candy, tobacco, Keeley cures, ventilation, poisonous dusts in industry, accidents, fire-prevention, garbage disposal, artificial resuscitation, vegetarianism, whole chapters on vaccination, and the latest gospel on vitamins, pages on constipation, woolen underwear and Freudian complexes which leave one bewildered to know what is biology and what is first aid, dietetics, home economics, industrial management, civics, or ordinary politics. From a biology designed to interest future citizens in the living world about them, and calculated to introduce those citizens to a scientific method, we are at best directing their attention to a species of toothbrush biology suspiciously fortified with the trappings of articles of personal faith.

The income from his high school text was considerable and provided the family with a measure of financial security they had not known before. Some faculty colleagues admitted that they felt mixed admiration and envy of Kinsey's quick success with his first venture into commercial publishing. In part, the royalties furnished funds to start the new home and to buy a first car, but most were put aside to be used later in meeting the costs of a college education for the children.

While the text was popular in style, it was not written to be easy for the pupils. A Lippincott staff member, Howard Bauernfeind, who assisted with the editing, felt that Kinsey was deeply concerned about the trend toward what he called "softness" in American education. Bauernfeind commented:

He was convinced that youngsters wanted to work and to learn if they were challenged by good teachers, good textbooks, and solid subject matter. He himself never made his books easy; they were scientifically accurate, stressed principles, and featured the illumination of difficult principles with appropriate illustrations and stories. No point was . . . insignificant [enough] to be treated casually. If material merited inclusion in the book, it also deserved painstaking preparation and full explanation.

Donald's illness and death at the age of three years and nine months was the family's first tragedy. His was an exophthalmic case, not recognized at first. In June, 1925, his parents took him to the Mayo Clinic, where his case was given intensive study. A successful operation on the thyroid was performed in September, and Kinsey left Clara in Rochester with Donald and returned home with twenty-month-old Anne to meet his classes and keep the household running. He would read to entertain her, put her to bed early, play the piano as a goodnight treat, and then leave the house in charge of a young student to catch up on his work at the laboratory. Although the operation on Donald had been successful, after the return to Bloomington he became seriously ill again. By the time his illness was diagnosed as diabetes, he had gone into a coma. Insulin had been discovered, but it was not yet in wide use. Diabetes in so young a child was not common enough for the symptoms to be readily recognized, especially since his true condition was masked by his earlier illness. Thus the family doctor was unable to make a diagnosis in time to administer the appropriate treatment.

The first edition of Kinsey's high school biology text was published the year of Donald's death. A friend and former colleague pointed out that the section on thyroid imbalance accompanied by illustrations of stunted laboratory animals has a special poignancy. "Few of those who read this calm, clear, objective discussion," he wrote, "realize that at the time it was written Kinsey's oldest son was suffering from a related condition."

Meanwhile Kinsey was vigorously pursuing the field of research which he had set for himself, the systematic classification of the many species of Cynipidae or gall wasps. He spent long days at the desk and in his laboratory classifying and studying his thousands of specimens. The field work necessary to collect adequate specimens was completely to his liking. Its chief difficulty was the problem of timing. It was essential to collect the galls at exactly the right degree of maturity—usually in the late fall—if they were to be bred successfully under laboratory conditions. This was rather awkward to fit in with an academic teaching schedule. By careful planning, however, he was often able to arrange regular late fall field trips of nine or ten days.

In view of his research work, his teaching load was often comparatively light. In February, 1924, for example, he wrote:

> The school has been mighty good to me here in regard to research. Last semester I had 22 hours a week of scheduled teaching, but this semester only five. That gives me much time for research. They have given me considerable assistance (three part-time people working for me in my lab now), equipment, and publication.

He had laid the groundwork for what he expected to be his lifetime study in his graduate work at Harvard's Bussey Institution and still further in his year of travel and field work after he completed his studies. Two short articles had already been published while he was still a student at Harvard, certainly a mark of distinction. They appeared in *Psyche*, a long established journal published by the Cambridge Entomological Club in Cambridge, Massachusetts. One dealt with fossil Cynipidae and the other described an unusual African species of gall wasp of which he had examined three specimens. (1, 2)

Just before Christmas of his first year at Indiana the findings of his graduate research appeared under three successive titles in the *Bulletin of the American Museum of Natural History*. (3,4,5) They covered well over one hundred pages of detailed description and taxonomic classification of gall wasps he had studied in the various collections to which he had access in the East. He identified new species, described their life histories, and set forth the phylogenetic position of genera. He also explored the implications of his material for evolutionary development, a theme further pursued later in his *Origin of Higher Categories* (21). Of special interest was the description of his methods of collecting galls and of hatching the insects under laboratory conditions. These methods were modeled after those used by the German scholar, Hermann Adler, but with some modifications of his own. Kinsey acknowledged warmly the help and encouragement of his Harvard teachers, particularly that of William Morton Wheeler and Charles T. Brues.

His next four major articles appeared during 1922 and 1923 (6, 7, 8, 10), and all dealt with the specimens he had gathered in the West during his year of travel on the Sheldon Fellowship. The last three of these four were his first publications to appear in the Indiana University Studies series. In them he warmly acknowledges Mrs. Kinsey's aid in that she "generously contributed encouragement, time, and skillful criticism," and again that she "helped in the proofreading and contributed the sort of encouragement and counsel which is of inestimable value."

A marked change of scientific approach appears in the second of these four papers, "Studies of Some New and Described Cynipidae (Hymenoptera)," on the Far Western field work. Kinsey admitted he had grown dissatisfied with his own earlier methods and declares: "Probably the most notable departure in this paper is the recognition of varieties." He goes on to point up the shortcomings of earlier practices in which closely similar forms were considered as haphazard variations of one species or in which varieties had been considered as distinct species. He continues:

> However, variations are usually orderly and abrupt, and much biologic data has been buried by ignoring minor differences. In many cases where the related forms were described as distinct it was due to ignorance of previously described forms, and they have been maintained as distinct by later workers thru continued ignorance of the meanings of the descriptions. Most of these descriptions are truly unusable because they make no comparisons with other forms, and usually fail to describe the very characters in regard to which there is any variation. Great confusion has been introduced by the reduction to synonomy of these related things; in the process much biologic data has been scrapped, not to be recovered without difficulty. I acknowledge

having copied all of these practices in my own previous publications.

Minor articles (9, 11, 13, 15, 18) were interspersed among these careful, scholarly publications. Some of them are book reviews; others deal with problems of teaching biology in high school; and still others give garden advice on pests and on iris growing.

In 1930 the first major study of his mature years appeared, ten years after his arrival on the Indiana University campus. It was entitled *The Gall Wasp Genus Cynips: A Study in the Origin of Species.* This weighty volume of over 500 pages with an almost equal number of illustrations appeared in the University series. Six years later, in 1936, he was to publish his second major work, *The Origin of High Categories in Cynips.*

These two volumes (16, 21), which he published during his second decade at Indiana University, firmly established his reputation both here and abroad as one of the leading authorities in his field; they are contributions not only to the taxonomy of the gall wasp but to genetic theory. They were the culmination of his earlier years of field work and study, painstakingly done and just as carefully seen into printed form. Kinsey's personal, bound copies of these two studies reveal, in their carefully inked marginal corrections and annotations, his straining for the unattainable goals of completeness and total accuracy.

Simultaneously with these scholarly pursuits Kinsey was intermittently at work on a revision of his elementary biology textbook and on the student workbook to go with it. Thus during the 1930's two separate revisions of his high school biology text appeared, in 1933 and 1938, and a short while later, a revised wookbook for each. In 1937, *Methods in Biology* was published, also by Lippincott. It was intended for college level work and especially for use in the training of science teachers. As the years passed the sales started to drop off as more recent texts superseded even the new and expanded editions of the popular Kinsey volume. The publisher was eager for Kinsey to again revise and update the text, but by this time he was far too engrossed in the opening avenues of his new field of sex research. The last record of advertising for the biology texts in his files is dated May, 1941. It was the end of one epoch for Kinsey and by then another already had a strong, lusty beginning.

Kinsey was a popular lecturer on campus and, in spite of his heavy work schedule, generously accepted invitations to speak before student or faculty audiences. The *Daily Student* reports many of these talks. That he enjoyed the role of speaker was evident to anyone who heard him, and his well organized material, clear-cut delivery, and incisive points left a strong impression on his listeners. These abilities served him well, when, ten years later, he went out stumping before scores of clubs, classes, and professional associations to ask for their cooperation in his gigantic task of finding willing subjects for thousands of sexual histories.

Among his early campus talks two are of special interest. The first was before the Psychology Club on December 16, 1926, on "Psychic Evolution." "My idea is," he is reported as stating, "that biologists cannot conceive any type of behavior, even the most complex of human behavior, which has not had its origin in the simpler type of behavior among lower animals." He concluded that it was desirable to study the simpler types among the lower animals "if we wish to understand the more complex behavior of the humans." In these words is a foreshadowing of his determination many years later to assemble and study films recording mammalian sexual behavior. There was often public criticism of Kinsey when he referred to man as "the human animal," but he came to sex research as a zoologist and deeply believed that many insights into human sexuality could be gained by the careful study of all forms of sexual behavior. Eventually he assembled a rare collection of such films covering seventeen species of animals for the archives of the Institute for Sex Research.

The other talk was on "The Revolt of Youth" at a Sunday afternoon Y.W.C.A. vesper service a few weeks later. Here he was reported as pointing out that youth's weaknesses were their attempts to get something without paying the necessary price for it in effort and self-denial, and their unwillingness to join the scientist in his search for the goal of absolute truth.

While Kinsey had by this time turned away from formal religion, he reflected here his adherence to the traditional work ethic and moral code.

In the mid-thirties Kinsey participated several times in the popular undergraduate course, "Life Views of Great Men of Science," a joint venture of the various science departments on campus. His two lecture subjects were the great French naturalist and man of letters, Henri Fabre, whom he described as having gathered the greatest body of facts on insect behavior that had ever been compiled, and Thomas Huxley, the British biologist. The *Daily Student* on March 18, 1936 reported Kinsey's second lecture as concluding on the note that Huxley was considered the author of the scientific "declaration of independence" because he bowed to none—church, colleagues, or tradition—unless his adversary would address sufficient proof to substantiate his contentions. It is revealing that Kinsey should have chosen these two particular figures as subjects for his lectures. They aptly mirror the contrasting sides of his own make-up. He was both the simple outdoor naturalist and later the iconoclast who challenged tradition.

In the mid-1920's three well-established Indiana faculty members, Professors Schuyler Davisson, William Moenkhaus, and Carl Eigenmann, had acquired a small tract of farmland in a newly developing area on the southeastern edge of town as a speculative investment. It was from them that the Kinseys bought a site for their new home in 1926. The plot had been part of an old orchard, and a few lone fruit trees dotted the area. The photographs of the unfinished house show a single persimmon tree in the front "L" of the new home. Otherwise the ground was largely barren. Skillful planning of the hillside-type landscaping necessary for the site was called for, and this was carried out in careful detail before breaking ground for the new house. Floor plans had been developed after long study of numerous books and magazines. Using his early engineering training, Kinsey prepared detailed drawings and blueprints. The unusual bricks he wanted for facing were found in nearby Martinsville. Since they were common brick which had been "overburned," they were a marked economy at $2.00 less per thousand than the standard ones. The knobbly, uneven effect of these virtual discards from the kiln is pleasing to the modern eye, but in this taste for the rustic and casual look the Kinseys were definitely ahead of their time. I can recall scornful comments about the ugly brick which had been laid so "crudely" and was so "unworkmanlike" in the new Kinsey house. The northeast portion of the wall is somewhat smoother than the rest. The story is that it was constructed before Kinsey had convinced the bricklayers as to exactly what he had in mind. The family moved to their new home in May, 1927.

The house was originally placed on a single lot, but other lots were added later, and finally the tract consisted of two and a half acres of skillfully terraced and heavily wooded grounds. A lily pond, wildflower garden, paths leading to sudden open spaces, and a fine combination of native and nursery-bred trees all contribute to the total effect of a splendid wild spot in the midst of town. Kinsey was well ahead of his time in his nontraditional ideas of how grounds around a home should be designed in a natural fashion, as well as in his taste for "overburned" brick. The Kinseys liked flowering weeds, and poke, snakeroot, goldenrod, Queen Anne's lace, and wild asters were given space along with the early flowering bulbs and later perennials. Day lilies and iris were two of their specialties. A wide range of fine-named varieties bloomed throughout the season in the generous, curving borders.

His great interest in iris, of which he at one time grew more than 250 kinds, developed into a modest business with his friends and acquaintances in Bloomington and its environs. A price list was printed up for several years (1931, 1932, 1933, 1935) by a local printing house, and forty to fifty persons ordered iris plants from him each season. Since iris must have sun, they were ideal for freshly established, shade-free gardens, and flourished in the clay that most faculty members found in the yards of their newly purchased homes. The Kinsey garden, with its many fine trees, eventually became too shady for such perennials. Even a new border, laid out and planted in the 1950's, soon gave way to the fast growing volunteer redbuds which seemed to spring up overnight in the rich woodland soil.

"The iris business never supported the hobby, which was an expensive one," Clara Kinsey observes in retrospect. "It was also a hard one to live down, as we would get calls many years later about possible purchases long after Prok had given up his sales," she added. But the then current folklore on this point is contributed by a former student who wrote: "We graduate students gradually came to the conclusion that Kinsey was very astute in money matters. It was our understanding that the monies gained from selling the fine iris in his garden more than paid for all that he invested in them and actually netted him some additional income."

Attendance at a meeting of the American Iris Society at Freeport, Illinois, in 1933, on which occasion grandmother Kinsey stayed with the three young children, gives evidence of Kinsey's strong interest in his horticultural hobbies. He also wrote a charming, informal article the same year for the *Bulletin of the American Iris Society* entitled "Landscape Picture with Iris" (18) in which he discussed the many varieties of iris he had used in his garden. He explained how they could be combined for the best effect in landscaping, either by using contrast or a subtle blending of colors.

A vegetable garden in which he did much of the work was another major enterprise. Before the advent of locker service and home freezers the Kinseys were growing green peas in market-garden quantities and having them quick-frozen and stored by the local butcher.

Kinsey's garden and landscaping interests also extended into the community. At one time a delegation of his students planted iris at the local courthouse under his supervision. On another occasion he planned and helped to execute the landscaping of a good-sized island oval in the newly developed fraternity quadrangle on south Jordan Avenue. His planning here stood the test of time, and today, many years later, it is still a pleasant oasis which divides the passing traffic. The nearby Theta Chi house also benefited from his gardening skills, when he not only helped redesign the landscaping of the grounds—the original design of which he had called "atrocious"—but also participated in the physical work involved in digging, planting, and transplanting.

Kinsey felt a need for strenuous physical exercise and was

never willing to just "putter" with his garden work as long as his health was good. He applied himself energetically to this, for him, recreational activity. He could always be seen in season on Sundays working in his yard dressed only in short trunks, which he first adopted for garden wear in 1934. He wrote to a friend that year: "Following your lead, I have adopted shorts—nothing more—as the garden costume, and have the best tan ever—more than I thought a bleached blond could have. And the most glorious feeling that my skin has ever known." He was often barefoot, too, but when digging, as a practical necessity, wore one shoe on the foot used on the spade. This was an unusual sight in those days, especially for a full professor. One of the coeds who worked on his laboratory staff at this period recalls:

> With the first days of spring one could always expect to see less of "the boss." He might rush in with great gusto a few minutes before class time and proclaim to the office at large that he had been out in his garden since 7:00 A.M. doing thus and so; that he had been, as always, stripped to bathing trunks and had gotten a good taste of sun; that he thought the neighbors were possibly getting used to seeing him so, although a few years ago he had used to shock them. (I think he rather enjoyed "shocking" people. When he spoke thus he was always, to me, rather like a small boy using a new word which he suspected might not meet with approval and then waiting rather hopefully for an explosion.)
>
> He took great pride in his garden. I can remember several times during the years that I worked for him when he reported that he "just bought another lot," and I remember his particular pride in a certain blue spruce which he planted.[3]

The garden was a refuge for the neighborhood youngsters, who were generously allowed to play there. They often cut through the wooded paths on their way to school. One boy of a neighboring faculty family well remembers how he guiltily ducked under the friendly overhanging branches of a huge forsythia bush when a police car cruised by to check out a neighbor's complaint of boys who were snowballing passing autos.

Kinsey's artistry and pleasure in arranging flowers for the house was an extension of his gardening skills. He once commented about iris, which were undoubtedly his favorites: "I can never paint with real colors, but I can with flowers."

An idiosyncrasy which made outdoor life and garden work easier for Kinsey than for most people was his immunity to insect bites and poison ivy. When others at the outdoor suppers in the Kinsey garden would discover themselves virtually covered with chigger bites the next day, he would have come through unscathed. Once I watched him while he casually cut down an inch-thick poison ivy vine which had grown up the side of Wylie Hall, where the Institute was housed at that time. He was using a pen knife he always carried in his pocket to cut the tough stems and his bare hands to rip the long vines from the brick walls.

With the buying of the first family car, a Nash, in 1927, picnics to nearby Brown County were easy to plan, a treat for an outdoor-loving family. Trips to other nearby places included one to Madison, Indiana, a scenic spot on the Ohio River, when grandmother Kinsey was visiting the household in 1930. The small car was well filled, as Bruce had been born by now. Other vacation trips followed as the children grew older.

Their childhood memories are of a warm and accepting relationship with their parents. The Kinseys felt that children were to be enjoyed and loved, and their children were taught to share and enjoy outdoor life with their parents. Swimming, hiking, picnicking, gardening all played their part in this picture. There is no memory, for example, of chores to be done in the large garden. Each child was given a plot of ground along the driveway, and they planted and tended it as they wished. If they wanted to earn extra money they could rake leaves, weed, or dig dandelions at twenty-five cents an hour, but no parental demands were made on their time in this respect. All questions they asked were patiently answered, those about sex as straightforwardly as those on any other subject. In fact the girls sometimes asked their parents such questions for their friends if they didn't know the answers themselves.

During the 1920's Alfred Kinsey, immersed in the life of a small college town, was absorbed with his young family and his professional responsibilities of teaching and research. As a result he was oblivious to the major changes in sexual and social patterns in this country in the decade following World War I. He once discussed these changes, which his own studies had by then clearly documented, with me. He admitted that he, like many others, had failed at the time to recognize what was taking place. The "roaring twenties" had clearly passed him by, unaware.

The Early Thirties —

Bug Collecting

O<small>NE OF</small> K<small>INSEY'S BASIC GOALS WAS TO DE-</small>
velop the true potential of taxonomy and to make it a respectable tool in the biological sciences. As early as 1927 in a formal
proposal for his research on the Waterman Institute grant, he
wrote:

> From our work on Cynipidae, in connection with a study of
> the published work in other fields of taxonomy, I propose to
> attempt a formulation of the philosophy of taxonomy, its useful-
> ness as a means of portraying and explaining species as they exist
> in nature, and its importance in the co-ordination and elucidation
> of biologic data. Taxonomy would long since have profited by a
> discussion of the usefulness and limitations of its tools. Such a
> study should bring the fields of taxonomy and genetics into closer
> understanding of their common problem of the nature of species.

In 1932 when Kinsey was seeking support for the botanical
journal, *Rhodora*, he wrote to Dr. Raymond Pearl of Johns
Hopkins University and again stressed this point of view:

The older systematic botany and zoology have not had much in them to commend them to other biologists. I feel, however, that there is a new day dawning in taxonomic research. The fields of genetics and taxonomy should have essentially the same goals. Each method of approach has its advantages and the taxonomists working with species as they occur in nature can make interpretations which are necessary for the complete utilization of the findings of the geneticists. This was a vision which geneticists had years ago, but which the taxonomists failed to bring into fruition.

With the publication of his major works (16, 21, 23, 25, 28, 31) during the 1930's he undoubtedly felt that he had made great strides toward achieving this goal.

Even Kinsey's fellow scientists stood in awe of his passion for collecting, which at times appeared almost an obsession to them. His long-time friend, the eminent botanist, Dr. Edgar Anderson, wrote:

Kinsey proceeded to collect galls, gall wasps, the oaks they lived on, the various insects which parasitized them, and the parasites of these parasites in quantities never dreamed of by any previous investigator. . . . Even with the help of devoted assistants, the preparation, care, and interpretation of such a collection would have chilled the ambition of a lesser man. The insects (and their parasites) had to be trapped and killed when they emerged from the galls. Each insect was glued to a snippet of stiff paper and impaled on a steel pin. Minute paper labels . . . were affixed to the same pin and thousands upon thousands of these exquisitely prepared specimens were pinned in insect-proof boxes. Hundreds of these boxes, together with field notebooks, collections of the actual galls, herbarium specimens of the oak trees from which the original collections were made were kept in orderly storage for effective cross reference. With the assembling of this vast collection the real work had just begun. The specimens were examined (and frequently re-examined) under a dissecting microscope. If they belonged to a known species and variety, they were so labeled; if not, the proper pigeonhole was worked out and elaborate descriptions were prepared and published, integrating all the newly collected material with the world's previous work on these insects, in whatever language. All this, to be sure, is the routine chore work of modern systematics, but where previous workers had studied a few specimens, Kinsey worked with them by the hundreds and thousands.

This tedious routine work of breeding and of preparation of the thousands of insects and then mounting and labeling them, often 800 to a single box, had to be moved ahead faster than one man could possibly do alone. Former assistants who worked under Dr. Kinsey in his laboratory[1] recall those days of delicate, painstaking, but routine work as a pleasant memory. Kinsey showed them in many small ways that he appreciated their loyalty and treated them in a kindly, paternal manner. They were a dedicated, tightly-knit group working happily in those post-Depression years for what would now seem to be the almost "slave" wages of thirty or thirty-five cents an hour.

The following account written by a former student worker has a rare flavor of verisimilitude, although it perhaps places more emphasis on the young coed's feelings than on her employer.

Dr. Kinsey's office . . . was filled on the window side from floor to ceiling with olive-colored metal bookshelves placed library fashion with two-foot aisles crosswise in the room. These were filled with books and journals except those at the ceiling, which contained the overflow of insect cases. (When he wanted something from one of the top shelves, Dr. Kinsey would climb up, straddling the aisle, hand over hand and with his feet on opposite shelves.) There was a wider aisle down the center of the room, lengthwise; the inner side of the room was filled with shoulder-high metal filing cabinets. There were two holes in this labyrinth; the first, about half-way back and on the window side, was Dr. Kinsey's "office," an opening just large enough for a large desk fronting a window, a swivel desk chair, a "visitor's chair," and a smaller table which might house a typewriter or a miscroscope. . . .

It was here that I first saw Dr. Kinsey. I cannot say positively that he was in shirtsleeves, that he was wearing a dark red bow tie, that his short, blondish-graying hair was standing on end, or that he greeted me with a somewhat boyish grin; however, I believe it is extremely likely that this is the case, for I can never remember seeing him in any other aspect in his office. (I remember that he always wore light wool socks and moccasins; that he kept two pairs of moccasins which he alternated day-by-day, and that when the older looked beyond repair, he ordered new ones exactly like the old ones from L. L. Bean's factory in Maine. I never saw him in a hat.)

He had a way, always, of setting a student at ease; and I remember feeling almost confident, as he led me around a second set of tall bookshelves to a large table in the rear, that it would not be too hard for me to learn to do whatever girls did with gall wasps. . . .

They were, it turned out, extremely small, winged insects (they didn't sting people, and anyway these were dead—this new knowledge brought a sense of relief!) that laid eggs in the stems or leaves of plants, which then swelled into a kind of malformation housing the developing larvae. To mount a gall wasp, one picked it up carefully, with tweezers, applied a transparent cement to the left side of the insect, and placed it on one of the clips of cardboard, which was then impaled on a two-inch long steel pin. The cardboards were mounted two deep and about three-quarters of an inch apart on each pin, and the pins were set about a quarter of an inch apart in cork-bottomed boxes and in rows about two inches apart. The important thing, was that the insects must not be broken and that they must all face toward the right. Would I like to try it? . . . I had lost track of time and had done nearly a row in the box when Dr. Kinsey came back around the corner and told me that the job was mine. . . .

Today it seems a little odd to me that for the next three-and-a-half years I continued in this same job without any particular feeling of boredom or resentment against the factory-production nature of the work. I learned to watch the window-screen collecting envelopes in the boxes outside the office windows for the emerging adult insects, to prepare and use a killing bottle, and later, using Dr. Kinsey's special lettering technique, with India ink to write minute, legible collecting data to label each insect: Species, place and date of collection, date of emergence, sex . . . "How do you tell?" I remember I asked. "The female's bigger," they told me. . . .

Once or twice I may have asked myself whether all this collection and the work it involved might be related to some of the make-work projects of WPA and NYA that sprang like Minerva out of President Roosevelt's mind to provide relief to the depression; no, I learned, scientific investigation can't yield valid results without lots of individual specimens—enough so that the statistical curve can't be changed by the addition or subtraction of a few hundred random individuals. It was terribly important to have lots of evidence.

Well, what did Dr. Kinsey expect to learn or to prove from all these cases? What was he looking for? Well—he wasn't quite sure. In fact, he wouldn't know until he had lots of insects and looked at them, just exactly what it was that he was looking for, or what he was going to prove when he looked at all the evidence. That, I gathered, was the scientific way of going about an investigation; and if what Dr. Kinsey needed for his scientific investigation was more and more and more mounted and labeled specimens of gall wasps, well, that was what he should have; and we were there to help him have them.[2]

Although generally kind and friendly, Kinsey was of the older school, inclining to be somewhat formal in his manner toward younger persons working under him, whether they were graduate students or laboratory assistants. The professor rather stood apart in those days. This relationship was shattered on at least one occasion in the mid-thirties. One of his graduate students has described it:

Probably one of the most priceless anecdotes in my memory of him concerned an April Fool's stunt that another student and I put a couple of his technicians up to. He had two freshmen girls who were mounting and labeling gall wasps for him who sat at a table in the back of his office. They were duly awed by Kinsey and held him in great respect. On April Fool's day, one of them brought some journals into the Graduate Library, and she mentioned the fact that she would like to April Fool Kinsey, but she didn't quite dare. We conceived the idea of having her discover dermestids* in one of his type boxes. After considerable urging, she said she would try it. Her description of what happened was something like this. She pulled out one of the type boxes and opened it, and said, "Dr. Kinsey, I think there are dermestids in this type box." She heard his chair shove back and hurried strides coming toward her. She did not have nerve enough to look at him, but as he towered over her, she managed in a faint voice to say, "April Fool." He stood looking at her with his hands on his hips, and finally said, "Hmmph!" and turned around and went back to his desk. He never said anything further to her about it,

---

*Dermestids are small beetles very destructive to dried meats, skins, furs, and insect collections.

but several days later, he told the two of us about it, and he said that he did not think a young, freshman girl would have the nerve to have done that to a full professor.

The question naturally arises whether Kinsey was on as comfortable terms with his colleagues as he was with his students and other subordinates. Some accounts[3] make the intra-faculty relationships sound almost ideal, but Kinsey's strongly independent streak actually stood in the way of his working as smoothly with equals or superiors as he did with those under him. When Kinsey was first on campus his youthful arrogance and frankly critical attitude of anyone who he felt did not measure up to his professional standards was the subject of comment. A certain professor came under his criticism, and a degree of animosity developed between them, as Kinsey bluntly let it be known that he thought the man should be replaced because, while a good research worker, he was a poor teacher. This critical attitude on Kinsey's part culminated when a few years later he began to find fault with Dr. Eigenmann, whose standing as a scholar in the field of taxonomy was beyond reproach. It is true that Dr. Eigenmann was at this time probably well past his prime as an investigator, and Kinsey's more recent training in the field enabled him to easily criticize the older man's work. The tables were turned when this antagonism led Dr. Eigenmann to decide that the young troublemaker "should be allowed to go." Other department members interceded on Kinsey's behalf and were able to persuade the chairman and dean to change his mind, but it was a close call, according to those who remember the event.

One former student, after pointing out that graduate students are busy developing images for their own future role in the academic world and hence are abnormally curious about the private lives of their professors, wrote this pertinent comment:

> I and my fellow graduate students had the definite impression that Kinsey was a prickly individual for fellow faculty members to live with. Certainly some of the botanists on the first floor of Biology Hall often gave every evidence, even to us, of being unhappy with Kinsey. The Department of Zoology, of course,

consisted of only four people at that time. Payne, with his consummate wisdom and understanding, appreciated Kinsey's abilities, and Scott always worked diligently to keep human relationships within the Department well below the boiling point. At least, that is how the graduate students saw it in the late 'twenties.

In the following decades Kinsey certainly mellowed in many ways. For one thing, he became increasingly urbane in his relationships with his peers. This probably developed from a wider experience with problems of interpersonal contact at many levels, as well as from the growing awareness of his own desperate need for public support from his colleagues and the University administration for his work in sex research. A month after the first volume of his findings on male sex behavior was published, Kinsey wrote a letter of appreciation to Dean Fernandus Payne thanking him for his years of staunch support of Kinsey's dual research in gall wasps and human sex, and he concluded with these sentences:

> It is a privilege to be able to record my indebtedness to you throughout our association of twenty-eight years. . . . You have continued to give your time and attention to finding ways and means for furthering my scientific work. . . . Throughout the years we have agreed upon most matters of policy; and when we have disagreed, we have continued to work together efficiently and comfortably. This is a measure of the considerable independence which you have allowed all of us on the Zoology faculty, throughout these years.

Kinsey was by nature totally unable to cast himself in the role of sycophant. To curry favor by the pretense of flattery was impossible for him. He had difficulty even in later years in curbing his direct and blunt manner. This inability to dissemble undoubtedly handicapped him in some of his relations with the press and public.

During the late 1920's and early 1930's Dr. Kinsey had various graduate students working under him on doctoral programs.[4] He trained them in his taxonomic methods and took them on extensive field trips by car, specifically to collect Cynipidae or gall wasps, but also to train them in collecting techniques. Alone or with his family he had collected many times in areas closer to Bloomington, but the first of these longer excursions was in the late fall of 1926. Ralph Voris accompanied him. Indiana, Kentucky, Illinois, and Missouri were on the itinerary, and the spoils included 20,000 specimens. Successive major trips are recorded in the fall of 1927, 1928, 1929, 1930, and 1934, and may have occurred at other times, although the trips to Mexico in 1931 and 1935 account for those two years. One of the early trips is well described by Herman Spieth, who was along:

> We always stayed in hotels at night, spending the long evening hours sorting and packing the day's collections; every other day or so we mailed these back by parcel post to Bloomington.
>
> For lunch, always eaten in transit, we feasted on peanuts, chocolate, and raisins. This diet did not agree well with Voris, and he was sick part of the time, a fact which the three of us did our best to keep unknown to Kinsey, thinking he would be impatient with such weakness.
>
> The car in which we were riding was relatively new. As I remember, it was Kinsey's first automobile and he was very proud of it. He had learned to drive it only the preceding summer —and I must confess that his passengers often had sinking feelings about their safety.
>
> This was my first trip to the Southeast, but Kinsey had known about the area from earlier collecting trips, and he regaled us with stories about moonshiners and hill people whom he had encountered. He pointed out to us with great earnestness that it was always safer to go unarmed, and advised us strongly never to carry guns when on collecting trips but to use every precaution to win the friendship of the native peoples.

Robert Bugbee, who accompanied him on the 1934 trip which covered the Ozark area, Louisiana, and Mississippi, also describes the chocolate, peanut, and raisin lunch "rations" and adds these details:

> I was always impressed with his knowledge of plants, as well as animals, on field trips for gall collections. His insistence upon a full day's work with an early, hearty breakfast . . . and a sumptuous dinner, plus hours after dinner spent in sorting and labeling the collections of the day, assured maximum utilization of time. His insistence upon a shower, even on the coldest mornings, always meant that we were wide awake, even though we some-

times felt that it was something of an injustice in unheated [tourist cabins] in late October or early November.

If the season had been dry in the area, there were fewer specimens, but this did not discourage Kinsey.[5] He loved the out-of-door life, and the days of freedom away from the college tasks provided an environment much like his early camp days when he was the knowledgeable leader and had willing novices to instruct. These trips were of necessity scheduled in the fall as at that point the galls containing the larvae were mature enough to be harvested and transferred to the laboratory where the breeding could take place. If they were collected earlier they would not emerge the following spring. Later than November the weather was inclement for field work. Some species actually took three to four years to produce a mature insect.

An interesting aspect of Kinsey's treatment of his graduate students is revealed in an account by Spieth of the preparation of his thesis. He had just been moved from a "bull pen" for graduate students on the third floor to a small basement office shared with Ancil Holloway:

> In the peace and quiet of the lonely basement room, my own research began to jell, and I spent most of the year writing my thesis. In the late winter and early spring it was in shape for Kinsey to read the first draft. He had read none of it before, nor had he even spent much time talking with me about it. This, however, was a studied part of his technique, i.e., to let the student work out his own fate. Only if and when something had been written down would Kinsey devote time to the student's method of procedure and writing. Kinsey liked my thesis when he finally read it. In fact, I had the distinct (and I must admit flattering) impression that he was quite surprised. He suggested few changes. In any case, from the time Kinsey read the first draft of the thesis, our relations were much improved and always extremely cordial. He continued to give me great help in many ways, a fact which gave me increasing satisfaction as the years went by.

It was clear that Kinsey was re-enacting his own earlier experiences with Dr. Wheeler, his graduate professor at Harvard; thus a pattern repeated itself.

A much later graduate student, Shelby Gerking, contributes an episode that throws light on Kinsey's passion for orderliness:

> It was Dr. Kinsey's habit, while teaching the evolution course, to have each student prepare a report on a small segment of interest to them and this report was to be given to Dr. Kinsey in oral form. I chose to report on the evolution of fishes and since his office was under repair, it was agreed that he would meet me in my office in the basement of the old Biology Building. The office was in a very unattractive location near the elevator shaft and it was never possible to keep it as neat and clean as I would like. I was engaged in my research at the time and bottles of fish were scattered over the room. My desk was unkempt and littered with paper. On this occasion Dr. Kinsey happened to be about a half-hour late, which was unusual for him, and I took these few minutes to straighten the office and my desk appeared in first class order when he arrived.
>
> Upon entering his eyes strayed to all corners of the room and particularly to my desk. He commented that I was very neat and he was glad to see a graduate student who took pride in his office. The interview about my report on the evolution of fishes proceeded, but it was obvious from the start that I had "passed" without answering any questions. From that time on I had a feeling that Dr. Kinsey and I were closer than ever before.

Dr. Kinsey was helpful and understanding with his graduate students if he liked them, but on the other hand, if he felt he had reason to criticize them, he could be unpleasantly tough. One candidate for a master's degree had been assigned the topic of the life history of the millepede. The coed established a colony of these creatures but, after months of observing them, could not obtain data on any changes. Kinsey was furious when it was suggested to him that he assign her a new, more promising topic. The issue of the departmental vs. the major professor's responsibility for such decisions triggered a real dispute, which of course simmered down in due time.

The promising career of Ralph Voris was cut off by his early death in 1940. He had been the first graduate student to receive his doctoral degree under Kinsey in 1928, and this was a great loss to him. There had been a close bond between them. He, according to Mrs. Kinsey, was the only one among all the younger men who worked with Kinsey in the field, either in "bug collecting" or in sex research, who showed personal concern for Kinsey's welfare and had an influence over him. Kinsey, prone to overtax himself, had such a strong temperament that it was difficult for anyone to step in and protect him against himself. Apparently Voris had this ability.

Kinsey made careful plans for his first field trip to Mexico in the fall of 1931, but it was full of difficulties he had not anticipated. Ancil Holloway and Donald McKeever took the trip with him. The latter was an underclassman knowledgeable about cars who had studied Spanish and hence could help in communicating with the natives. The rebuilt Nash car he used for the tour was not equal to the strain it was put to, and it was crippled en route by twenty broken spring leaves and several cracked oil pans. According to Mrs. Kinsey, the amount the University had allotted for the trip ran out, and Kinsey ended up by paying the extra cost out of his personal funds.

At the border the party experienced an unforeseen delay of a week's precious time. Kinsey had carefully packed enough canned goods to last them for the entire three-and-a-half-month trip. The Mexican customs officials looked at this stock with great suspicion, and it was finally necessary to hire a customs broker to arrange the matter of crossing into Mexico with the reserve canned groceries intact. It was at this time that Kinsey decided to learn to smoke in order to fit in with the Mexican male culture. He reasoned that since all Mexican men were smokers he would have a better chance of dealing with them successfully if he smoked too. Holloway, the graduate student along on the expedition, was his mentor in his practice sessions. Kinsey never really took to smoking, however, and after his return home, the only times his wife can remember seeing him smoke was when he wished to drive the mosquitoes away on a summer's evening in the garden. Much later he smoked now and then when taking sex histories, especially those of the prisoners at the penal farm, where limited bathing and change of clothing led to a typically ripe odor. On the advice of one of his Institute colleagues, he finally gave up smoking as an aid in gaining rapport with his interviewees. This was the result of Wardell Pomeroy's frank observation that Kinsey looked so inexperienced and awkward in the way he handled a cigarette that it did more harm than good in the interviewing relationship.

In both this first Mexican trip and his later one in 1935–36 contacts had been made in advance with the proper authorities in Mexico, who gave their approval and support to the research project. Little entomological work had been done in Mexico on gall wasps, and Dr. Alfons Dampf, an entomologist in the Mexican Ministry of Agriculture, was delighted that this American scientific team was collecting specimens in his country. Later Kinsey named one of the new species he had found (Amphibolips from Oaxaca) in Dampf's honor.

The second Mexican trip was financed by a grant from the National Research Council and also by funds from the University. This trip was more ambitious, and Kinsey was better prepared this time both in transportation and in equipment. He had bought a new half-ton International truck and installed a second gas tank which could be connected when needed by a switch. Back of the seat was a water tank with a connecting pipe and faucet on the outside. Specially built springs had been added. The transmission for a ton-and-a-half truck was installed in Texas after difficulties with the roads in the Big Bend. Four thousand cloth bags for use in returning specimens were included in the supplies. The plans were to cover the eastern and southern Sierra regions of Mexico, shipping the truck by rail on a flatcar from Cordoba, Mexico, to the Guatemala border; and then continuing into Guatemala, where they would board a United Fruit boat, truck included, for the return trip. Kinsey was accompanied by Osmond Breland, his graduate student, and by James H. Coon, an I. U. senior. Coon's parents were good friends of the Kinseys and his father taught classics at the University. The group of three left in October, 1935, and returned in January, 1936. Coon later wrote this graphic report:

> The trip was really an exciting adventure. Kinsey was of course by that time an old hand at such expeditions, but this one was more ambitious than most. To go into the remote mountains

of Mexico and Central America in those days of primitive roads was not a Sunday afternoon jaunt. But Kinsey knew how to plan it so we could travel and eat and sleep and collect galls. The biggest effort of the expedition was travel. Although the trip was planned for the "dry season," the rains and mud were terrible. On one occasion we worked for three hours filling in a stretch of muddy road with branches and rocks. Then Kinsey got a running start and drove thru it. It was nearly impossible to get information about road conditions ahead. The Mexicans would always reply with "Muy bueno" when asked how the road was, even when it was miles of deep mud. And if it wasn't mud, it was a mountain boulder road which you had to crawl along at five miles per hour. Then there were the streams to be forded; the engine must have stalled out dozens of times. Usually if we just waited 15 or 20 minutes, the engine would dry off and we could drive out.

The most exciting event of the trip was the crossing of the suspension bridge we reached soon after entering Guatemala. The bridge was really intended only for carts and pedestrians. But on the map this route was marked Pan American Highway, and it was the only way to proceed. So we hand-carried across every item we could remove from the truck, including the spare tires. Then, with the river gorge 100 feet below, Kinsey got in with a wave and a smile and started driving across. From where Breland and I stood at the far end of the bridge, the sag of the bridge under the weight of the car looked like disaster, but he made it.

In addition to the work involved in traveling, another major occupation on the trip was camping and cooking. We camped out every night except for a few nights when we passed thru big cities: Monterrey, Mexico City, Guatemala City and a couple more. The cities made Kinsey unhappy, partly because we were not among the galls, but also because we were likely to pick up stomach bugs, which apparently we did more than once. When camping, Kinsey was always "chief cook," and he did a fine job of it. Breland and I helped out some and always cleaned up afterward. Typical dinner was macaroni and cheese, cut from a tremendous 40 pound cheese that lasted us most of the way thru the trip. But a couple times Kinsey had a big surprise for us. We had passed thru Quezaltenango, Guatemala, on the day before Xmas, and Kinsey picked up food for a Xmas eve banquet at the camp table: pressure cooker chicken, creamed carrots, rice and gravy, lettuce-asparagus salad, cocoa, plum pudding with lemon sauce!! In contrast with our usual austerity diet it was a real banquet.

I should have said that for lunch we never stopped, just kept moving while we munched on rations of peanuts, raisins, and chocolate—which got pretty tiresome in the course of two-and-a-half months. Kinsey took great delight in handing out these things to the native kids whenever he got the opportunity, and trying to make friends with them. He had also taken along quite a few cartons of cigarettes to help make friends with the Mexicans. His Spanish was quite a bit better than mine or Breland's, so he did most of the communicating with the natives.

Coon comments in closing: "My strongest feeling about Kinsey is that he was in his element when out in the wilds fighting adversity."

After the three men returned to Bloomington they celebrated by entertaining their families at Kinsey's home at a Mexican dinner. They acted as cooks and hosts, and the aluminum serving pans from the trip were once again put to use. Fried bananas were one of the main dishes, but this was not too well received, especially by the Kinsey children, as the variety available locally was not adaptable to the Mexican recipe.

On his return Kinsey wrote his friend Voris:

We are just back from the second Mexican trip with some nine thousand miles to our credit in that country and in Guatemala. It was a very difficult trip, for we were handicapped by unseasonable rains for the first month and a half and by the expected poor roads throughout most of the trip. The mountain grades in Guatemala are terrific, so our average rate was well under ten miles an hour. Again, we discovered to our surprise that oak species are not as abundant in the Eastern Sierra as they were in the Western Sierra and that the White Oaks began to give out in southern Mexico and Guatemala. From the small number of complexes which remained we secured as much of the material as we would from any similar number of complexes in the Western Sierra, but because of the reduced abundance of complexes we brought back only about fifty thousand insects. The two boys on this trip were splendid. Breland is a remarkably good field man with a great flair for bug hunting.

These two trips led to the publication of three journal articles on gall wasps (25, 28, 31), all of which followed his large 1936 volume on the origin of higher categories, in which some of the earlier Mexican material had already been utilized.

In the summer of 1934, when he was in the midst of work on this major study, he had with high enthusiasm sketched out what he anticipated would be his final conclusions after the detailed analysis was complete:

> The complexes and subgenera, and even one genus which is far enough away from Cynips in the U.S.—all run together in southern Mexico until it can be established, I think, that the higher categories are nothing but sections in a continuous chain of species—the divisions between the categories purely arbitrary unless one has limited his collecting to an incomplete portion of the range, or unless nature has obligingly exterminated some of the older species. There is no tree of life—the simile should be to the creeping vine or plant with runners. The first species of the new genus is as closely related to the last species of the old, as any two species are to each other within the genus. Higher categories arise merely as species—by mutation or hybridization and subsequent isolation—with no greater degree of difference than is involved in the origin of any other species.
>
> Amen.

Two of the three articles on the Mexican data were published in the March and October, 1937, issues of *Revista de Entomologia*, a Brazilian journal (25, 28), and the third, a summary paper, the following year in the *Proceedings of the Indiana Academy of Science* (31). In introducing his detailed data, Kinsey wrote that—since Mexican gall wasps represented the continuation of the same phylogenetic lines which are known in the United States—until studies of faunas and floras became continental in scope, ultimate solutions of the evolutionary problems involved could not be arrived at. The fifty-three new species and five new genera he lists in the first two of these papers on the Mexican material brought the total list of Mexican Cynipidae up to 131 species. These will become significant, he cautiously concluded, "as they are fitted into the phylogenetic chains which we are building in an attempt to discover the nature and origin of species, and the nature and origin of the several biologic peculiarities shown by those species. The final studies must, however, await complete revisons of the genera involved."

The actual publication of his final entomological volume, *Origin of Higher Categories*, hung in the balance for more than a year. The publication committee of the University Science Series had doubts as to its merits, and submitted it, in Kinsey's words, "to a taxonomist and a geneticist for criticism. Taxonomist said the taxonomy was O.K. and important, but the genetics unprintably bad. Geneticist said the genetics was sound enough, but the taxonomy certainly not in accord with current work in taxonomy." Annoyed with this uncertainty, Kinsey stored his manuscript in his bank vault while he was in Mexico in 1935–36, and upon his return was able to "include the winter's collections" by a six-month further delay. At this point the committee's doubts had been satisfied, and publication proceeded.

Origin of Higher Categories is a handsome book. Its pages are interspersed with beautifully detailed drawings of insects, which are in some cases superimposed on maps showing the areas of distribution. Many excellent photographs of galls and carefully drawn figures illustrating Kinsey's evolutionary theories appear throughout the text. The bulk of the volume is devoted to a systematic presentation of seventy new species of gall wasps. This is preceded by a sixty-page discussion of Kinsey's new insights into evolutionary theory which he had developed from the study of these and other species. In his summary he wrote:

> Our previous studies have shown that species are realities in nature. But the conclusion is now reached that all of the higher categories are artificial conventions useful for cataloging biologic data, but hardly real either in manner of origin or in their intrinsic qualities. The evolutionary pattern is not that of a "tree of life" in which the main branches represent ancestral stocks which disapppeared as they gave rise by radiate evolution to the species at the ends of the tree. The pattern is that of an infrequently dividing chain in which the oldest species may remain coexistent with all of the derived species. The most diverse ends of such a chain (the higher categories) may be united by series in which each element is a geographic or host isolate of the next in the chain. Apparent discontinuities in such series, due to the

extermination of some species, do not indicate discontinuities in the evolutionary history of a group. Higher categories are not necessarily groups of similar units (e.g. genera are not groups of similar species), and higher categories are not groups of units with a common origin. Higher categories are merely sections inclusive of the smaller sections (the lower categories) in a chain of species. Higher categories may best be defined as arbitrarily limited groups of related species in a phylogenetic chain.

A gift copy was sent in November to his friend Edgar Anderson at St. Louis, who with his light touch and sharp pen replied:

> Just now I am deep in your Olympian thunderings in regards to Cynips. With most of what you say I am in hearty agreement, and most of my disagreements are really in the nature of qualifying phrases. As I read I am making pencilled notations, more or less legible, in the margins. When I finish, if you should have any use for or interest in my precious volume of Kinsey and Anderson, you may obtain it by sending me a nice clean copy of Kinsey.

Kinsey complied by forwarding the "nice clean copy of Kinsey" a few weeks later.

By January the volume had reached the reviewers, and he was elated with its reception. The journal comments were largely favorable, and he mentions in one letter the "lavish praise" of one writer. He continues:

> The geneticists are strong for it—have had most interesting correspondence with a lot of them. Dobzhansky, Sewall Wright, Blakeslee, Anderson, Banta, etc., etc., all quite convinced. Anderson has objected for all these years that I had a very special case in these bugs—that such major mutations were not to be expected in most groups. Now he writes he is quite convinced that it is my method that is unique—that he can believe that the use of as diverse means for recognizing relationships in other groups might show relationships that we have overlooked because of our dependence on morphologic similarity. He was handsome in his acceptance of this at the Atlantic City symposium. A number of the paleontologists have testified that their fossil connecting links make higher categories just what I find them. Even a number of the taxonomists are enthusiastic—tho they as a group offer the most objections. You are going to see a day when taxonomic

contributions will be accepted as a fundamental part of biologic science.

When this 1936 study, which he described as "having been in brew for five years," had been sent off to the press, Kinsey, who was never satisfied with past accomplishments, immediately started a study of a new genus of gall wasps, Xystoteras. He writes about his new project:

> I will finish this in a year or 18 mos. at the rate it is going—and it will cover more ground than the 2 Cynips volumes on which I spent nine years. At long last I may be able to convince somebody that I have been laying a foundation in all those 18 years—on which the finished structure may now rise rapidly. While on Cynips I had to take a year and a half to lay the foundation of the generic rearrangement of the whole family—a matter of 6 months to solve the long-wing, short-wing riddle, much time over many years to make catalogs and accumulate literature—endless technique in preparing collected material for future study. Now, suddenly, it has all come to a head—everything is ready for the new study, and I am writing thousands of specimens and ten or a dozen new species into the manuscript each week. That is the fruition of the dream I have had about building for a life-time of research. But it is a dangerous program if one gets bumped off prematurely!

This description rounds out his image of his life-plan. In fact, it was to be abandoned in a few years, though not by his being "bumped off."

Modern genetics is a very different science from the one that Kinsey knew. But he evolved his theories strictly from his data, and according to authorities, his "hunches" were basically correct in a farsighted way. As newer theories in the field evolved—based not on subsamples but on major populations—Kinsey had lost his interest in these problems.

One of Kinsey's own pleasures which he shared generously with his students was his interest in music and his ever-growing record collection. A fair number of his former assistants and graduate students, as well as colleagues, recall with pleasurable nostalgia the evenings spent in his home listening to good music. The programs varied, but usually had a theme, with a musical style, period, or instrumentation to link the selections. Later Kinsey formalized the occasion by prefacing each record with a brief introduction about the composer, period, or composition itself. By then the evening's music was carefully pre-timed, with the heavier, more imposing selections played first, before refreshments, and the lighter part after. Kinsey rarely played a record on demand, except to illustrate a point under discussion. He disliked anything that destroyed the unity of his planned program. Some of the first of these sessions were held following student seminars at his house on Sunday evenings. Later, Wednesday nights were reserved for students and Sundays for his interested friends and acquaintances. Finally, the student group was dropped after he had less and less personal contact with them.

At times he helped out by taking selected records over to the Alumni Hall in the Union Building, where record concerts for larger undergraduate groups were held. On one of these evenings, around 1938 or 1939, as a participant recalls it, with the large hall about a third filled with a student audience, he had played some classical waltzes among other selections. Next, she recounts:

> When he had finished, he remarked with his zestful smile that we ought to have the experience of dancing to Strauss, that he had no official clearance to hold a dance, but that if we'd fold up the chairs and stack them, he'd spin the Strauss records for us. Some twenty (at a guess) couples of us danced and danced and danced, in an exciting gaiety at the slightly mad speed of concert waltz time, while Dr. Kinsey chuckled and patiently replayed records till we were all breathless and very happy.

Some of his young protégées in his laboratory were not inclined to become involved in the evening record concerts even though they appreciated the invitation to join the group. Thus one coed of the 1930's writes in retrospect:

> We were also invited to the "music nights"; and although I think I never went to but one of these, he never failed to extend the regular, informal invitation: "Music tonight, remember. Mrs. Kinsey and I both hope you'll be able to come." Sometimes he would remark upon a new recording which he had just ordered or received and which he would play that evening. . . . I remem-

ber asking my co-worker after the first of these invitations what sort of affair "music tonight" was. "No one can describe it to you exactly," she said. "You'll have to go, once, and see for yourself. It's kind of nice. Everybody just sits around in a circle and listens to music. You know, classical music. Records. Dr. Kinsey tends the record player. He's very particular about it. He always uses a cactus needle of a certain kind and I think he counts the number of times he uses it. Nobody talks. Some of the graduate students try to be dreadfully highbrow and appreciative. There's always at least one not very pretty girl wearing glasses who listens with her eyes closed and her mouth soulfully open. . . . And afterward Mrs. Kinsey serves refreshments on the Mexican plates. It's really rather nice. You'll like Mrs. Kinsey."

I went once, as I said, and she was right. It was rather nice. Mrs. Kinsey served persimmon pudding. . . . I admired the lovely design of the Mexican plates. And I did like Mrs. Kinsey. Very much. But youth is self-conscious. I was not educated enough to make highbrow remarks and I would not be one of the soulful, mouth-open listeners.[6]

Kinsey, like many other professors, exerted himself to help his newly-graduated students find satisfactory teaching positions. This activity on his part was mostly during the 1930's when the pall of the Depression still hung over the land. His personal letter files of these years are filled with the records of his often futile efforts to assist these highly trained men in finding decent jobs at living wages. An $800 a year salary offered by a tiny teachers' college at a Western outpost has him aghast, and he loans small sums from his own funds when financial situations become unendurable. He writes: "I have really felt depressed over your difficulties for several years," to one whose salary failed to be paid because municipal taxes supporting the college had shrunk. To another he offers financing for an expensive trip East to be interviewed for a better position. The students' letters glow with grateful thanks for his help and encouragement.

At times Kinsey did yeoman's service on the interminable standing committees with which all universities seem to be plagued. He served, for example, on the committee which recommended the establishment of a University Council—forerunner of the present Faculty Council—and served on the

Council itself from 1929 to 1931. He was a hard-working member of the committee which, during 1929–30, drafted the newly required program of studies for students in the College of Arts and Sciences, and his name is among those assigned to present proposals for a new system for departmental chairmanships.

An anecdote from a former assistant shows Kinsey's occasional intolerance for wasting his time on such matters. She wrote: "Dr. Kinsey was equally impatient of faculty behavior at committee and other administrative meetings. On occasion he came back to the Lab after such a session, exclaiming, 'What nonsense!' "[7]

When plans for a University Ten-Year Program were initiated in 1927, faculty members were canvassed for their ideas on how the larger interests of the University could be promoted. Kinsey's answer is a remarkable document. Its recommendations incorporated much of the future thrust of the University. In his forward-looking suggestions he placed particular emphasis on library expansion and the need for staffing the graduate school with "men who are moving ahead of the scholarship of their own day."

Kinsey concerned himself with several campus organizations. One of these was Phi Beta Kappa, the other Sigma Xi. In the late thirties he served as president of each of them. One of his chief concerns in his Phi Beta Kappa work was the noneligibility of the student who had graduated with a B.S. rather than a B.A. degree. He felt that this ruling unfairly eliminated many superior students who expected to be doctors or college science teachers. Kinsey argued that it should make no difference what degree they received as long as they had the required credits in language and cultural subjects. He was ahead of his time on this matter. A former associate of his on the executive committee of the organization commented: "His clear and logical presentations of the facts year after year were a delight to hear, even if they fell on some deaf ears. His ideas are generally accepted now." Somewhat earlier he led in a broader movement against the general tendency to award Phi Beta Kappa election to graduate students for work done on their advanced degrees, and to emphasize rather the recognition of undergraduate achievement.

Kinsey's style of writing was closely related to his speaking style. He was a master of clear, direct expository prose.

He tutored the graduate students writing under him to follow the same path. One states: "I remember his wisdom in suggesting the elimination of unnecessary modifying adjectives and greater economy of statement. His own style was terse and lucid." Editors who worked with him on his textbooks similarly recall "the meticulous care with which the copy was prepared." As Mrs. Cecilia Hendricks, a long-time associate of his in the work of the Indiana chapter of Phi Beta Kappa, commented:

> His ability to use language clearly, accurately, and succinctly was admirable. I have often thought this clearness of thinking and expression was his finest achievement. Of course he knew the subject matter accurately, but no one could state a point or defend a position with his clarity and brevity.

After his return from his second Mexican trip and a few months before the end of President Bryan's administration, Kinsey, somewhat disillusioned, grew increasingly dissatisfied with the administrative situation on the campus. In a confidential letter to a close friend he wrote: "The President is seventy-five years old and unwilling to settle any question, large or small. The whole University is in a mess; we get nothing done apart from the ancient routine—I would leave at the first opportunity offering comparable recompense and research opportunities." He was forty-one years old at the time and probably at the apex of his career as an entomologist, with two major works behind him and a large part of his Mexican collected specimens still to be examined and classified.

By June, 1937, President Bryan had retired. A few months before doing so he sent a letter with this handsome tribute to Kinsey:

> I never urge anybody to go in for research. A man should not go in for it unless he cannot help it. When a man has the mind and the will for worthwhile research, everything should be done to clear his path.
>
> I have rejoiced always in what you have the ability to do and what you do. It is an extreme satisfaction for a man in my position to aid such a man as you to do his work.

With the advent of the new administration of Acting President (later President) Herman B Wells, the picture shifted and Kinsey took heart. His more hopeful, yet cautious, attitude is reflected in this passage in a confidential letter to a friend during Wells' first year:

> I am not yet certain that I want to fix my future here. If it comes out right in this shuffle, I. U. will be a good place to stay; if it is screwed up as some things threaten to be, I shall be in the market for another job. Some place where there is active genetic work, and a graduate program that allows a better grounding for taxonomic-cytologic-genetic studies. Perhaps we can build that here.

A few weeks later he sounds more certain of the new administration:

> The new president is giving us an opportunity to get things done that were never interesting to the old administration; there is a faculty survey committee of men of my own age, and it is a great oppprtunity for men of my generation to put ideas across. Lots of time being spent with them.

Various honors came to Kinsey during this period. In the fall of 1937 he became a "starred scientist"; his name in *American Men of Science* would be starred to indicate this coveted distinction. Such names were chosen by a vote of the outstanding biologists in the country. In April of 1938 he was elected to the executive committee of the American Association for the Advancement of Science at their meeting at Columbus, Ohio. One of the duties of this committee was to survey contributions of science to college cultural programs and to evaluate methods of college teaching.

Attempts were made several times to get Kinsey admitted to the National Academy of Sciences, but he was always blackballed by someone. Many felt that he well deserved this honor and was clearly a better candidate than many who were selected. While Kinsey never admitted it, he felt this slight keenly. Now and then he would take occasion to make fun of the Academy and its stodginess.

Vacation trips with his family interspersed these years of the early 1930's. In the summer of 1931 they traveled to Colorado to give Clara and the children their first view of

Western mountains. Mesa Verde National Park was the goal. They followed the Million Dollar Highway, from Ouray to Silverton, so named because of the gold-bearing gravels used in its base. Car trouble developed at Pinkerton's Springs, close to the east edge of the Continental Divide. Repair parts had to be ordered from Denver and sent by train to Durango, where the dismantled car waited. The impatient family was marooned for several days in the Pinkerton Springs tourist cabins and lodge. It was just as well, since there was time to mend the ugly blisters on Kinsey's heels, which he had acquired on the fourteen-mile tramp back from Durango after leaving the car there.

In 1936 the family set out for the familiar White Mountains in New Hampshire, traveling through Canada. They camped with the sturdy truck and other equipment that had been used on the second Mexican expedition earlier that year. Anne, then twelve, remembers it especially well because the children had their first encounter with finger bowls at the summer home of their "Aunt Bartie" at Lake Charleston in Leeds County, Ontario. This was the aunt who was a nurse at St. Luke's Hospital in New York and after whom their mother had been named. She and a longtime friend, Miss Webster, who lived together, were at their lakeside summer home. The contrast between the Kinsey family's grubby camping style and the superelegant table service struck them as very funny and became a family joke. Later Miss Webster, after looking into Kinsey's first volume on male sexual behavior, remarked that "fish were the only decent animals."

The next year brought a tour to the Smoky Mountains, where they climbed Mount Le Conte and explored Cades Cove. Of this trip Kinsey had written in anticipation: "Only 1000 miles to drive in all the 10 days—leaving plenty of time to climb mountains and browse thru the deep forests." In 1938 the family drove to Florida for their late summer vacation. The camping equipment went along but was used only once during the fifteen-day trip. Kinsey wrote to a colleague:

> We had a glorious stretch of hot sunshine and endless ocean beaches for bathing. I, for one, am glad that we did not come

north, for at that late date in the summer we too have found the northern lakes just too cold for comfort.

Kinsey took his last real field trip to collect gall wasp specimens during the summer of 1939. For the first time Clara, as well as his ten-year-old son Bruce, accompanied him. Their goal was to revisit sites where he had found samples of an exceedingly variable species ten years earlier. The hope was that these more recent specimens would serve as a revalidation of his original findings and possibly reveal new variations within the species.

The three-week trip took them first through Missouri and Kansas to Denver and on to Steamboat Springs, Colorado. Crossing over into Utah, they passed through Ogden, Salt Lake City, Provo, and Tooele, collecting specimens at specific sites as they went. Near Castlegate they sought in vain to sample the species collected there a decade earlier. Stops at Manti and Richfield led the way to Bryce Canyon and the North Rim in Arizona. The trip home took them through Holbrook, Arizona; Amarillo, Texas; and Springfield, Missouri. Motels were substituted for camping, as a time saver, but outdoor lunches were still part of the daily routine. Photographs from the trip show the young Bruce with cloth bags bulging with specimens piled high around him.

In all but one case the galls were just as abundant as they had been ten years before. For Kinsey this threw an interesting light on the continuation of local colonies. Of the total of twenty-one collections "more than half were made in a cold rain," he wrote to Voris, who had accompanied him on the trip ten years earlier. "So Mrs. Kinsey and Bruce got a typical introduction to our bug collecting," he added.

Although the material was successfully gathered it was never fully studied. Other interests and new responsibilities were by now absorbing more and more of Kinsey's time, and his hope of finding a competent technician to whom he could relegate the task of making twenty painstaking measurements on each of the tiny insects failed to materialize. This was the final family trip to the West. Commitment to research in human sex behavior would soon demand a very different kind of field work.

6.

The Pivotal Years (1938-41)

T HE LATTER PART OF THE 1930'S WAS THE
turning point in Alfred Kinsey's professional life. Hitherto
he had followed a fairly typical course for a hard-working
academic biologist. Graduate training, a teaching job, marriage and family, field work, professional publications, textbook writing—all of these could be duplicated in the lives of
hundreds of college professors. He had won considerable success in his chosen field, but so had many others. The events
that led up to his spectacular shift of research fields at age
forty-four are worth careful examination.

Kinsey came to the study of human sex behavior as a
biologist, not a social reformer. Essentially a taxonomist, he
gradually became aware of a new, little cultivated field that
lent itself perfectly to taxonomic exploration. Eventually this
new field absorbed his entire interest, and his gall wasps were
neglected. But though primarily a scientist, he was well aware
of the human, social, and educational implications of his new
scientific labors.

The beginning of his active work in sex research is usually, and correctly, traced to a marriage course initiated at Indiana University in the summer of 1938, in which Kinsey took a leading part. Yet there are earlier evidences both of a concern with the problems of sex behavior and of the crusading spirit with which he pursued and defended his studies in this field.

In 1919 Kinsey's graduate professor at Harvard, William Morton Wheeler, wrote a famous article comparing the society of termites with that of human beings, to the detriment of the latter.[1] Wheeler's parable thinly masks a sharp criticism of social ills that could be ameliorated by scientific means if approached in a totally rational fashion. In 1919 no reputable scientist could have spoken out openly on the topics he treated—euthanasia, birth control, eugenics, and prohibition. Wheeler successfully used his fable to level barbed shafts at society's illogic in facing problems of its own making. This essay pleased and amused Kinsey, and he remembered it long after he had left Harvard. Several of his associates at Indiana have recalled him chuckling over it at his desk and lending a reprint of it to favored graduate students.

But by far the most solid evidence of Kinsey's interest in and awareness of sex research as a field for scientific investigation prior to his work in the marriage course is found in his first letter to Dr. Robert L. Dickinson. Their contact began in June, 1941, after the appearance of Kinsey's earliest article on sex, "Criteria for a Hormonal Explanation of the Homosexual," which was published in the *Journal of Clinical Endocrinology* (34). Dr. Dickinson, a famous New York gynecologist, had long been a leader in sex education, maternal health, and birth control work. He wrote that he was impressed with Kinsey's "scholarly and important contribution to the study of homosexuality." The letter is written in longhand and Dickinson comments, "You see I do not even wait for a stenographer before greeting the discovery of a discoverer." Kinsey responded: "It was your own work which turned my attention to the purposes of research in this field *some 10 or 12 years ago* although circumstances were not propitious for starting the work until three years ago."* If

*Italics added.

this statement is accurate, Kinsey was *already* aware of such studies *in 1929 or 1931*. Since Dickinson's first book, *A Thousand Marriages*, was published in 1931, it would be reasonable to assume that this was the date Kinsey had in mind. Later, after the two had met in New York, Kinsey wrote: "Be assured again that your published work was one of the original sources of inspiration for our own study." This evidence clearly indicates that the germ of a sex research project was present in Kinsey's mind some years before he began his marriage course in 1938.

Campus lectures furnish further clues to his basic concern for society's impact on man and the resulting problems and dislocations. A discussion club to which Kinsey belonged provided him with a sounding board of friendly colleagues for his ideas on these subjects. Since he typically spoke from brief notes or none at all, only one of the more than a dozen talks given to the club exists in manuscript form. It was delivered in April, 1935, and is titled "Biologic Aspects of Some Social Problems." This is a strongly worded but thoughtful exposition of the influence of social institutions on sexual and reproductive behavior. It predated the marriage course by three years, and it provides convincing evidence of his early interest in and concern for the problems arising from the social restrictions on man's biologic nature. Two passages in particular are significant. On page ten he cites "the ignorance of sexual structure and physiology, of the technique fundamental in the normal course of sexual activities, and the prudish aversion to adequate participation in the one physiologic activity on which society is most dependent, as the chief sources of psychic conflict and resulting broken marriages." He also refers to the works of G.V. Hamilton and of Katharine B. Davis in 1929, as well as to the study by Robert Latou Dickinson and Lura Beam in 1931, showing his familiarity at that time with these early pioneering studies in sex behavior.

Later, after a digression on eugenics and differential fertility, this pertinent passage occurs:

Most of the social problems and the sexual conflicts of youth are the result of the long frustration of the normal sexual activities. Thus delayed marriage, especially among the educated classes, is likely not to occur at all. Biologically, delayed marriage is all wrong. Every increase in the enrollment in our institutions of higher learning, every encouragement toward additional work for advanced degrees, every economic factor which makes it difficult for the young man and woman to get along, every cultural trend, every Union Building and fraternity house which elevates their standards as to the comfortable minimum on which they care to found a home, contributes to the extent of the biologic disturbance.

Finally, two events of the 1920's are evidence of Kinsey's sympathy for students' problems and his zeal in what he considered a good cause. On two separate occasions the student literary magazine tangled with the University administration on an issue of censorship. The editors attempted to publish material that did not meet faculty standards of propriety, and their cases were brought before the proper disciplinary bodies. The exact circumstances of the earlier event seem lost in time, but it involved young Phil Rice, now dead. He was a promising, brilliant student, who went on to an outstanding academic career. He was befriended by Kinsey when he came up before the student affairs committee for discipline on his too free editing of the *Vagabond*, and he often mentioned his debt to Kinsey for interceding in his behalf.

The second incident occurred in the spring of 1927, when, as the story is reported, the term "phallic worship on campus" along with other unacceptable phrases had appeared in the magazine. Charges were presented by the Dean of Men to an assembly of all male members of the faculty. Since not all of those present understood the meaning of the term "phallic worship," the classics professor was asked by the Dean to explain it. One now retired faculty member who was present recalls the scene vividly. Kinsey stood up to voice a strong defense of the two culprits. He argued eloquently that young people had a natural impulse to try their elders by exhibiting their animal spirits, and felt that suspension or expulsion was far too severe a punishment for a mere prank. He failed to influence the outcome, however, and the academic career of a young writer was blasted. It is clear from these early incidents that Kinsey, when he felt the issues at stake were worth it, was not intimidated by the solidly conservative elements in the faculty and administration.

In the summer of 1938 a noncredit marriage course, at that time a pioneering venture, was introduced at Indiana University. The first session was attended by ninety-eight curious seniors, graduate students, faculty members, and faculty wives who signed up to attend the twelve lectures. A petition to institute such a course for college seniors had been presented to the Board of Trustees by the Association of Women Students that spring. According to a letter of July 9 from President Wells to Dr. Kinsey, the trustees agreed that the course should be offered. Its content, method, and material were to be placed in the hands of a seven-member faculty committee, of which Dr. Kinsey was asked to serve as chairman. Three important recommendations had been included in the student petition. They were that it should be a noncredit course for seniors only; that it should cover a wide range of topics, including legal, economic, biological, sociological, and psychological aspects of marriage; and that men and women should attend the lectures, together. The committee from the Association of Women Students, headed by Miss Cecilia Hendricks (now Mrs. Henry Wahl), evidently had worked out these stipulations in meetings in Kinsey's office the preceding spring.

Before working with the students in planning the course, Kinsey had conferred with Mrs. Cecilia Hendricks, Cecilia's mother and a member of the English Department, to make sure that, in her words, "the girls and their elders were in accord on the subject." Mrs. Hendricks' account of their conference continues:

> His chief question was whether or not the planned lectures should be forthright and scientific, or merely avoid the subject. I assured him my idea was that a course that avoided any of the necessary material was worth little or nothing, and that I approved heartily of a course that gave all the anatomical information as well as the legal and philosophical details on marriage. He was interested in my account of a series of such lectures given by an Indianapolis woman doctor to the women students in 1905 and thereabouts when the information was veiled and garbled, with no real value except to frighten the weak. A regular staff had to be on hand to carry out the ones who fainted each time. Those

of us who had hoped for real information ceased attending after the second lecture and spent the hour playing tennis. I assured Dr. Kinsey such lectures were wasted time by all concerned. He agreed, and the lectures he gave were direct and clear for the purpose of giving exact information to both men and women on physical relations and changes.

Thus Kinsey's appointment to chair the committee, which, in the words of President Wells, "will be given full responsibility for the handling of such a course," could have come as no surprise to him. The final provision in the President's letter, that all material in individual conferences "is to be considered confidential, and that it is not to be available to the disciplinary deans," is of special significance. It may have slightly tilted open the lid of Pandora's box. Kinsey wrote a note of acceptance to President Wells including these oddly prophetic words: "Thanks for all the support which you have lent to the consummation of this program. I trust that the history will justify its existence."

Eight faculty members served as staff for the first session of the course. These ranged from Dr. Edith Schumann, Director of the Student Health Service, to Fowler Harper from the law school, Harvey Locke in sociology, and Edmund Conklin in psychology. Economic aspects of marriage were presented by my husband, Carroll Christenson, while Alfred Kohlmeier of the history department lectured on the ethical aspects of married life. That the emphasis, however, would be primarily on the biologic background might have been foreseen. Kinsey's three lectures—"The Biological Bases of Society," "Reproductive Anatomy and Physiology," and "Individual Variation"—plus two by Robert Kroc, his colleague in the zoology department, on "The Endocrine Basis of Sex and Reproduction" and "Human Sterility," gave a strong biological and physiological bias to the course. A carefully tallied attendance sheet shows a ninety-four per cent attendance at the twelve lectures.

In September Kinsey wrote to a friend:

The Marriage Course was a huge success. The students filled out detailed questionnaires at the end of the course, and we have their reactions to each item. This provides some guide for some modifications; but particularly gives us assurance that we are on the right track in meeting their needs.

To the President he sent a summary of the student answers to the questionnaire and added:

> You will be interested to know that the personal case history work bids fair to become one of the most significant parts of our program. The 32 cases handled by the biologists this summer was a startling indication of the need of such work on the campus. . . .
> We appreciate the interest you have taken in the course, and I should be glad to tell you more about it whenever you wish.

These first case histories which Kinsey collected were apparently in the form of self-administered questionnaires. Students who had questions were asked to cooperate in a scientific experiment by answering some questions themselves.

On September 30, 1938, he wrote to one of his first respondents: "We have over fifty case histories—complete questionnaires of the sort you filled out for us—already in our files. They help mightily in giving us backgrounds. We must accumulate more. If you know 'victims' for additional questionnaires, refer them to us."

Kinsey was handicapped by the lack of privacy in his office —a desk blocked off by cabinets in the corner of an open laboratory room. How he met this problem when he was interviewing for a sex history is described by one of his former lab assistants:

> I do know that upon occasion even before the "conferences" that resulted in great number after the institution of the marriage course, we girls were asked to take our work into an adjoining room after a sudden lowering of voices in the course of a routine sort of conversation with a graduate student; and during the first months after the course began we began to find for the first time that we might come to work and find the office door closed. Knocking, we were requested to take our work into the other room; and while we collected our materials, great silence reigned —accompanied perhaps by some, to us, more or less obvious discomfiture on the part of Dr. Kinsey's companion, particularly if he happened to be an acquaintance of ours, as frequently

happened in those days when the campus population was smaller.[2]

Thus, while the emphasis in his letter to Wells was on the consultation part of the interview—which included answers to questions raised by students—there is no doubt that even at this early point the collecting of sexual data from his conferees was of significant interest to him. It was soon after this that he shifted from the questionnaire format to the personal interview. Kinsey and Kroc worked together in this early period developing the questions used in the interview. They would try out the exact wording and sequence of questions on themselves during their lunch hours together in their offices. Kinsey also designed an efficient positional code for recording the answers. A single blank sheet of paper, ruled off into nearly three hundred spaces, sufficed for most cases. A second sheet was later developed for more extensive and elaborated histories.

As he worked with the face-to-face interview Kinsey came to believe strongly in its great advantages over the questionnaire.[3] He cited the development of rapport, the steady assurance of the investigator's objectivity by his manner and voice, and the increased trust in confidentiality as the recording in code is observed. In addition, the interviewer could shift his vocabulary to suit the locale and the educational level of the respondent. This was particularly important as Kinsey recognized very early that many people, especially at the upper educational levels, lack an adequate sexual vocabulary. Cross-checks could be used to determine veracity or accuracy while the interview was in progress. Personal interviewing shortened the time required to take a history, resulting in a higher level of attention and lessened fatigue. The interviewer could also shorten the interview time by skipping over nonpertinent sections at will. Counterbalancing these advantages was the difficulty of finding and training competent interviewers and of standardizing their approach. Since for several years Kinsey himself was doing all the interviewing, this did not present a problem in the beginning.

When the marriage course was offered during the fall semester of 1938, it had been expanded to sixteen lectures. The attendance was more than doubled with 207 persons signed up. Another sociologist, John Mueller, had been added to the staff as well as a visitor to the campus, Dr. Raymond Pearl. Pearl, an eminent biologist from the Johns Hopkins University, who had been appointed to deliver the 1938 Patten Foundation lectures, gave five public talks based on the general topic, "Man the Animal," during the month of October. He also served as a guest lecturer before various campus groups, including the marriage course. The Pearls were entertained by various faculty families and Mrs. Kinsey recalls that the Pearls attended the musical evenings at their home. She and Dr. Kinsey also took them with friends to the Abe Martin Lodge at nearby Brown County State Park for dinner. Kinsey wrote:

> Raymond Pearl is with us for six or eight weeks. . . . He is a very pleasant individual to get along with, and Mrs. Pearl is charming and most brilliant. I begin to suspect that much of the pep in the *Quarterly Review of Biology* is due to her editing. His hobby is music, and so we are seeing a good deal of him at our house. It is an especially rare opportunity, because I am starting work on this variable-winged Utah species. A good part of it is going to be a purely biometric study of individual variation, and there is no one in the world better equipped to guide me on that than Raymond Pearl. He seems very much interested in my research. When I told him that someone else would have to handle the mathematics of the material, he told me that when one has such quantities of material as I have it needs very little mathematical manipulation. He points out that statistical theory is largely a substitute for adequate data. All of this encourages me greatly. We are scheduled for a long session together on the subject of sampling, pretty soon.

Thus, while it is doubtful if Pearl played a decisive role in encouraging Kinsey to center his interest in sex research—a field which Pearl had already touched on in his population studies—he undoubtedly did make an imprint with his advice on sample size and statistical theory. He also suggested Frank Edmondson from the University astronomy department as a first-rate person to turn to for statistical advice. Pearl generously invited Kinsey to come to his laboratory at Johns Hopkins to work on his gall wasp data. He wrote later, reissuing the invitation:

> I hope you have not forgotten the tentative plan, which I had hoped by this time would be by way of becoming definitely fixed, to come along here with your material and settle down in the laboratory for a while next autumn. I am sure we could help you in the work on your problem. In particular I am in the midst now of working out quite a novel approach to the biometric treatment of data such as yours. I feel certain that this new technique would be particularly useful in your problem.

By midsummer of 1939 Kinsey, already swept up into his sex history field work, decided that he could not afford to be sidetracked by such a visit, and he answered:

> I fear that I shall not get to your laboratory this next fall. I have a bad habit of carrying several strings along at the same time; ultimately it all gets done, but there are too many things that need attention here right now to allow me to get away for any time. . . . I still hope that I may come to you later for help.

Kinsey had earlier avoided statistical analysis in his gall wasp studies and seemed uncertain of how to approach the problem. Pearl died at sixty-one, two years after his stay on the Indiana campus. Thus Kinsey's hopes of a visit to work out details of his analysis of data on his variable-winged species in Pearl's laboratory never materialized.

The marriage course was given six times in all in successive school terms with Dr. Kinsey as the chief lecturer and coordinator. In the final session, with fourteen lectures, it reached a peak enrollment of almost four hundred. Over the two years it was changed somewhat in format. Dr. William Reed, a Bloomington physician, as well as Bernard Gavit of the law school, C. M. Louttit, a psychologist, and J. E. Moffat of the Department of Economics joined the staff. Father Thomas J. Kilfoil presented "A Catholic Interpretation of Marriage" in the fall session in 1939, and to balance this the Reverend William E. Moore from the local Christian Church gave the Protestant point of view in the spring of 1940. Freshmen and sophomores were by now allowed to enroll with their parents' written permission.

This new program would have had small consequence for

Kinsey's future except for the "conferences" he was holding in increasing numbers with students who wished to ask questions or to discuss their personal problems. The exact number of such interviews connected directly with the course which Kinsey himself held is not recorded, but they were many. In a letter to President Wells in the spring of 1939, after the close of the third session of the course, he explained:

> The personal conferences between students and the staff have increased considerably during the year. A number of the staff have rendered service in this connection. Naturally, I have had the largest number of questions concerning sexual adjustments. So far during this one semester, I have met 258 students in personal conferences. This has given us a wealth of experience which should make us increasingly valuable to our students, and has at the same time provided some of the data which will determine our future program in presenting biological material to the Marriage Course.

Just when Kinsey grew to realize the real long-range potential of the research material which these individual conferences produced is difficult to pinpoint. The shift of viewpoint from seeing the conferences in the light of information and counseling sessions to considering them primarily as a source of research data was probably gradual. He actually stopped giving advice to subjects in 1939–40 and would only suggest in response to questions that they look at the data together. To collect data while giving therapeutic help in the course of a single interview presents obvious difficulties. Persons close to the early period of the research have been struck by the fact that Kinsey really took little interest in the element of therapy. The time-consuming character of treatment—if he had assumed the responsibility of providing it—they observe, would surely have bogged down the whole effort to gather data. Kinsey was well aware of the lack of scientific information on sex questions, and there were earlier instances of his graduate students asking him questions that he could not answer. The original aim in the interview was certainly a combination of giving out information or advice and fact-finding which would aid him in furnishing valid answers to further questions. In order to furnish such answers he discovered that he usually needed to ask the student further questions to gain insight into the real dynamics of individual sexual behavior. Even though his findings were based on very small samples at this early point, he soon started summarizing the results in his marriage course lectures. Thus he achieved an immediacy and significance which he felt added greatly to his presentation.

While Raymond Pearl was a visiting lecturer on campus he was well aware that Kinsey was starting to gather sexual data in his student interviews. Robert Kroc, the zoology department colleague who assisted with the marriage course lectures, recalls that Pearl urged Kinsey to formalize and systematize this information with a view to ultimate publication.

Pearl's *The Natural History of Population* was published by the Oxford University Press early in 1939. In March Pearl sent Kinsey an autographed copy inscribed "With warmest regards." In his chapter "The Biology of Fertility" Pearl summarized the available statistics on the frequency of human coitus and included data from cases he had gathered himself. This presentation must have served as a further incentive to Kinsey to push ahead with the gathering of his own case history material. Pearl, a top ranking biologist, clearly contributed toward opening the door for a scientific approach to the statistical study of human sexual behavior.

A recognition of the possible research value of the data Kinsey was collecting is reflected in a letter written to Pearl a year after the start of the marriage course program. Kinsey explained that the interview material was being systematized with "something like 250 items on each student," and that at this point there were "over 350 complete histories." Then follows the rather diffident remark: "This should be of some scientific interest someday."

But only a week later in a more informal letter to a former graduate student he admits a much greater sense of the future importance of his interviews: "The personal conferences are giving us a set of histories that are invaluable, and I begin to wonder if this is not going to account for the largest volume of research I will yet publish."

Just before Christmas, 1939, he wrote again: "Our case

histories have proved a gold mine," and to another friend he termed them "a scientific gold mine." He continued: "I have developed numerous contacts outside of the University which are bringing us histories. I have made 5 trips to Chicago, where I am getting a variety wider than is possible within the college population."

It was clearly during the interval between these letters that Kinsey developed and put into execution his idea of incorporating a larger and more varied sample of subjects than the marriage course enrollees or convenient students could furnish him. His first out-of-town trips for the histories appear to have been to Chicago, beginning in June, 1939. He would leave Bloomington after his last class on Friday, drive the more than two-hundred miles to Chicago, work straight through the weekend, and drive back to Bloomington in time for an 8:30 class on Monday morning. This matched his later program of interviewing at the Indiana State Farm, a state jail for misdemeanants at Putnamville. By the end of the year he had made six trips to Chicago. He was now working in a community where he had few contacts and it was an uphill job at the start to establish himself. He recalled in a letter six months after the event that it had taken him "five days to persuade three people to contribute. Now I can pick them up at five to seven per day," he continues, "as fast as I can get time to make the records. Each case leads to other introductions; there are half a dozen centers from which I am making contacts on this trip."

Some of these interviews were primarily for homosexual histories, but along with them was a mixture of divorce cases made available to him by an investigator for a state committee, and also histories of big-city prostitutes. Of the homosexual histories he wrote that they were "the most marvelous *evolutionary* series—disclosing as prime factors such economic and social problems as have never been suggested before, and a simple biologic basis that is so simple that it sounds impossible that everyone hasn't seen it before." It is clear that his heterosexual-homosexual rating scale, to be published in his 1948 volume, was already evolving in his thinking.

By this time his enthusiasm was unbounded and he describes his work as a "research project that is growing constantly more exciting." There was a total of 570 histories by now, 500 of them added in the past twelve months. He writes:

It is the most complete, exhaustive record ever had on single individuals, and already 2½ times as much in quantity as the best published study has. While agreeing with previous studies as far as they go, our data go much further. Since we are getting entirely new types of histories and still new slants on interpretations, as we get additional histories, it becomes clear that we need many more before we have begun to tap the true study of human sexual behavior. Will get my first thousand men in another year or so, when I will publish the first findings. The thousand women will be accumulated a bit more slowly.

To another correspondent he explained that his work was "developing into a long-time research project that should command attention from biologists, psychologists, sociologists, and others."

In the beginning of his work in this new field Kinsey had few associates to whom he could turn for support and encouragement. He had formerly leaned heavily on Ralph Voris, the first graduate student to complete a degree under him. Voris' death in May, 1940, as mentioned earlier, had a heavy psychological impact on him. After Kinsey had returned from the Voris funeral in Springfield, Missouri, he wrote to a mutual friend:

It is a very great loss to me. I had traveled more miles with him than anyone else. I so regret the fact that there were not more contacts in the last ten years. It has greatly broken me up. ... I never had a chance to discuss with Ralph the endless things that this new study of mine has developed. He would have understood so much better than almost anyone else. Now it becomes increasingly imperative that you help me in my thinking on this.

He is clearly seeking to counterbalance his sorrow over Voris' death by reaching for a new allegiance, a groping that would not have been revealed except for his shattering grief.

Later in May he wrote regarding his August plans: "If I get the funds, I shall probably take my vacation in Chicago or St. Louis gathering histories." It would appear that the die as to where he would place his energies had really been cast.

Mrs. Kinsey recalls the origin of one of his important early off-campus contacts for interviews. A routine conference was held with a student whose home was in one of the northern Indiana industrial towns. The young student, who was taking courses in the government department, was confused and upset because his own experiences in city politics and underworld patterns were so at odds with what his professors were talking about in his classes. Kinsey became interested in the young man's firsthand account of illicit sex and commercialized vice. He accepted the student's invitation to visit his home town and to be introduced to shady characters of a type he would not be likely to meet in his academic environment. His subsequent trips for interviews, made alone on weekends and financed out of his own funds, opened another new world to him.

It was this spill-over into off-campus interviewing that made it feasible for Kinsey's taxonomic approach to be applied to his new field of investigation. Dr. Frank N. Young of the University Department of Zoology pointed out in a 1955 paper that Kinsey's success in studying human behavior resulted in part from the application of such taxonomic methods as "an insistence upon massive series, wide geographical coverage, and detailed analysis of every biological aspect of an organism."[4] "He insists, and rightly so," Torrey wrote of Kinsey, "that he is still a taxonomist working with a taxonomic problem. The methods remain the same; only the material has changed."[5]

Kinsey's concept of wide variation and extreme range in individual sexual patterns, all to be tabulated in great number and to be sheltered under the label of a biological norm, was his first major contribution. To this he added an analysis of the social factors that operated in part to create these differences: education, religious devoutness, and decade of birth. These items could never have been envisaged or developed without wider sampling than the campus provided.

The questionnaire format of the very early histories was embryonic, and some of those gathered in the first year were later discarded from the sample as too incomplete to go into the tabulations. They did from the beginning, however, cover questions on the major sexual outlets: masturbation, sex dreams, petting, and coitus. The latter was subdivided into categories based on the identity of the sexual partner. These classifications included premarital, marital, extramarital, or postmarital coitus, and intercourse with prostitutes. Added were the two almost unexplored areas of homosexual relations and sexual contacts with animals. Such a variety of factual questions on sexual activities had never been asked systematically of any sample, much less of such a large one. Further refinements were to come later.

The marriage course was clearly successful with the majority of students who attended the noncredit lectures. Kinsey reported to a friend:

> Students would do anything to defend us, their appreciation is so great. . . . We have tapped fraternity house gossip and find the course treated most considerately. The Gridiron banquet brought only one reference to it—a reprimand to a couple of the boys for having engaged in biologic activities "without benefit of Kinsey's course in connubial calisthenics."

But during the second year there was growing criticism from other sources. Some conservative faculty members felt it was an inappropriate program at the University for various reasons. Kinsey mentioned in a letter that there were "a few flurries with unfavorable criticisms from older faculty who had no firsthand knowledge."

Someone protested about the course to Mrs. Nellie Showers Teter, the first woman trustee of the University. She asked Wells if he thought it was "proper in every way." He suggested that she visit the lectures to see for herself. After a talk with Kinsey followed by attendance at a few of the sessions, she was satisfied. She reported back to the trustees—"very ladylike and quiet," according to Wells, but definitely approving—and they raised no further questions about the propriety of the series. To Wells she also remarked, "I wish I could have had these lectures when I was young, when I was in college."

But others felt differently. A few faculty members of the School of Medicine took the stand that if such a course were to be offered, it should be staffed primarily from their ranks. One doctor was quoted as saying that Kinsey was practicing medicine without a license. A second referred to it as "the smut course." Another was fearful lest the legislature get wind of the topics covered in the course and cut off funds to the University. A group of local ministers expressed concern over the "moral and social implications" of the lectures. The first break in the ranks of participants and supporters was, surprisingly, in the sociology department. Its members voted to request their staff to withdraw from the panel of lecturers, and Dr. Edwin Sutherland, chairman, so informed President Wells and Dr. Kinsey in January, 1940. The first reason given by Sutherland for this action was that "the importance of the work of the sociologists in the course is much less than had been anticipated." This was, it was explained, because the sociological materials were already familiar to a large proportion of the students enrolled. But more significant was their second reason: "The sociologists must share the increasing criticisms of the course with the other participants, although few of the criticisms are directed specifically at the lectures by the sociologists."

There may have been additional reasons. Certainly some held the opinion that Kinsey was using the lectures given by the members of other departments as "window dressing for his own show." His counseling with students and making a clinical record of their sexual histories were criticized as being in conflict with his role as coordinator of the course. His off-campus interviewing was not generally known about at this time, although it was well under way. Kinsey had actually gone ahead with his research for almost a year before discussing it with his own department, fearing that a premature announcement would perhaps kill the work. About the same time Kinsey took occasion to break the news of his new project to his faculty discussion club. His talk to them was entitled "Student Sex Problems." In describing their reaction to his report on his work in collecting sex histories he wrote: "nearly bowled some of them over—but they were game and objective and most encouraging in their approval of further investigation."

By March, 1940, he had settled down to an almost constant schedule of being out of town the last few days in the week. He explained:

It is this research on human sex behavior that has piled on the extra load. At the start it was a problem to get contributions to our histories; now it is a scramble to find time to record all of those that are offered. The students here on the campus are increasingly getting the habit of coming over. I recently had two whole fraternity groups offer 100%. That is invaluable because it gives us the nearest substitute that seems possible for a random sample.

Every day's mail brings requests from the outside for conferences whenever I travel their way. Within the past month I have lectured at the request of a clergyman in a small town where I picked up ten histories on the day following my lecture. I have given a series of three lectures to a group of 180 parents at A————, and during the past month staying over in the town for a day following each lecture, and getting histories of every variety from parents to high school boys and girls. The people in the high school are so enthusiastic that they promise me 1,000 histories there if I want to take the time for them.

Two weeks later he elaborated:

Connections at the Y.M.C.A. at Indianapolis started me on a series of histories there, and I suppose I could get several hundred out of that building if I could find the time. My Chicago and St. Louis connections are spreading like the branches of a tree. We now have over 700 histories, and our tabulations, curves, correlation charts, etc. are beginning to be impressive. There continues to be a stray dissenter among the older members of the faculty who objects to all this, but an increasing number of the faculty are offering a very definite cooperation. The people in physiology, psychology, and sociology have had long sessions with me, and are offering definite cooperation on their aspects of the matter.

By the end of March he had talked to Dr. Edgar Allen, the endocrinologist from Yale, and wrote that Allen had suggested "several foundations that would be glad to cooperate with their resources." Kinsey adds naively: "It looks as if it was going to take a full-time assistant to help out on that end of the thing. Ideally, it should be an older married person, but whether I will find the right one is difficult to guess."

Matters came to a head in the summer of 1940, after the project had completed its second year. Following complaints from the local ministerial association, President Wells called Kinsey to his office and placed a choice before him. He could continue either with the marriage course or with his research project of collecting the case history studies in human sex behavior, but not with both.

Two faculty members recalled clearly meeting Kinsey on the day that this choice had been put up to him. He was greatly agitated over the turn of events. One of them gives this account:

> I am not sure if it was on a very hot night in '40 or '41 that one of my most vivid memories of Dr. Kinsey takes place. We were both working in our yards about dusk. He asked me if I would come in for a cool drink and music. I accepted. Almost before we reached the house he began talking in a very excited way about action against his Marriage Course. It seems that earlier that very day the Bloomington ministerial association and the university administration had agreed that in the future Dr. Kinsey must choose between giving the course and/or interviewing students and members of the university community. He resented this action deeply and did not hesitate to say so. He also did not hesitate to compare himself with such historical pioneers in science as Galileo! I recall that I felt sorry for him but also felt that he was not reacting too sensibly.

Kinsey next conferred with his committee, and he countered shortly with the request to Wells that a qualified faculty committee be appointed by the President to "investigate the Course and make recommendations to the whole faculty as to the continuance, discontinuance, or modification of the program."

Wells' prompt answer is an example of adroit administrative handling of a thorny situation:

> I am sure the chairman of the present committee will remember that the course was not instituted in the beginning by faculty action, but rather, at his request, was inaugurated by action of the Board of Trustees. If therefore seems to me inappropriate for the matter at this late date to be referred to the faculty.
>
> Quite aside from this consideration, I am convinced that it would be unfair to the marriage course at this time to submit it to the general faculty for discussion. It is in such ill repute with

the members of the faculty that unquestionably it would be eliminated by overwhelming vote. I believe such action would be unfortunate.

If it is your wish, after the course has been reconstructed and the members of the faculty have gained greater confidence in it, to have a general faculty discussion at that time, personally I would be agreeable.

A month later Kinsey had made up his mind. He wrote Wells that he must "as a research scientist, choose to continue with the case history studies," and he submitted his resignation as chairman and lecturer in the marriage course. In a note to a friend he described his "forced resignation" from the lecture course and predicted its demise if turned over to the medical school. He also surmised that the ministers were more afraid of the conferences than of the lectures in the course, and that they had thought to curtail the conferences by his threatened expulsion. He added: "Most of them (for instance those who do not know me) thought I would choose the lectures and stop the research." His parting shot in his letter of resignation to Wells reflects his staunch conviction that he had taken the right course:

> The possibility which you offer of my lecturing in the Course while refraining from answering inquiries which the students bring, or making studies on the students in the Course, does not appear to me to be a possible solution of the problem. No scholar will voluntarily waive his right to disseminate information in the field in which he is especially qualified.

In a statement found in his files which he drafted to the President and the Trustees of the University, but which he never sent, Kinsey expressed these convictions even more strongly. After two pages, in which he sets forth the merits of the marriage course as presented at Indiana, the student success with which it had met, and the approval from groups outside the University, he ended with these unambiguous words:

> Objection to a scholarly analysis of the problems of marriage is a challenge to the University's right to engage in research, and to transmit the results of such research to our students. Obviously it arises in a fear that some of the problems which have hitherto been considered theological may become matters for

legal criticism, for sociologic study, and for biologic investigation. It is no new thing to have these rights challenged by clerical authorities. The right to investigate the shape and the rotation of the earth, the nature of organic evolution, the forces which are basic in our social and economic organization, have been challenged by one or another group ever since the founding of universities. But in the long run matters that are legal, economic, or physiologic will be submitted to students of law, economics, or biology for study. We have arrived at a day when these aspects of marriage are being subjected to that very sort of investigation. It is best that the ethical aspects of marriage should be presented, as they are, by clergymen in our Marriage Course; but, interference from clergymen with studies by students in these other fields is a challenge to the University's right to provide the scholarly leadership which the people of this state have a right to expect.

Kinsey had conviction and determination and he would need a good measure of both. The marriage course continued on the campus for a short time under medical sponsorship, but interest in it dwindled. With the coming of the war the campus tempo changed and the marriage course was soon dropped.

With the decision regarding withdrawal from the marriage course behind him and thus freed from its restrictions, Kinsey started in the fall of 1940 to pour his tremendous drive and energy into furthering his off-campus field work. In an October letter he said:

> I have been going to the State Penal Farm at Putnamville two or three times every week for the last two months and shall continue so through most of the winter. I have 110 histories from inmates there and can get as many hundreds more as I want. The prison authorities are dumbfounded that I have been able to win the confidence of the men. I have the complete confidence of the five men who are the inner circle of inmates who are in the institution, and their tips to the other men result in their willingness to tell me everything without fear of exposure to the prison authorities. This will give us the first real study on sexual adjustments in prison. I find the actuality is considerably different from the guesses in the current criminology literature. More important than that, these histories are giving me a look-in on a lower social level, and the patterns of sexual behavior are totally differ-

ent from those of college students. After all, our college students constitute less than 1% of the population and it is the great mass of the population which is reported in the group that I am now working.

These were his first prison histories and the start of his interest in the problems of sex offenders and of sexual adjustment in prison. Taking sex histories from prison inmates had several clear advantages, he found. If one can gain the confidence of the prisoners—as Kinsey was phenomenally successful in doing—there is a steady supply of readily available subjects who have plenty of free time on their hands. Thus the investigator wastes no time in making contacts or trying to work out convenient interview schedules. There are no canceled, late, or forgotten appointments, and few interruptions. Furthermore, the inmates are chiefly from a social-economic level that is difficult to tap in the outside world. These are some of the practical reasons why Kinsey early sought prison cases for his sex histories. As he was financing the field trips entirely out of his own funds at this time, there was an especial urgency to do it as economically and efficiently as possible.

Strange circumstances arose sometimes in the prison interviews, and Kinsey enjoyed telling this joke on himself. During the late fall of 1941 he had interviewed a black prostitute, Delores, in the women's prison. She was about to be released after serving her term, and since her pimp was currently under surveillance, her friends were worried that she might be rearrested. In trying to plan how this could be avoided one of the women prisoners suggested to Kinsey, "Doc, why don't you just take over Delores?"

One of the reasons why Kinsey was so successful in gaining the full cooperation of the inmates in the women's prison was explained in an amused but appreciative account which Mrs. Marian Gallup, Superintendent of the Indiana Woman's Prison, gave to Mrs. Kinsey: "When one of the women prisoners entered the room to give her history, he always stood up, pulled out the chair for her to sit down, and offered her cigarettes."

Kinsey had another experience about this same time that

Kinsey in the field: Filming animals with
Dellenback in Oregon, archeology with Gebhard
in Peru, interviewing at San Quentin

Porcupine film, apples, and lollipops for staff children

Viewing animal films with McKenzie and Shadle

With President Wells and Corner

Entertaining the journalists, 1953

The Kinsey team: L-R: Martin, Gebhard, Kinsey, Pomeroy

Cook-out

Final staff picture, 1953

In conference: Christenson, Kinsey, Pomeroy, Gebhard

A Kinsey gallery 1948–1956

"Mr. Tilby is in the Kinsey Report."

HAZEL

he often recounted. A certain underworld character that he had met in his prison interviewing promised to help him make contacts in the ghetto area in the city after he had been released from prison. Kinsey had his address, and when later he tried to follow up on the lead he had no success. No one in the neighborhood would admit that he had ever heard of this person. He went from place to place without any clues. Finally, one woman admitted she had perhaps heard of him after Kinsey explained he wanted to find him because he had a "job" for him. She agreed that she would try to get a message to him, and did. Later it turned out that she was his sister! It was just like Catfish Row in *Porgy and Bess*, Kinsey would comment. They would play completely dumb to protect any-one against a stranger they didn't know or trust.

Two handwritten letters to Clyde Martin, then his stu-dent assistant, written in November, 1940, from a small town in northern Indiana, portray some frustrating experiences typical of his early field work. He had been invited to give three of his marriage course lectures to a group of "young and married people" and also to speak before the luncheon meet-ings of the local men's service clubs. His first morning in town he explained his project to a meeting of the local minis-ters, but failed to get any volunteers for histories from them. In spite of his subsequent five lectures, the offers of townspeo-ple to volunteer as subjects were tantalizingly slow in com-ing. "All told then, damn few histories yet," was his terse comment. He describes one group as being "a royally cordial group of precisely the older age that we need in our histo-ries." He adds: "Got no takers on the invitation to contribute tho some talked to me and they may come across later. At any rate, it gives me a better idea of my talk in approaching a group that seemed more uplift even than the ministers. It is going to be hell to get older, well-established business men to jeopardize their positions by confessing even to me." In the next letter he enlarges on this point:

The business men are very wary about exposing themselves—extramarital coitus is the rub—they fear economic and social ruin if exposed. I expect extramarital coitus is in 80 percent of the really successful business man's history. They talk around for a half hour with me, asking questions—refuse to sign up—call back the next day, only finally to come across. . . . God, what a gap between social front and reality!

The American Association for the Advancement of Science meetings at Philadelphia over the Christmas holidays of 1940 gave Kinsey a splendid opportunity to follow his now dual track. To the Genetic Society he presented a paper on local populations of gall wasps. Clyde Martin had painstakingly prepared, in Kinsey's words, "some splendid drawings with large gall wasps in color," which provided a "stunning exhibit" on the variable-winged Utah material (Biorhiza eburnea). A second paper, "A Scientist's Responsibility in Sex Instruction," given before the National Association of Biology Teachers, stirred up considerable controversy. (See page 209.) "I shall aim to distinguish the scientific data in this field from the moralistic claptrap which has invaded our school room," he wrote to a colleague. "Morals masqueraded under the name of science," was his further, unflattering description of current instruction in sex education.

His most important part in the Philadelphia programs, however, was the paper he presented to the psychology session, "Criteria for a Hormonal Explanation of the Homosexual," a summary of the article which was later to appear in the *Journal of Clinical Endocrinology*, and which began his friendship with Dr. Dickinson. This paper was an impressive first performance. It is an attack on a hormone level study made by three Harvard medical research workers, in which they claimed to have found that androgen-estrogen ratios in seventeen clinically diagnosed homosexual males were significantly lower than in "normals." After presenting his own findings on homosexual behavior among the 1,058 males he had by then interviewed, Kinsey expressed doubt as to whether it was likely that any hormonal factors could be identified as a basis for homosexual behavior. He concluded that if there is to be a hormonal explanation of the homosexual, it must take into account the variety of patterns of such behavior as he had found them in his case histories. This paper served notice to the world of science that a new figure of stature was emerging from the murky hinterlands of sex research. The author was challenging the stereotyped views on homosexual behavior with strong new data which were going to be difficult to controvert.

Kinsey later described the reception of the paper thus:

> The psychologists received the material most respectfully, asking a great many interesting questions, and offering no adverse criticism. Meanwhile I had applied to the National Research Council Committee on Sex for funds for expanding our program, and Yerkes, psychologist from Yale, was present at the Psychologists' meeting and gave me several hours of personal interview later. His reactions were all to the good, and it looks as if we are going to get rather ample funds from the National Research Council for furthering this human study. That has added a great deal to the awakened interest of Dr. Payne and recently of President Wells in this study, and things begin to look easier for us. We have 1,747 cases now.

It was clear that he was on his way.

By the following April, at which time he made his 1940–41 annual report to the graduate school, he was able to announce that he had added over 700 case histories during the past twelve months and that the grand total was now "more than 1,900." "In gathering these histories," he wrote, "I have traveled 106 days at my own expense to St. Louis, Springfield, Missouri; Chicago, Peoria, Illinois; Indianapolis, Elkhart, South Bend, Anderson, Indiana; Philadelphia; New York; Winchester, Indiana; and to the Indiana State Penal Farm." Elsewhere he estimated that he had put from $800 to $1,200 a year into the project from his own pocket. "I did this," he explained, "in order to get the thing started without interference, and in order to prove to people that the job could be done before I asked for help."

Outside financial support was soon to come, however, and in the spring of 1941 a grant of $1,600 from the Committee for Research in Problems of Sex of the National Research Council was announced. The University supplemented this grant with $1,200.

The summer of 1941 was a quiet interlude. Kinsey writes:

> Mrs. Kinsey and I have had a sort of vacation because it is the first time in twenty years that we have been at home without any

of the children. We took a few hours off now and again in a day or two of trips but not longer vacationing. My research is pushing very hard and I am trying to use this end of the summer for concentrated work.

During the fall his traveling was steadily intensifying, and he was also still hoping to push ahead with his gall wasp studies. In October, while on a field trip, he wrote to his assistant, Clyde Martin: "Hope the weekend vacations prove good to you—God knows when we will dare ease up on work again," and adds: "Get ready for a grand job with new histories when I get back." In December, he described their both "working intensively" and carrying "a terrific load." "People are volunteering faster than we can take the histories," he added. "It is a great opportunity."

One of his first out-of-town visitors who came specifically to find out more about the research project was the biologist, Dr. Carl Hartman, who was then at the University of Illinois. He came to Bloomington early in December, 1941, and following his visit to Kinsey's laboratory, wrote that he was calling the attention of the National Committee on Maternal Health to Kinsey's work and its importance, "commending it as a project which the NCMH might well adopt and place on their budget." Before returning home he visited at the Carnegie Institution at Baltimore, where he gave to a luncheon group a firsthand account of Kinsey's research, eliciting their interest in the program.

In December the 1941 AAAS Christmas meetings at Dallas, Texas, provided Kinsey with an opportunity to take part in two final symposia on gall wasps. He and Clyde Martin drove to Texas. At Dallas he appeared before the psychology section for a second time, presenting a paper on "The Frequency of Sexual Outlets," based on his fast growing sex history data, which he now described as having become "tremendous in its scope." A familiar word, "outlet," had suddenly acquired a new level of meaning. This was his first professional presentation of the total range of his data, which by this time included over 2,500 cases.

After the Dallas program and the discussion it provoked —neither of which seems to have been made a matter of record—a significant shift took place in Kinsey's treatment of his frequency figures. He decided to change from a current rate basis to a rate for each of the five-year intervals of the subject's life span. Yerkes had actually suggested a modification somewhat along these lines in a letter following their conference in Philadelphia at the AAAS meetings the year before. His idea was that one-year intervals should be retained during the important 20-year span from age 10 to 39, five-year intervals should be used from 40 to 59, and ten-year intervals thereafter. He pointed out that this would simplify the analysis and cut down on the sample needed. The change to five-year intervals was a big undertaking, and the following August Kinsey wrote:"We have recalculated all of our data on a much sounder basis." Clyde Martin, his earliest statistical worker, explains:

> The shift was very helpful in many ways for it meant that more close attention had to be paid to securing in the interview age at onset and early, as well as late, frequencies in order to incorporate changes in frequency over time. Simply, these two statistical requirements did a great deal to focus the questioning in a way that revealed new aspects of the life history, especially the picture over the course of marriage.

He continues:

> I think this attempt to look at frequencies in the past also helped reveal the fact that the very early frequencies soon after puberty in the male tended to be rather poorly recalled, and also revealed that while age at first experiences of masturbation, coitus, homosexuality, and animal contacts was likely to be fairly well remembered, the first experience of nocturnal dream to climax often was not.

This change meant that the frequency of an individual's sex experience was now tabulated in each five-year age period up to the age at which he had been interviewed. Obviously it greatly increased the count in each category.

Through the period from 1939 on one can trace the gradual move away from gall wasp research on Kinsey's part. It was with great reluctance that he gave it up; his hopes of keeping both fields active finally faded as he saw the immensity of the new project he had become involved with. The following mileposts on the road give a glimpse of the inevitable shift that took place:

January 17, 1939: "So I am all set up about the possibilities that lie in the work" (a statistical analysis of gall wasp measurements).

December, 1939: "I have kept the Cynipid work going, tho it has slowed because of the other research problem."

March 29, 1940: "I am going to have to make some drastic reorganization of the gall wasp work in order to concentrate on the study of the material we now have. Without any expansion of program, there is enough material to be studied for a long time to come."

As late as March 11, 1943, he wrote: "We will keep up gall wasps, but there is no question that the Sex Behavior Research will take precedence."

One seeks the reasons why the study of human sex behavior won out over the study of gall wasps during these pivotal years in Kinsey's life. In part it was doubtless the freshness of a different field and the excitement of new, vital discoveries that tilted the balance in favor of sex research. Surmounting the difficulties which had defeated others who had tried the same path certainly had a strong attraction. He once wrote to Dr. Dickinson:

> For more than twenty years I have worked on individual variation in population of insects. . . . In the course of that work I have explored throughout the length of the continent in the most remote desert and mountain areas. This unearthing of the fact in Human Sexual Behavior proves a much more difficult and more dangerous undertaking; but the very difficulty is one of the things that leads me on.

These sentences reveal the paramount importance to Kinsey of the challenge of the new field. There were undoubtedly many reasons why Kinsey turned to sex research, but this sudden insight of his own furnishes a crucial clue to his biographer. Kinsey was not an introspective person, and one searches the thousands of letters he wrote for self-revealing passages. When they occur, it is like a flash, and then the curtain is drawn. He is once more into his role as objective scientist, friendly graduate professor, or eager promoter of his research endeavors. He must have felt a kinship with Dickinson, a respected older doctor, who had trod the same path he saw ahead for himself. This closeness is documented by Dr. Robert W. Laidlaw, a mutual friend, who observed:

> I particularly enjoyed the many occasions in which I was able to listen to Kinsey and RLD talking together. Here were two "greats" talking about the subject nearest and dearest to them, and always in the simplest and most unassuming manner. I feel that in the early days of the study, RLD contributed significantly to Kinsey's confidence in himself in turning to the study of human beings, and that RLD opened many medical doors to Kinsey which a doctor with less stature would not have succeeded in opening. Each had a deep admiration of the strong points and an understanding of the weak points of the other.

Kinsey and Dickinson were both trail blazers over rugged terrain, and one can surmise that Kinsey's dogged field work in "bug collecting" well fitted him for the endurance he needed in his new field.

Most important, however, was his realization of the need which people, especially young people, had for the sex information he was collecting. He once wrote Dickinson: "The research is not for myself but for the elucidation of a badly neglected field." He saw that there was a problem to solve and a job that needed to be done. By examining the previous studies, he realized their many limitations. A moralistic bias was implicit in many of them. Unwarranted conclusions based on inadequate samples faulted others. In some instances Victorian inhibitions prevented the crucial questions from being asked or shrouded the real problems involved.

"I hope to prove to the world someday that any subject may be a profitable field for scientific research if zealously pursued and handled with objective scholarship," he stated. Kinsey's aim was clearly to provide data upon which a start for a new science of man and sexuality could be built.

One of his laboratory workers during this transitional period described her reactions to the events she watched:

> At this time Dr. Kinsey was still carrying a full teaching load; something, of course, had to give way. We girls continued to kill, mount, and label gall wasps, and Dr. Kinsey even hired a new girl

or two; the number of boxes in the collection grew as before, but the extensive project of the microscopic measurement of individual differences was laid aside. Who could blame Dr. Kinsey? Not we. How could a race of insects compete with the infinite variety of Man![6]

His alter ego, Edgar Anderson, put his astringent blessing and amen on Kinsey's new role with these words:

It was heart warming to see you settling down into what I suppose will be your real life work. One would never have believed that all sides of you could have found a project big enough to need them all. I was amused to see how the Scotch Presbyterian reformer in you had finally got together with the scientific fanatic with his zeal for masses of neat data in orderly boxes and drawers. The monographer Kinsey, the naturalist Kinsey, the camp counsellor Kinsey all rolling into one at last and going full steam ahead. Well, I am glad to have a seat for the performance. It is great to have it done and great to know that you are doing it.

7.

The Male Book and

Full Course Ahead

So much has been written about the two books, *Sexual Behavior in the Human Male* and its companion, *Sexual Behavior in the Human Female*, which Kinsey and his staff produced during the ten years 1943–1953, that it is hardly necessary to detail their content. Their principal impact lay in the fact that science for the first time had been provided with a wide, systematic, and detailed body of knowledge on human sex activity. This opened whole new areas for investigation in related sciences. In the words of Dr. Alan Gregg in his preface to the first volume, "In so far as man seeks to know himself and face his whole nature, he has become free from bewildered fear, despondent shame, or arrant hypocrisy." The lifting of some of the ancient taboos on the discussion of sex by the Kinsey books meant that sex could now be considered openly and objectively in many places where it had been a closed topic before.

Many applauded Kinsey's bold approach and liked the frankness of his biological terminology. This part of his public—largely males—took the attitude that Kinsey was just revealing by his survey methods what they had known, or at least strongly suspected, was true in regard to human behavior. Others were shocked and offended that the curtain should be drawn aside to expose such a rude scene. To many of the latter it was almost as if Kinsey had invented sex and all that they found distasteful about it. Even if the things he wrote were true, they felt he should not bring them to the attention of the general public.

While his fame in this country was great, it was more than equaled by the popularity he achieved in England, Germany, and the Scandinavian countries. In all, his two books between them were translated into thirteen different languages: German, French, Spanish, Dutch, Italian, Portuguese, Norwegian, Swedish, Hebrew, Finnish, Greek, Chinese, and Japanese. The new herculean effort from America was well received in Europe in part because earlier writings there had prepared the way. In the late nineteenth and early twentieth centuries Krafft-Ebing, Moll, Hirschfeld, Rohleder, Stekel, Havelock Ellis, and, of course, Freud, had written on sex, presenting material chiefly in case-history format. French readers were probably the coolest toward the Kinsey work of all the major European countries. The story was told that the French comment was: "Numbers are all right in the counting room, but not in the bedroom." But even in France a translation appeared and imitative "Little Kinsey Reports" sprang up here and there in the wake of the Institute for Sex Research publications.

During the seven-and-a-half-year interval between July, 1941, when the first outside funding was received, and December, 1948, when *Sexual Behavior in the Human Male* was published, events crowded into Kinsey's life in an ever-increasing tempo. Two staff members were added to help in the interviewing work, but this only served to raise his sights as to the goals to be aimed for. The world was his source of data, and as one associate expressed it, he had a need "to devour life, to gulp life, to look, and experiment and record."

Since he had set out with no definite hypothesis to test, all data on all kinds of sexual behavior of all kinds of people were grist to his mill. The findings were to evolve from tabulations of the mass of data. Early in 1944 he wrote: "The technique we are using in this study is definitely the same as the technique in the gall wasp study." He was still a collector. The variety and range he found astounded and excited him as it would any scientist in search of the new. But it also endlessly complicated his analysis, and to reduce his findings to meaningful statistics in the days before computers were available was a backbreaking job. As early as 1938 hours were spent by Martin in hand tabulations with Kinsey reading off the data from the coded histories. The hand punching of Hollerith data cards began by 1942. When the decks were complete, they were fed through a sorting and tabulating machine. Next, tables and graphs were drawn up to summarize the results. After inspection and study it was not uncommon to decide to analyze the data in a somewhat different fashion, doubling the work for all. Many such false starts were made, and the leads Kinsey followed—sometimes on the advice of others—were not always profitable.

Frank K. Edmondson, chairman of the Department of Astronomy, had become interested in Kinsey's data on his variable-winged species of gall wasps when he found they presented a statistical phenomenon called a "double-drift" distribution. He also provided advice on how to handle the calculations for the human sex data. The Edmondson and Kinsey families were close for other reasons, as they shared a deep interest in listening to classical music. Frank and his wife Margaret were long-time "regulars" at the evening record concerts at Kinseys'. For several years Edmondson contributed a great deal of time in aiding Kinsey's thinking on the statistics of his research; later he was given a small consultant fee. His fine professional training in astronomical statistics on the population of stars did not always lend itself well to human populations, however.

Raymond Pearl's advice—that if one had enough cases, the statistical treatment was of little concern—doubtless haunted Kinsey during these years. In 1945 he wrote in his annual report that his goal was to amass 100,000 cases. This, he felt, would furnish him with the cases he needed for each of the one hundred to two hundred specific homogeneous groups which constitute the major portion of the population and which he felt were important to study. Twenty years, he estimated, were needed to reach this goal. Later, this unrealistic figure was forgotten. At the time of his death there were about 18,500 cases in the files.

For thirteen years the Committee for Research in Problems of Sex of the Division of Medical Sciences of the National Research Council provided financial support for the Kinsey research. The original grant of $1,600 for 1941–42 was token help only; and with the growing complication of the war, Kinsey became genuinely uncertain as to what the future held. He was determined, however, to push forward. In March, 1942, he confided to his friend Carl Hartman at the University of Illinois:

> I shall, of course, not allow the work to be stopped under any consideration. If money is not available from one source, we must find it from some other. The material is too important to go unpublished and the project too far along to stop. The present National emergency calls for earlier publication than we had originally planned.

But, as it turned out, Kinsey was needlessly worried.

At this point a committee of the National Research Council visited Bloomington to investigate at first hand the skills and methods which Kinsey was employing in his work, to look at his preliminary findings, and to find out about his future plans. It was also important to test the degree of support he had from the administration of the University. The visiting committee included Dr. Robert M. Yerkes, the Yale psychologist, as chairman, Dr. George W. Corner of the Carnegie Institution of Washington at Baltimore, and Dr. Lowell J. Reed, Dean of the School of Hygiene and Public Health at the Johns Hopkins University. Kinsey was pleased when they arrived in December, 1942, as he had never before had the opportunity to show his research to anyone in such detail. He wrote later:

> They were with us for nearly five days on the campus. They went into everything in minute detail . . . saw histories being taken in our penal institutions, went into the slums of Indianapolis and saw what contacts I have.
> As a result of it we are promised unlimited support for an

indefinite period of years. If we can use it, we can have $20,000.00 to $25,000.00 per year, or more, for a long period to come. While the specific appropriation is still to be made, there is no doubt of their enthusiasm about the research.

This report was decidedly overoptimistic, but it is true that the visitors were well impressed. Corner's letter of thanks called it "one of the most interesting and instructive trips I have ever had!" Yerkes termed it "memorable" and expressed his "satisfaction in what you told and showed me." The official twenty-five-year history of the Committee reported it thus:

Having made an initial grant to Kinsey for 1941–1942, the Committee made a careful investigation of his plans and methods for the study of human sexual behavior by the interview method, and in 1942–1943 entered upon a program of gradually increasing financial assistance to his work.[1]

Kinsey had, in fact, a ready-made, successfully operating project which fitted perfectly into the Committee's plans. This is underlined by excerpts from two letters. Kinsey had written Hartman about his hopes for further funding and thanked him for his encouragement. Hartman replied in an informally scribbled, handwritten note:

Dear Kinsey,
Man alive, you don't need encouragement. You've got what it takes—except money. This should be thrown at you and probably will, now that you've put it over. I have a feeling that the Yerkes committee will be glad to get on the bandwagon. Committees like to know what is a good bet.

In a report to Dean H. T. Briscoe Kinsey notes the success of the visit of the three committee members:

They tell me that they have tried a dozen or more times to get this done in the last twenty years, and they assure us that this is the most successful development of the program that they have yet had. They are planning a long-time support of our project in trying to lay plans for its still more permanent subsidy directly through one of the national foundations.

The grant that followed the site visit was for $7,500 for 1942–43, which allowed for additional research staff as well as funds for travel expenses. This represented well over a quarter of the total income, $26,900, which the University received in that year from outside funds.

During the following years the Medical Division of the Rockefeller Foundation, through the NRC Committee for Sex Research, continued ever stronger financial aid, the amount reaching $23,000 in 1943–44, and $40,000 by 1947–48. The Committee's official history published in 1953 sketches some of the background of this period up to 1947, at which time one-half of their entire annual resources was allocated to the Kinsey group:

> The Committee's support of this enterprise, which seems to fulfill so clearly the need for research in human sex behavior that was stated at the beginning of this history, has not been a matter of course or always unanimously voted. All the objections that have been raised against the propriety of the research, against its isolation of sexual from other aspects of life experience, and against its techniques of sampling and calculation, have been discussed at Committee meetings, where indeed some of them were first expressed. Consultations between Dr. Kinsey, the Committee's chairman, and officers of the Rockefeller Foundation have been frequent and earnest. The Committee, however, has constantly been impressed by the importance of this study and by the competence and honesty of Kinsey and his associates. Well aware of the difficulties imposed upon its sponsored investigators and upon the Committee itself by emotional and moralistic attitudes with regard to this delicate topic, it has staked its reputation for wisdom in judging research programs and research workers on uninterrupted and increasing support and encouragement of the Kinsey program.
>
> The administration of Indiana University has shown equal confidence and has strongly supported the work.[2]

It is impossible to overestimate the importance of this consistent support in funding from responsible outside sources. Kinsey cited it again and again in his letters, lectures, and writing to indicate that it was not his judgment alone that set the seal of approval on his investigations into sexual behavior. The University's support was in turn strengthened by the outside endorsement of the work.

The grant continued at the level of $40,000 annually until

July, 1954. At that point it was cut off except for the token support of $3,000 to $5,000 given annually directly by the NRC. The exact causes for the withdrawal of support have never been fully explored. It is certain that pressures had built up from various sources and that there was also some feeling that the Institute had by now made enough money from its books to finance its work from royalty monies. Kinsey felt very bitterly about it and made every effort to explain why annual budgets of nearly $100,000 could not be supported entirely by the proceeds of publications.

During the entire period President Wells and the administration of the University were unstinting in their help and moral support. Kinsey's salary as a research professor in the zoology department came from University funds. The University also supplied quarters, equipment, supplies, and general services. Other expenses such as salaries for staff not directly involved in research—librarians, translators, and a photographer, acquisitions for the library of books and journals, and any additions to the collections and archives, as well as all extra travel costs—were covered by royalty income from the publications. Kinsey estimated that his work had been supported approximately in equal parts by the three sources—the University, outside grants, and income from publications.

That Kinsey had early projected the expansion of his staff and the ultimate cost of his work is revealed in a carbon copy of a routine questionnaire on public service projects at Indiana University which he filled out in 1944. He listed his sex research work, and he wrote under "Estimated Cost," "1 million dollars." Under "Completion Time" he inserted "20 years." After "Staff Members Required," he filled in "16." For "Estimated Receipts," he typed "None." He apparently did not at that time envisage any sizable income from the publication of his work.

As the professional staff was expanded, the first to be added was Wardell B. Pomeroy, a young and energetic clinical psychologist, not yet turned thirty. He had been working in South Bend for the St. Joseph County Department of Public Welfare and was hired at the modest salary of $3,000 in February, 1943. By this time Clyde Martin had completed his undergraduate degree and was working for Kinsey full time, and adequate secretarial help had been added. Paul Gebhard, an anthropologist with Harvard graduate training, joined the staff in August, 1946. He is now the director of the Institute. These three persons—Martin, Pomeroy, and Gebhard—were the backbone of Kinsey's team, and all became trustees of the Institute and were recognized as co-authors of the books.[3]

One of Kinsey's difficulties was that it was almost impossible for him to really delegate responsiblity. He was so exact and meticulous in all he did himself that he could not quite believe that anyone else would do a job as well as he could. He had, in fact, carried on the work virtually alone during the years that he was getting it established. He liked to keep a close eye on the work of his subordinates. This personal supervision seemed to give him a sense of the extension of his own powers. At firsthand observer in the office at this time (1947–49) remembers:

> He did not allow any other staff member to do anything independently. . . . Even the most mundane of the routine tasks of the office were checked and rechecked by him. . . . The nature of the man made any sharing of responsibility unthinkable. . . . His staff was capable; this he knew and appreciated; yet his own self would not let him lean back for five minutes and let someone else do the job.

This meant that while he shared credit for authorship of the books, he himself assumed the real responsibility for both the text and the statistical presentation. It also meant that his working hours were long and he was not one to stint on that.

That Kinsey was a hard taskmaster cannot be denied. He demanded a great deal of his associates, but also asked a great deal of himself. He was generous with credit and in his praise of the contributions of his coworkers. There was a sound mutual respect between him and the staff members. But Kinsey could also be sharply critical, and this naturally led at times to tensions. If he were especially pleased with someone's work, his face could break into a magnificent smile.

As the books were published and funds were available for developing the archives and library facilities, it was also necessary to staff these areas. The first professional librarian was Jeanette Foster, who was aided by part-time translators in the many foreign languages represented. Danish, Swedish, Russian, and Japanese sex studies particularly intrigued Kinsey, and translating these called for special skills.[4]

Kinsey was very rigorous in his choice of persons who he felt were capable of doing the right kind of job in interviewing in the field. He described the qualifications thus:

> It is going to take someone who is capable of achieving absolute objectivity in interviews. There can be no approval or disapproval of anything that appears in anyone's histories or else the subject will cover up. It is going to take somone with the personality which can win the cooperation of all sorts of people, of all social levels. If we can find such a collaborator, either male or female, we very much need him.

In addition he realized fully that the staff had to follow a fine line between avoidance of disapproval of any sort of sexual behavior and regard for social convention.

Reliable, nonshockable, and close-mouthed secretaries were also necessary, but hard to find. One faculty wife told me that in the early 1940's she had alarmedly refused an offer of a secretarial job with Kinsey during her first months as a young bride in Bloomington. She was reluctant to be associated with research dealing with such a questionable subject as sex behavior. Kinsey succeeded, however, in securing a succession of secretaries who met his requirements.[5]

Another point which Kinsey emphasized in hiring all his staff was the paramount importance of keeping all material collected absolutely confidential. His elaborate code system for assigning a number to the case history to key it into the proper list number in the separate name card file was set up with this precaution in mind. Name lists had to be kept to avoid duplication of histories, particularly in prison interviewing and when different staff members were involved. Since at the lower economic levels there was a small payment of money to repay the subject for his time, there was some temptation to try to collect more than once.

In hiring Pomeroy in 1943 he spelled out the long-term commitment to maintaining confidences:

We have discussed the nature of the position here and the conditions of confidence imposed upon any of our staff at sufficient length in the past. There is only one point which I should like to have in black and white. It must be understood that all confidences attained from our records must be maintained not only while you are connected with our staff but at all times in the future. . . . I am putting this in writing because I want to protect you as well as ourselves if you are ever in future years put in a position where your future employer might want information out of our records.

Kinsey's emphasis on security in the Institute always impressed visitors. The "lab"—as we always called it—presented a uniform, trim, antiseptic appearance of green file drawers and metal cabinets, all well-locked. At Wiley Hall, where the Institute was housed on the ground floor, windows even with the campus lawn outside were carefully fitted with strong metal grills in preparation for the move there in February, 1950. All doors to private offices had to be soundproofed and special locks were installed to insure privacy in discussion and interviewing.

Pomeroy was the first to be trained specifically by Kinsey to do interviewing. He had had two years' experience at the Indiana State Reformatory, which furnished him with a good background. By April, 1943, two months after he had joined the staff, he was taking histories. Kinsey had worked intensively with him for eight weeks and commented in a letter to Yerkes that "it was a slow job to train anyone to take histories that are precisely coordinated with our own." The research staff had short periods of work in the laboratory in Bloomington interspersed by long treks out of town to amass more data. In hiring his staff Kinsey was always specific in explaining the schedules he expected the men to follow. They were told that they would be home at least one week out of any month, that no trip would be over three weeks in duration, and that approximately half of the year would be spent in travel. It took a devoted young scientist to be willing to live within these strictures, but Kinsey succeeded in finding them.

Certain locales proved to be very successful in providing ready sources for histories. New York and Philadelphia were two of these. Key figures such as Dr. Robert L. Dickinson in New York and Emily Mudd in Philadelphia aided in arranging lectures to professional audiences, which led to ever-broadening contacts. Specialized sources for histories were also utilized. Among these in 1943–44, for example, were the Indiana state prisons, the Ohio Bureau of Juvenile Research, an exclusively Negro township in a sparsely settled section of Kansas, and a Michigan state home for the retarded. Social workers, school counselors, conscientious objectors, hospital staffs, and school administrators were other clusters that were tapped. Some of these were small groups in which a one hundred per cent sample could be tried for. Much of the travel was now done by air, and a rule was followed not to have two staff members on the same plane. Since Kinsey took pride in the fact that the code was a memorized one and not recorded anywhere, this was a reasonable precaution.

One of the early crises in the interviewing work occurred in 1941 while Glenn Ramsey, a former student of Kinsey's who was teaching in Peoria, Illinois, was collecting case histories from young boys on a project he had started there. Even though the interviewing, which had continued for three years, was done away from the school and on Ramsey's own time, the president of the school board, a physician, wanted to stop it. Ramsey finally resigned over the matter. No charges were ever suggested against his conduct or his teaching. The issue turned on the propriety of the investigation, and it was asserted that questions were being asked of the boys which no one except a physician had the right to ask. Kinsey tried by various means to back up Ramsey so that he could win out in the controversy, but was unsuccessful. The material he had collected led to the publication of several papers by Ramsey, and was later incorporated into the Kinsey findings. The lesson in a minor defeat of this kind was to lay better groundwork for interviews in the future by preliminary contact work. Ramsey joined the staff at the project in Bloomington after this, but soon went into the army.

It is clear from his successive Progress Reports to the NRC and to the University that Kinsey originally had in mind the publication of short papers dealing with segments of his findings before the release of his major volumes. These never materialized. Whether he was dissatisfied with the adequacy of the sample or uncertain of his analysis is hard to say. The facts are that in 1942 he already listed an article, "Frequency and Sources of Sexual Outlet of White Males" as "ready for publication this spring." In the 1944 report he again wrote that he planned to publish it in the "calendar year." This paper was to be a reworking of his Dallas 1941 talk to the psychology section of the AAAS. It was never published. His reach was ever more than his grasp.

As a sequel to this, one might inspect the nine prospective studies listed in the 1945 Annual Report. These are described as "full size volumes," and start with the study on the male and the one on the female, and then continue with: "Sexual Outlet in the Negro"; "Sex Offenses and Sex Offenders"; "Sexual Factors in Marital Adjustment"; "The Hetero-Homosexual Balance"; "Sexual Adjustments in Institutions"; "Sex Education"; and "Prostitutes." The first two of these he published. One other, the sex offender study, came to fruition nine years after his death. The remaining six are unwritten.

World War II had its impact on the work. Great efforts were made to protect the specially trained research staff from the draft, and in general the appeals, which were in some cases carried to higher authority than the local boards, were successful. "We now have all of our staff exempt from military draft for some time to come, and we have every reason to believe that we will have no further difficulty on this point," Kinsey wrote in his June, 1944, report to the University. Wartime gas and tire rationing were problems in traveling. In February, 1942, for example, Kinsey described his dilemma:

> I am well fixed for tires right now. I think I can get perhaps 30 or 40,000 miles out of what I have, but if retreads are not available then, my traveling after case histories will be at an end. I am going to New York . . . and to Bugbee's place to lecture to Kansas Academy on the Sex Behavior study. . . . I am beginning to fear that I should make both trips by train in order to save rubber, and that will make it expensive. I must keep up my traveling to the two penal institutions, to Chicago, Gary and other places where we have contacts that are netting us abundant histories.

This lecture in March, 1942, to the Kansas Academy at the Fort Hayes State College was his first open lecture on a college campus. There was some apprehension on his part and also by Robert Bugbee, who was on the local faculty and who had made the arrangements, as to how frank he could be in a talk at a small state teachers' college in this locality. The title of his lecture was cautiously announced as "Studies in Human Behavior," the term "sex" being carefully avoided. The program was well received and netted him a fair number of histories of older persons, which pleased him, as contacts for these histories were difficult to make. After two return trips, he ended up with over one hundred cases for his research from the community and the small college.

A specially arranged NRC conference in New York late in August, 1943, on "Patterns and Problems of Primate Sex Behavior" brought Kinsey, Pomeroy, and Martin together for the first time with the entire membership of the NRC Committee for Research in Problems of Sex. At this time the Committee included: Walter B. Cannon, Harvard Medical School; George W. Corner, Carnegie Institution; Karl S. Lashley, neuropsychologist from Harvard University; Adolph Meyer, psychiatrist at the Johns Hopkins Medical School; Carl Moore, zoologist at the University of Chicago; Lewis Weed, representing the NRC Division of Medical Sciences; and Robert Yerkes from Yale, the chairman. Guests were also invited and the final group represented the outstanding scientists in the field. Kinsey had provided each participant in advance with a copy of the items he covered in his standard interview, as well as with a list of suggested questions for discussion. The sponsorship by Yerkes and his committee of this conference to allow Kinsey to present his program of research was a landmark for him and his staff. "Our New York trip," he wrote shortly after, "was one continual series of successes."

Visitors to Bloomington now began to appear more regularly. They sometimes came primarily to give a professional lecture but would stay over an extra day or two to inspect the operation of the Kinsey research and to examine its resources. These scientists were usually a source of information for the staff as well.

Frank Beach, who had met Kinsey at the August NRC conference on primate behavior, and who specialized in animal sexual behavior, stayed in Bloomington for four days in February, 1944, as Kinsey's house guest. He was then on the staff at the Museum of Natural History in New York. He had, before his visit, been skeptical of Kinsey's accounts of his ability to obtain full rapport with certain lower-income social groups. He recalls:

> Kinsey met my train in Indianapolis. The train was two hours late and he hastened to phone Bloomington to arrange for a two-hour shift in my program for the next two days. Immediately thereafter we toured the slum sections of Indianapolis and visited several colored houses of prostitution. I was tremendously impressed by the ease with which Kinsey communicated with the women working there, and the apparent respect and even affection with which they regarded him.

Kinsey was invited to Washington in April, 1945, to present his findings in advance of publication to a small, select conference on "Human Sex Patterns." Pomeroy and Martin accompanied him. The meeting was held under the auspices of the Division of Medical Sciences of the National Research Council and was attended by NRC committee members, by officials of the Armed Services and of the Selective Service with their civilian consultants and by Public Health Service representatives. His data on his more than 8,000 cases were considered of top level importance at this time because they provided basic information needed for establishing policies pertaining to the behavior of large groups of men such as were then in the armed forces. Most of the group were appreciative and enthusiastic, but Dr. Adolph Meyer, the eminent psychiatrist, took issue at certain points.

Several other public appearances during these years preceding the publication of the volume on the male are worth noting. In March, 1946, at the first conference on Physiological and Psychological Factors in Sex Behavior held by the New York Academy of Sciences, "Sex Behavior in the Human Animal" was Kinsey's topic. The two-and-a-half-page summary of this talk (38) indicates that his major points dealt with the prevalence of childhood sexuality; the early fixing of sexual patterns in individuals; the contrast between males and females in their development of sexual responsiveness; and the biological origins of the so-called sexual perversions. All these themes were to be adequately documented in his later publications. At the annual meeting of the American Association for the Advancement of Science held in Boston at Christmas, 1946, he spoke before a symposium held jointly by the zoologists and geneticists on "Sources of Human Sex Behavior," and two months later in February, 1947, "Studies in Human Sex Behavior" furnished the lecture topic for a special session of the American Orthopsychiatric Association meetings in Cincinnati. These and other such appearances all served to strengthen his position with the scientifically trained sector of his public. Little general notice was given to them, however, and he often requested that his talks be "off the record."

By 1947 matters had proceeded to the point at which it seemed advisable to incorporate the Institute, which comprised the framework within which the research work had been going forward. This would clarify its legal status as well as assign ownership of the case histories and library. The articles of incorporation were filed on April 8, 1947. The purposes listed were to continue research on human sexual behavior; to accept, hold, use, and administer research materials, a library, case histories, and other materials relating to the project; and finally, to acquire, own, hold, rent or lease such real estate and personal property as might be reasonably necessary to carry out the general purposes of the Institute. Two days later Kinsey signed a deed of transfer of the case histories and research materials he owned to the new corporation. As part of the considerations for this transfer of property, if the corporation were abandoned, its properties were to go either to the Rockefeller Foundation or to an educational institution of repute where the research could be continued. This legal move had various advantages, not the least of which was that in the event of withdrawal of University support or of Kinsey's death, the corporation would continue the research elsewhere, if not at Indiana. The first trustees of the newly incorporated Institute for Sex Research were Kinsey, Martin, Gebhard, and Pomeroy. Later, during Kinsey's lifetime, Douglas Short, a California lawyer, and Alice Field, a writer and social worker from New York, were added.

As the male volume neared publication date Kinsey became more and more troubled by the problem of public relations—how to handle the newspaper and magazine publicity in connection with the book's release. He explained the problem to Hartman:

> For several years we have been hounded by journalists who wanted to write on the material. We held them back with a promise they could have it when the book came out. Consequently, a number of the magazines such as *Look, Life, Reader's Digest, Science Illustrated,* etc., will carry articles in their December issues concerning the research.

The NRC was also concerned with the methods of release, and conferences were held in which matters such as publisher's contracts, advance reviews, and advertising copy were discussed. The final selection of the old-line medical publishing house of W. B. Saunders Company put many fears at rest. Half of the manuscript was sent off to press July 2, 1947, and the rest late in the summer. Helen Dietz, the Saunders editor who worked on the book with Kinsey, has described how his meticulousness made him an ideal author to work with. "He was extremely conscious of his writing style," she added, "and believed that a book should read well aloud, paying special attention to the cadence of his sentences. I recall several times finding him sitting at his desk in Bloomington reading the manuscript aloud to himself."

George Corner, the newly appointed chairman of the NRC sex research committee, which had supported Kinsey's program over the past seven years, visited Bloomington in September and read the manuscript. He wrote shortly: "My confidence in your program and admiraton for the great progress you and your colleagues are making scarcely required strengthening; but I feel I have added greatly to my comprehension of your program and needs." Science writers were by this time reading the book in proof and preparing articles on it. Corner noted in a memorandum to the members of the NRC committee that when the book was released the scientific knowledge of human sex behavior would be "augmented to a revolutionary extent" and that this would be likely to result in "a great deal of comment." "In some quarters," he added, "there may be reactions of surprise, even of shock." Because of this he stated it would be better for the work to be introduced to the public by trained science writers than by "ill-informed, sensational journalism." So much for the high hopes.

On January 5, 1948, *Sexual Behavior in the Human Male* by Kinsey, with Pomeroy and Martin as co-authors, was published. The almost cataclysmic results were largely unexpected. The publishers had consulted a public opinion poll as to the sales prospect for the book. Their "considered scientific opinion" was that it would not sell well. Kinsey, on the other hand, judging from his experiences with the public interest up to this point, predicted a big sale. The press it received was unprecedented for a scientific book. It was on the best-seller nonfiction list within three weeks of publication, and stayed there for twenty-seven continuous weeks. By mid-February it had climbed to first place, and by mid-March the seventh printing had been run off and the 100,000th copy had been sold. British, Swedish, French, Spanish, and Italian editions had been contracted for by the end of May. Kinsey's name had become a byword over night.

While the quantification of many types of sexual behavior based on a large sample was the book's greatest contribution, the most significant single finding was the marked differences in sexual patterns between males of varying social and economic levels. Similarly, the decade of birth and the degree of religious devoutness of the individual were also shown as relating to sexual behavior. Other important points which the Kinsey data established were the almost universal incidence of masturbation in young males and the early peak of their sexual levels, which occur typically in the late teens. Also, individual variation in sexual behavior was found to be much greater than had been previously thought, leading to the conclusion that formerly accepted norms were often inapplicable. Cases and figures were used to dispute the accepted theory of sexual sublimation. The concept of the total sexual outlet, the sum of all orgasms from any source, first proposed by the Kinsey team, was used to study the differences in sexual patterns and to tabulate sexual levels. A heterosexual-homosexual rating scale was another new concept presented by the authors. It was designed as a continuum on which the individual was placed at the proper point depending on his degree of psychic response and overt behavior during any period of his life in these two diverse forms of sexual activity. Childhood sexuality, petting to climax, and sexual contact with animals are other significant subjects that were developed in depth in the volume.

When the book was published President Wells was in Europe as a Cultural Affairs Adviser in the European Command Headquarters, where a copy was forwarded to him. Kinsey briefed him with this enthusiastic report on events:

> The reception of the book has been phenomenal. The magazine articles have all been favorable and, while there has been more varied reaction in the press, fully ninety-five per cent has been objective or definitely favorable. From about a thousand letters which we have received, we have six or eight complaints, nearly all of them from cranks who say very little about our book but talk for pages about the mysterious forces of the universe. . . .
>
> There apparently have been no complaints registered with the University (except from one faculty member), nor with the publisher, nor with the National Research Council. As far as I know, the only complaint the Rockefeller Foundation has received came from Harry Emerson Fosdick, brother of the president of the Rockefeller Foundation, who complained that the advertising was not dignified enough. That complaint is, of course, quite groundless.
>
> There will be complaints ultimately, without doubt; nevertheless, the flood of approval seems clear evidence that the public wanted such an objective scientific study of sex made. As scientists and educators, I think we have underestimated the public's capacity to look facts in the face.

On the following July 12 Kinsey was scheduled for a free lecture on the Berkeley campus of the University of California. The Harmon Gymnasium was filled by six-thirty for the eight o'clock program, and two other halls were pressed into use with loudspeakers installed. After over twenty years it is still a record attendance for the building. While this kind of reception was gratifying, the success of the book also brought many problems with it. The correspondence to be handled and the demands for radio appearances, lectures, and interviews were unending. The newspaper and magazine coverage was mixed—some of it was exaggerated and sensationalized, while other accounts were straightforward. The scientific and professional reviews were the crucial ones, of course.

The more serious criticism centered on what were perceived as the three chief weaknesses of the research. They were the lack of an adequate sample, too broad projection from the data to a larger population, and the use of a mechanistic "orgasm-counting" approach to the sexual experience. In addition, many reviewers named special areas that they felt Kinsey should have covered in his survey. These ranged all the way from depth analysis and levels of hormones in the urine to an exhaustive treatment of the subject of love. Another favorite, but basically trivial, criticism was of the wording of the title of the book, *Sexual Behavior in the Human Male*. Some nonscientific readers felt that the author was claiming his findings as applicable to the total human race. Actually the wording was acceptable by time-honored scientific practice. Studies with such titles as: "Maze Behavior in the White Rat," or "Mating Patterns in the Guinea Pig" are common. The flood of publicity which accompanied the publication was another point of attack. Few persons realized that it had been spontaneous and that Kinsey had not consciously sought this for his work. One critic stated that he was sure that only prostitutes would have been willing to be interviewed for the female part of the sample.

Some persons from a wide range of professional groups came strongly to his defense. He was probably most severely attacked by the ministers, the psychiatrists, and the statisticians. One of his favorite explanations for this was that these individuals were emotionally disturbed, and that they reacted violently because they felt threatened by his findings. His work carried broad implications for many disciplines: anthropology, sociology, psychology, psychiatry, and law. At times Kinsey may well have wished that he could have exchanged his biological hat for another one.

While Kinsey claimed that his only aim in his investigations of human sexual behavior was to record hitherto unexplored facts and relationships, he also had a strong streak of the social reformer in him. Discovering facts is good, but if they are not used to correct what one sees as social ills, such work loses much of its attraction and import. Since he was careful to divorce these two elements and consistently turned his scientific face toward the public, those who were moved to criticize him had difficulty in finding this suspected chink in his armor. The resulting frustration may have been the basis for some of the bitter personal attacks he suffered. Confronted with his eminently respectable scientific backing and wide public support, his critics often struck out wildly in an attempt to repudiate his work, and the ensuing onslaught was ruthless. In retrospect it has at times an almost ludicrous aspect. One of the most widely quoted intemperate comments was that of an Ivy League president who wrote: "Perhaps the undergraduate newspaper that likened the reports to the work of small boys writing dirty words on fences touched a more profound scientific truth than is revealed in the surfeit of rather trivial graphs with which the reports are loaded."[6]

According to those who knew him best, Kinsey was thin-skinned, and he smarted under these attacks. He had really expected workers in these allied scientific fields to accept his findings gratefully, since they had so many implications for their own sciences, but this was not the case. A psychiatrist who was a friend of Kinsey's observed some years after his death that it seemed to him an unusual phenomenon that he so rarely met an American physician of any kind—psychiatrist or other—who sincerely said "Dr. Kinsey gave us some valuable information" or "Dr. Kinsey gave us something valuable to work with." Both physicians and laymen, he added, will smirk, criticize and make jokes. "I believe this is because the name of Dr. Alfred C. Kinsey came to mean sexual curiosity," he explained. "Few people," he concluded, "realize that Dr. Kinsey's sexual curiosity was a constructive and creative curiosity."

When Kinsey was rejected as an outsider who was meddling with things he didn't really understand and was considered by some as professionally unqualified to study, he tried in various ways to counter this criticism. One means he turned to was to use a variety of professional consultants on his second book.

Dr. Fernandus Payne very wisely urged Kinsey not to be distracted into defending himself against his critics, but to let his friends do that for him. Kinsey, he felt, should bend all his energies toward pushing ahead with his research. While it is true that, with very minor exceptions, Kinsey did not try to answer his critics in lectures or in print, to ignore them entirely was for him impossible.

Proof that their barbs cut deep is in a thick pack of file cards in the Institute records. Mrs. Dorothy Collins, an assistant, was asked to collect the most scathing criticisms of both books that she could find and to type the exact quotes on the cards. Such denunciatory phrases as the following are typical: "Mr. Kinsey's animal books" (a college president in a chapel address); "In effect, he equates a good husband with a stud animal" (a gynecologist's remark in a newspaper interview); "Instead of admitting that they are compiling pornographic literature for the money they make out of it, these depraved characters offer it as scientific research" (a newspaper editorial); "I don't like Kinsey; I don't like his report; I don't like anything about it . . . the Kinsey Report might well be called the Kinsey Inquisition" (a university biologist); "It is impossible to estimate the damage this book will do to the already deteriorating morals of America" (a well-known minister). Whether he had in mind that at some grand finale he would make this vituperation a matter of record is uncertain. He did carry the cards with him for ready reference on some of his lecture and interviewing trips. He was never one to spare the lash on himself. Dwelling on these extreme examples of abusive invective was the equivalent of twisting the knife in his many wounds.

That during this period he often felt embattled is clear from his letters. To assume the burden of work which he did and then to be continually aware that he had also to defend his right to do it was unnerving and exhausting. He reassured himself sometimes by sending on endorsements of his work to friends. As these were worked into his conversation or passed over his desk, they would tend to become somewhat magnified. By these small means he bolstered his courage and strengthened his conviction in the essential right of what he was doing.

The annual conference of the American Psychopathological Association in June, 1948, gave the Kinsey team of four its first opportunity to present a joint paper, which was published the following year under their authorship in the volume reporting the conference (40). Entitled "Concepts of Normality and Abnormality in Sexual Behavior," it developed further the point of view that some nonreproductive sexual activities—such as masturbation, mouth-genital contacts, and homosexuality—which were traditionally, legally, or socially, proscribed as "crimes against nature" have behind them a strong biologic heritage. This often leads, they pointed out, to a conflict for the individual involved. The general conclusion was:

> Whether such biologic inheritance is an adequate basis for considering any activity right or wrong, socially desirable, or undesirable, is an issue which we do not raise, and one which we have never raised. We do contend, however, that sexual acts which are demonstrably part of the phylogenetic heritage of any species cannot be classified as acts contrary to nature, biologically unnatural, abnormal, or perverse.

Crank letters were not infrequent at the Institute. Some were obviously written by unstable persons. Others were direct expressions of an honest conviction that such sex research was the work of the Devil. One lady from Delaware wrote to President Wells protesting Kinsey's employment at the University. She ended with the suggestion that he "be imprisoned for life," since he was doing all he could to "push this civilization down the hill." The accompanying sardonic note by the President's assistant who forwarded the letter to Kinsey must have brought a smile. It read: "There is nothing like knowing what your public thinks of you. I would say that this lady sits pretty far back in your rooting section."

8.

The Female Counterpart

I N THE FIRST PROGRESS REPORT TO THE NA-
tional Research Council in April, 1948, following the publication of *Sexual Behavior in the Human Male,* Alfred Kinsey
paused to take stock of what he had accomplished in his ten
years of sex research, to answer certain issues, and to forecast
his future path. He first discussed the reasons why other sex
surveys had been unsuccessful, citing chiefly timidity on the
part of the investigators, who doubted public tolerance of
such studies. He and his staff had learned through "sometimes
unpleasant experiences" to take care of awkward situations
which they met. "By staying with the project, we did learn
how to meet the public, and to win support from a great
diversity of people," he continued. Giving credit to the backing of the National Research Council and that of Indiana
University as a great help in gaining general acceptance, he
noted that a Gallup Poll had reported that five out of every six persons in the country approved the idea that such a
study should have been made. Few other questions of social

impact have received such wide approval, he pointed out.

On the touchy issue of whether data such as Kinsey's should have been made available to the general public, he made this unequivocal statement:

This is a question which scientists, of course, will not debate. Moreover, it is unrealistic to propose that it would have been possible to have published this material, and to have kept it out of the hands of the general public. The courts have recognized this, and there are court decisions which clearly establish the right of a scientific investigator to make such material available to persons who are not technically trained.

Next, he took issue with the psychoanalysts' claim that it is impossible to secure sufficient data for a sex survey in an hour-and-a-half interview. He pointed out that with two interviewers—the number he had on his staff—about seven hundred years would have been required to obtain a similar number of the type of case histories they recommended. He further explained:

We undertook the present project with the idea that an overall survey of human sexual behavior, divorced from questions of therapy, would help orient the psychiatrist, the clinical psychologist, the physiologist, and all other specialists dealing with problems of human sexual behavior. We should welcome intensive studies that might be made by students in each of these fields, but we cannot conceive of a psychoanalytic approach which is set up to provide the sort of general survey which our program calls for.

Finally, he outlined his plans for new staff members qualified to investigate the physiology and psychology of human sexual behavior. This would lead, he hoped, to research in these neglected fields.

After the first furor died down following the publication of the male volume, Kinsey and the staff returned to another period of intensive travel to gather new histories—this time chiefly from women—to enlarge the sample for the next study. In 1948–49, trips to New York, Boston, Washington, Miami, Chicago, Berkeley, San Francisco, and elsewhere netted more than 3,000 new cases, most of them for the new volume. Often there were reports of trouble with impostors who claimed to be gathering interview data for Kinsey. One man is said to have gone through most of an office building in New York soliciting and obtaining interviews before he was found to be fraudulent. In various localities police headquarters and Better Business Bureaus cooperated by giving publicity to the Institute statement that no Kinsey interviewing was done by telephone or by doorbell-ringing.

As a counterpoint there is a letter Kinsey wrote late in 1948 to Anderson, his long-time friend at St. Louis. After receiving a copy of Anderson's new study in plant genetics, Kinsey thanked him and wrote with a tinge of wistfulness: "I wish such a book had been done in the days when I was working in this field. I do long to get back into it sometimes, but I know that it is more important to stay with the thing I am on."

Interspersed with travel was an influx of visitors at the Institute at Bloomington—if they could schedule a day when they could catch Kinsey in town. Some came to learn about the research at first hand; others were consultants for the female volume, which was rapidly taking shape. Requests for popular lectures poured in, but Kinsey cannily set up a general rule which allowed him to avoid many of these without offense. This is how he explained his practice:

> We have to adopt a strict rule in declining all invitations to lecture, except to groups with which we are working for the purpose of obtaining histories. We can be of more use to science by continuing our basic research. . . . We lecture for the sake of securing histories or to technical groups where the scientific interpretations of our data are involved. I am sorry that our schedule is so full that we cannot take on your group as one to work with for histories.

In March, 1948, the American Social Hygiene Association devoted two days of their Conference for Social Hygiene Executives to a discussion of various aspects of Kinsey's book. They scheduled Dr. George Corner to speak, as well as representatives from the fields of psychiatry, sociology, law, medicine, anthropology, and statistics. They did not invite Kinsey to attend, however. Later, they asked him to write a rebuttal paper to be included in the printed report of their program, but he refused to do so.

The American Association for the Advancement of Science honored Kinsey at their 1949 meetings in New York by holding a symposium on "The Kinsey Report and Its Contribution to Related Fields." Those speaking included Morris Ernst, lawyer, Dr. Manfred Guttmacher, psychoanalyst, and Ralph Linton, anthropologist.

One of the first public addresses given by Kinsey on his own campus was sponsored by Sigma Xi, and was delivered before a capacity audience in the Chemistry Building auditorium in the early 1950's. The first ten minutes were spent in describing the male and female orgasm. This sort of straightforward talk caught many of his audience unaware. But he registered no reaction and seemed insulated from the embarrassed giggles and other manifestations of uneasiness among the audience. "He gave the impression of an evangel, totally absorbed in his message," one listener recalls. Since Kinsey went on to present his statistical findings, which were primarily based on orgasms, his introduction was a sensible one. None of his listeners could profess ignorance of the meaning of the term.

Although Kinsey had early made a strict rule not to charge fees for lectures, expenses of the trip were sometimes covered, and any honorariums freely offered were accepted with the understanding that the money would be added to the Institute reserve funds. These funds, which also included the book royalties, were used to help defray the costs of continuing the research, especially servicing and maintaining the library and archives. The fact that no one on the staff personally profited from the income from either the book sales or lectures certainly helped in some quarters to influence opinion in favor of the research.

Among the engagements that Kinsey did accept, the 1952 Jake Gimbel Lectures on Sex Psychology at Berkeley and Stanford are memorable. One of the four Berkeley lectures was repeated at the Medical Center of the University in San Francisco and one at the Stanford campus. At Berkeley, Wheeler Hall proved far too small, and the series was moved for the last lecture to the men's gymnasium for the crowd of 5,000 students. The topics covered included concepts of normality and abnormality in sexual behavior as well as physiological, psychological, and hormonal factors in sexual response.

Early in the research Kinsey had become aware of the insights to be gained by a study of the erotic element in art. He felt that the representations of sexual themes—either in fine art or in amateur pornographic scribblings—were indispensable sources of data for any scientific study of sex. In line with this he had begun a series of interviews with established artists which explored the relationship between their work and their sexual patterns. When he started to expand the library of the Institute, books on art were among the first of his extensive purchases. He sought advice on acquiring erotic art for the archive collection from artists, art historians, museum staff, and dealers both here and abroad. One of his chief purposes in adding a photographer to the staff was to make an archival record of original art which was too expensive for the Institute to ever hope to acquire. William Dellenback, the staff photographer, often spent months away from Bloomington photographing erotic art which was in the hands of dealers or owned by museums or collectors. Friends traveling to foreign countries were asked to keep their eyes open for erotica for the Institute. Some collectors and artists found it convenient to donate individual items. Pictures drawn by children and a wide range of pornography confiscated by prison authorities augmented the files.

In 1950 material which the Institute for Sex Research was importing for its archives and collections was unexpectedly seized by a United States Customs official in the Indianapolis office. Previously, Kinsey had by special arrangements been able to have such erotica cleared for importation. The regular customs officer who usually expedited this matter was on vacation at the time. The substitute who opened the packages was thoroughly horrified to find what he considered very offensive pornography being collected by a research organization of an Indiana state institution of higher learning. Showing the contents of the package to reporters and then to the governor's office sealed the matter; the cat had leaped completely out of the bag. Part of the material in the original Indianapolis seizure was shortly forwarded to Bloomington, but the remainder was impounded in New York. As other shipments came through the U.S. ports of entry—books, photographs, art objects—they were likewise held.

Some months later as the controversy grew, Kinsey made this statement to clarify the issues:

> In response to a recent inquiry, the Institute for Sex Research, at Indiana University, explains that it has inevitably had to gather data and materials which, under other circumstances and in other places, would be considered obscene. Investigators of human sex behavior have always had to deal with these things. Otherwise it would be impossible to understand the full reality of human sexual interests and behavior.
>
> There have of course always been attempts to control the distribution of materials which when publicly circulated might arouse sexual interests and activities. So-called obscenity statutes, however, have always been difficult to frame because, as court decisions have repeatedly emphasized, concepts of obscenity have varied from time to time. . . .
>
> Consequently, many states have made specific provisions for the admission, possession, and utilization of so-called obscene materials for clinical and scientific use. In the same way, the courts have admitted socialistic, anarchistic, and other materials which scholars needed in their investigations of other social problems.
>
> The obscenity clause of the Customs Act makes an exception for works of artistic or scientific merit. The wording of the Statute, however, is not wholly clear, and the Institute's present conversations with the Customs Officials are designed to secure a clearer interpretation of this part of the law. The material immediately in question was imported by the Institute in good faith for the furtherance of its scientific investigation. The Institute believed that the importation of such material was based on precedents from several previous Federal Court decisions. No final decisions have yet been reached in these discussions.
>
> The Institute feels that the issue is much broader than that of the importation of a specific object at a given time and place. It considers that the issue is one which concerns all scholars who need access to so-called obscene materials for scientific investigations which in the long run may contribute to human welfare.

This dispute was never settled during Kinsey's lifetime although he made repeated efforts through various high-ranking state and federal officials to get a favorable out-of-court ruling on it. When in 1957 it finally came before Judge Edmund L. Palmieri in the United States District Court, Southern District of New York, with the University acting as *amicus curiae* (friend of the court), the case was decided in favor of the Institute. The importation of such materials was to be permitted when they were for the purpose of scientific research and so would not in all reasonable probability appeal to the prurient interests of those who would be using them. The scientific cause had won a victory, but too late for Alfred Kinsey to relish it.

Because of the widespread discussion and criticism of the statistical aspects of *Sexual Behavior in the Human Male*, it was decided jointly by the National Research Council and the Institute for Sex Research to ask for a critical appraisal of the statistical methods used in the book. At their request a committee was appointed by the American Statistical Association to make such a study and to submit a report. They came in the fall of 1950, three strong, to acquaint themselves with the Institute and to evaluate the statistical problems. William G. Cochran, Johns Hopkins University, served as chairman. Frederick Mosteller from Harvard University and John W. Tukey from Princeton were the other two members of the committee. The Institute staff chiefly involved were the three authors of the book, although others, especially Dorothy Collins, who had a mathematical and statistical background, were called upon for help with the detailed analyses necessary. Since the male volume had been published over three years before and the next book was well along, time was of the essence if the recommendations were to be used to improve the presentation of the data in the female volume.

A five-page summary of the final 331-page report was released to the public in June, 1952, twenty months after the committee's first conference in Bloomington. The report, entitled *Statistical Problems of the Kinsey Report*, was published in full late in 1954 by the American Statistical Association. While Kinsey and his associates in their response accepted many of the committee recommendations as sound, they pointed out that with improvement of their own facilities they had already incorporated a large number of the suggestions into their program. Thus the appraisal, they felt, was not currently valid. The real point of difference, however, was over the practicality of an ideal statistical approach in terms of money, time, manpower, and more particularly, of overall goals.

The statisticians granted that such a complex program of research involved many problems, "for some of which there appear at the present to be no satisfactory solutions." Many of the basic dilemmas, they admitted, were currently inherent in any study of sexual behavior since its taboo subject matter hinders probability sampling as well as the gathering of data based on observed rather than reported behavior. Pointing out that the Kinsey team had received limited statistical help, the committee commented that they "deserved much credit for the straight thinking which brought them safely by many pitfalls. . . . The sort of assistance which might resolve some of their most complex problems," they added, "would require understanding, background, and techniques that perhaps not more than twenty statisticians in the world possess."[1] The sampling bias which is inevitable in such a study, they concluded, should have been better compensated for by greater caution in the conclusions and more frequent warnings to the reader.

In a point-by-point comparison of the Kinsey book with seven other earlier sex studies, it came off with flying colors, being ranked first when examined on sample and sampling methods, interviewing methods, statistical methods, and checks. It was also described as unquestionably covering more ground of a specific variety than any of the others.[2] One might conclude that while Kinsey's work was clearly the best, it was still not as good as they felt it might have been.

The newspapers, as Kinsey had feared, fastened largely onto the critical aspects of the summary. Later, a listing was compiled of the 120 headline captions which appeared over the news story in papers across the country. Although they were all based on similar material released by the wire services, they ranged from the simple, "KINSEY FAILED" (*Times-News*, Burlington, North Carolina) and "STATISTICIANS RAP KINSEY REPORT" (*World-Herald*, Omaha, Nebraska) to "STATISTICIANS SAY KINSEY DID AN EXCELLENT JOB" (*Journal*, Elizabeth, New Jersey). The three authors of the report had been correct in sounding a warning in their introduction that the mixture of praise and criticism in their findings lent itself to widely varied overall interpretations, depending on the predilections of the reader.

The confrontation with the Cochran, Mosteller, and Tukey committee appointed by the American Statistical Association was undoubtedly therapeutic for the research in that it focused the attention of the staff more sharply upon the intricacies of the statistical problems they were facing. The National Research Council seemed satisfied with the results. The whole investigation was time-consuming and disrupted the work schedule on the forthcoming volume. Kinsey deeply resented this, but he felt that the challenge was one he had to meet. The detailed report was too technical to be read widely, but it served the purpose of putting the statistical problems faced by such a survey as Kinsey's in proper focus. It must also be pointed out that at the time Kinsey was collecting his data and planning his analysis nonprobability sample theory was largely undeveloped.

The pressure for advance releases on the findings of the new volume grew in intensity as the news spread that the manuscript was nearing final form. In his 1950 Progress Report, Kinsey had anticipated some of the problems:

> The appearance of our second volume will involve a public relations problem which is, in some ways, similar, and in many ways more complex than the problem which we met on the publication of our first book. Considerable interest has been shown, and in some cases threatening attempts have been made, to obtain advance information on the content of the volume; and it is obvious that there will be a flood of magazine articles and review volumes appearing as soon as we get into print. It will take a special effort on our part to keep the condensations and commentaries from appearing before we get into print.

Attempts were made by various magazine writers to outwit Kinsey in his refusal to release preliminary findings on his new book. Several articles appeared which purported to be "sneak previews" of the data. Two of these appeared in *Focus* and *Redbook*. The story in the latter appeared as early as May, 1950, and was written by Morris Ernst and David

Loth. Its subcaption claimed: "The authors of this vitally significant article have long worked closely with Dr. Kinsey and his associates. . . . Here they present for the first time the facts to be revealed in the new report." In view of this the Institute issued a press release stating that the authors had not been given any special access to the material for the forthcoming book and that what was accurate in the *Redbook* story had been available in print since 1948. As for the predictions made, the Institute press release pointed out that preliminary calculations did not substantiate many of them, and that others were totally unfounded as no data had been collected on these questions.

However, by May, 1953, a note from Kinsey to Carl Hartman read:

> The news now is that the book will be coming out early in the Fall. It has nearly killed us to do it but we have finished it the way we thought it should be. We think it is a great book and I hope you agree with us when you see it.

This book was indeed a more ambitious undertaking than the first one. The mass of data presented in it was enormous. There was also the added job of constantly contrasting the findings for the female with those reported earlier for the male. All the statistical material was worked out carefully in a much improved form. The new data were extensively footnoted to pertinent material published by others. This ranged from the *Ananga-Ranga*, the Talmud, and the Koran to Freud, Katharine Davis, and Simone de Beauvoir. The significant sources of data in allied fields—medicine, law, sociology, psychology, anthropology, demography—were carefully sought out and cited to strengthen and supplement the interpretations. This reference work was done by the staff, largely by myself, but Kinsey edited it painstakingly, culling each unnecessary word.

The work with a number of outside consultants was another time-consuming job during the final stages of writing. A New York psychiatrist, Dr. Robert Laidlaw, who, with Emily Mudd, a Philadelphia marriage counselor, and Dr. Sophie Kleegman, a Manhattan gynecologist, spent time in

Bloomington serving as consultants on certain chapters, describes these sessions:

> You will recall that Emily and I would be closeted in separate rooms in the laboratory and each of us would go over the same chapter, making notes as we did so. Then we would meet with Kinsey and the staff and would raise questions, make suggestions for new material or for changing existing material. I was deeply impressed with the way in which Kinsey handled this. Here was a manuscript on which he and all of you had worked so diligently and here were the two of us bringing in a point of view from the outside which at times differed quite markedly from the text. In this situation Kinsey admirably demonstrated his scientific objectivity. If he felt that he was right and we were wrong he staunchly defended the text, but in many instances where we were able to make a reasonable presentation, he instantly accepted it and made appropriate changes in the text.

"Both of the women did an excellent job with our two chapters and the chapters are much better for it," Kinsey wrote to Pomeroy, who was studying for his advanced degree at Columbia at this juncture. Other consultants went over chapters which were mailed to them. In all ten persons outside the staff aided in this way.

Kinsey was a master of the generalized, well-rounded, but not always completely accurate, statement, and it sometimes got him into trouble in his writing. It made him a striking lecturer, a dramatic storyteller, and also a vulnerable target for critics. Necessary qualifying phrases in his text were not infrequently suggested by others. These hobbling restrictions were accepted with fair grace, as Kinsey could recognize this weakness once it was pointed out to him. Because of staff suggestions, the second book certainly had fewer flaws of this sort. Kinsey was in general reasonable about criticisms from his staff or those who were trying to help him. In contrast, he often seemed "almost physically wounded," in the words of a former staff member, by criticisms from outside.

The advance stories on the new book were prepared in May and June when copies of the page proof of *Sexual Behavior in the Human Female* had been made available to about fifty journalists who came to the Bloomington campus for a stay of several days. They were scheduled in three groups, and

Kinsey briefed them on the research, arranged for his secretary, Eleanor Roehr, to serve them a luncheon in the office conference room, entertained them at dinner in his garden, and gave them a tour of the Institute. They were then sent back to their hotel rooms with the book proofs under their arms, pledged to write only one 5,000-word article, to hold it for an August 20 deadline, and to submit their reviews to a check for factual errors before publication. To read and digest the 761 pages of tables and text in a few days, to take adequate notes knowing you could not refer back to the original as you wrote your final draft was a demanding assignment. Some of the reporters decided to be interviewed for their own histories in order to better acquaint themselves with the methods of the research. Personal conferences with Kinsey were also scheduled by many of them.

These three weeks, with a Monday through Thursday stint during each, were an enervating period for the staff, and particularly for Kinsey. Many of these writers had been put off earlier when they had requested a firsthand visit to the Institute and an interview. Kinsey felt obligated to play the role of generous host and to make them feel that the postponement had resulted in equalized and more advantageous opportunities for all. Kinsey wrote after the first book that controlling publicity and public relations had entailed "sometimes nerve-racking work." This term certainly applied this second time around. On August 20, or "K-Day," as it was dubbed, the newsstands were filled with magazines carrying banner headlines about the Kinsey Report on their covers. Practically every newspaper in the country carried a news release on the findings, and many published either reviews or detailed summaries of the forthcoming volume by wire service science writers. Kinsey's strenuous efforts to direct the unprecedented journalistic interest in his unique findings to dignified and conservative channels were of little effect. The widely publicized reviews and news stories flooded the country, alarming his many well-meaning supporters and making them fearful of the repercussions on the research and the University.

The center of the storm, *Sexual Behavior in the Human Female*, was actually published three weeks later, on Septem-

ber 14, 1953. The first printing was 25,000 and the sixth printing was in press within ten days, which carried the total to
185,000. While there was talk of sluggish sales and overstock-
ing, the fact was that the sales of this book very closely paral-
leled those of the earlier volume. By December it had been on
the *New York Times* best-seller list for eleven weeks, hovering
between second and third place most of the time. Each of the
two books sold roughly a quarter-million copies.

A few days before the release date on the magazine articles
Kinsey had flown to San Francisco for a respite from the
pressures he had been under. A short handwritten note, dated
August 24 and sent to me from his California hide-out, reads:
"Hold everything tight—NO COMMENTS to the press—until I
get home." A first-hand account of his hideaway is provided
by Douglas Rigg, then a warden at San Quentin:

> He returned to San Quentin just as the female volume was
> released. As he put it, "This is the last place anyone will look for
> me." He enjoyed hiding out—the prison was a sanctuary from
> the hustle and bustle of the Female Volume birth. I was in San
> Francisco with him that week. His face and name were on every
> national magazine cover. He got a kick out of wandering around
> en route to one of his favorite restaurants, the bow tie and shock
> of hair showing and being so seldom recognized; or if recognized
> not being bothered!

On September 2 he returned East and spoke to a capacity
crowd at the Women's National Press Club in Washington,
D.C., where he denied that his books were intended as a
"prescription for any social policy." "We have never suggested what should or what should not be done in human
behavior," he added. "We have never made recommendations
that there should be new sex customs or laws."

The most important contributions of the volume on
female sexual behavior, aside from the incidence and frequency figures on various kinds of sexual activity, were the
exploration of basic male-female similarities and differences
in sexual behavior and response, and evidence of the lesser
effect of certain social factors on sexual behavior in women
than in men. The anatomy, physiology, and psychology of

erotic arousal in both males and females were delineated in a detail which had never been presented before.

This shift in attitude is well reflected in an incident which Kinsey was fond of telling. He had been invited to give a Sunday morning address at a Quaker meeting. He faced the morning with some misgivings as he knew that there had been considerable discussion among the members on the propriety of having him appear. His talk, giving a straightforward account of his work and its findings, was followed by a dead silence for several minutes. One of the very dignified older members of the congregation then stood up and exclaimed, "Praise the Lord that such things can be discussed in our meeting house and in such a proper manner." Kinsey knew the day had been won.

At the beginning Kinsey was highly optimistic about the reception of the new book. For example, about two months after publication date he wrote:

> There has been an occasional protest and an occasional letter from a psychotic, but well over ninety-nine percent of the letters that have come here, to the publisher, to the administration of the university, to the magazines that have written the review articles, etc., etc., have been in high approval. Apparently the world has wanted this thing done, much more than even we realized.

But then the attack began, and for various reasons, not all of which are clear, the criticism became more violent than after the publication of the volume on the male. In the heat of the dispute highly derogatory statements were frequent. A London clergyman termed the work "pseudo-scientific snoopings," while one in Indianapolis stated that Kinsey had degraded science and publicized his books "like a cheap charlatan." A rabbi in New York considered the findings "a libel on all womankind." These and similar statements were given wide publicity in the news media. Kinsey was dismayed and saddened. A year later he wrote in retrospect:

> I am still uncertain what the basic reason for the bitter attack on us may be. The attack is evidently much more intense with this publication of the female volume. Their arguments become absurd when they attempt to find specific flaws in the book and basically I think they are attacking on general principles. There

is a segment of the church that believes that sex morality is the most important thing in all morality. Honesty, charity, plain ordinary decency toward one's fellows and a hundred and one other virtues sink into insignificance when they are considering sexual morality.

He added in an even more melancholy vein:

There is nothing that disturbs me more than the fact that there is practically no scientist outside of yourself [Hartman] and the National Research Council's committee that has commended any aspect of any single item in our volume on the female. I have no doubt that there are many scientists who have seen some importance in what we have done, but the only ones who have bothered to go into print are those who are objecting.

Kinsey has somewhat overstated the case, but it is true that criticism dominated the scene. The degree to which the professional world challenged many of the published findings and pointed out their shortcomings is difficult to realize currently, when practically every textbook and piece of scientific writing in the field makes constant reference to the data in the Kinsey studies. Some of the findings which were under particular attack were the low rate of frigidity found; only about nine per cent of the women interviewed had never had an orgasm. This differed widely from what the psychiatrists had held as true. Another result that met with disbelief was the rapidity of erotic response of women to physical stimulation, which Kinsey data showed as comparing favorably with that of men. This was based on timing in masturbation, a criterion that had been largely ignored in other studies. The counting of multiple orgasms, the equating of the clitoral and vaginal orgasm, and the unexpected aging curve—so different from that found in the male—were other points of controversy.

Much second guessing has been done as to why the book and its authors suffered such a vitriolic attack. As one reads the now yellowed newspaper stories of eighteen years ago, various explanations come to mind. The figures on premarital and extramarital intercourse were taken by many as a besmirching of American womanhood. The revelation that the range of women's biological sexual capacities was greater than man's may have been felt as an affront to male sensibility. There was a fear that the curtain of conventional sexual morality would be permanently pushed aside. The backlash from the excessive advance publicity, which many again assumed Kinsey had masterminded, certainly played a role.

The interval between the late 1940's and the early 1950's—the period when Kinsey's works were published and discussed—was characterized by a generally conservative political climate. There was a strong insistence on patriotic orthodoxy, a marked trend toward conformism, and a shying away from controversial issues. Thus it was a time less favorable to the acceptance of such a radical departure from ancient taboos than the 1920's, 1930's, or 1960's might have been.[3]

The controversy took on a literary and philosophic tone as well as a scientific and theological one. An influential essay by the literary critic Lionel Trilling, entitled "The Kinsey Report," which was originally published in 1949 in the *Partisan Review*, is a case in point. His line of attack was impossible to refute, since his assumptions were outside of the scientific framework. He was trying to draw the "champ" out of his class. This essay was reprinted many times in various formats over the following years and became a minor classic on the subject of Kinsey's naiveté and shortcomings. The assault by the theologians was spearheaded by Dr. Henry Van Dusen, President of the Union Theological Seminary, and by Reinhold Niebuhr, also of the Seminary. Van Dusen had thrown down the gauntlet to the Rockefeller Foundation in 1948 for having supported the Kinsey research, and now republished his statements, somewhat modified, in an editorial in *Christianity and Crisis*. Originally he had written:

> The most disturbing thing about the current vogue of *The Sexual Behavior of the Human Male* is not the facts it set forth; although as a recent editorial in this Journal pointed out, if they are trustworthy, they reveal a prevailing degradation in American morality approximating the worst decadence of the Roman era. The most disturbing thing is the absence of a spontaneous, ethical revulsion from the premises of the study, and the inability on the part of its readers to put their fingers on the falsity of its premises. For the presuppositions of the Kinsey Report are strictly animalistic. This bias underlies the Introduction and controls the interpretation of the data at every point. Few have

raised ethical queries regarding the sponsorship of this study by a responsible national research body, and its financing by one of the great Foundations dedicated "to promote the well-being of mankind throughout the world."[4]

In 1954, Van Dusen quoted the first part of his earlier statement and added, "the *response* to the Kinsey premises reveals how far advanced is ethical nihilism and irresponsibility in the contemporary American consciousness."[5] Nor was it long before Congressional forces added their voice to the mounting tide of criticism. New York Congressman Louis B. Heller in a public letter to Postmaster-General Summerfield proposed that the book should be banned from the mails until Congress could investigate it. "He is hurling the insult of the century against our mothers, wives, daughters, and sisters," Heller said of Kinsey, "under the pretext of making a great contribution to scientific research." There were strong rumors that the Reece congressional investigating committee would call the Rockefeller Foundation to account for its support of sex research.

This special House Committee, head by B. Carroll Reece, Republican from Tennessee, was established during the McCarthy era to investigate the use of funds by tax-exempt, nonprofit foundations. Early in January, 1954, papers carried the story that Kinsey would be called in to testify regarding the finances of his research. He countered with the statement that the accounts of the Institute for Sex Research were a matter of public record. They were handled by the University and audited by state examiners.

In March, 1954, Kinsey was officially informed that further support from Rockefeller Foundation funds channeled to the Institute for Sex Research through the National Research Council Committee for Research in Problems of Sex was highly unlikely. The current grant was to expire in a few months. Kinsey could not have been taken entirely by surprise. Dr. Corner had warned him five years earlier that financial support by the NRC committee might not continue after 1952. But later it was extended two years beyond that date. The duty of his committee, Corner wrote Kinsey, was "to promote risk projects, venturesome but promising new activities." Kinsey's work had been "exactly in that class when Yerkes was first attracted to it," he explained. This purpose had been carried out in the committee's long-term support of Kinsey's work, which he felt was now well established. Thus Kinsey had been forewarned of this eventuality—the loss of major grant funds—but was not in any way prepared to meet the crisis. Reserve funds would last only a short time and rushing ahead with another best-seller or searching out a willing millionaire to endow the Institute was not feasible. The withdrawal of support at the exact time that the tax-exempt foundations were under fire from congressional investigators clouded the entire issue, however.

In August, 1954, the axe fell officially. Newspapers carried the story of the Rockefeller Foundation's second-quarter grants for that year. The announcement of a three-year grant of $150,000 to the Committee for Research in Problems of Sex of the National Research Council was accompanied by the statement: "Some of the projects formerly supported by the committee, including that of Dr. Kinsey, are now in a position to obtain support from other sources." Dr. Keith Cannon, chairman of the Division of Medical Sciences of the National Research Council, when interviewed was quoted as explaining that the funds for Dr. Kinsey were dropped as of midsummer because the Institute for Sex Research did not request a renewal of support. He added that the presumption was that Kinsey's work was now well endowed and did not need further help from the Council.[6] This was, of course, far from the case.

In spite of this public pronouncement, it was clear to those who observed the sequence of events that political pressures and public criticism had played a role in the withdrawal of funds, although how decisive a one could not be accurately assessed. The previous May, however, Kinsey had spoken to the American Psychiatric Association meeting at St. Louis and had charged that religious and other groups were exerting pressure on Indiana University and on the Rockefeller Foundation to end their support of his studies.

Once it was clear that foundation funds were not available for the Kinsey research, the NRC committee sought a means to show that it, at least, was not deserting an old friend whose work was under fire. They had modest research funds from other sources on which they could draw. Their token grants to the Kinsey project from National Academy of Science funds continued for several years, showing where their heart was in the matter.

The public hearings of the Reece committee, which received wide publicity, had started the previous May and lasted for sixteen sessions. The foundations were not given an opportunity to testify on their side of the story, but were permitted to file sworn statements with the committee. The final Majority Report was issued in December, 1954, accompanied by a strongly dissenting minority statement. The Majority Report, as might have been anticipated by anyone who had followed the hearings, charged that the foundations had used their tax-exempt monies to foster programs and studies which were "directly supporting subversion." The Kinsey Reports were termed unworthy of the foundation aid they had received. The report considered them "as good an example as any of the extremely limited positive value—combined with extremely grave possibilities of adverse social effect—of much of the empirical research in the social sciences." All of these arrows of misfortune were exceedingly distressing to Kinsey, not only because he could not understand the real reasons behind them, but because they had apparently led some of his backers to scatter for cover.

It is plainly in the record that President Wells and the University unwaveringly stood by Kinsey and the research during the period when violent criticism was being leveled at them from many sources. This was most clearly exemplified when, during the previous September, Mrs. Harold Brady, the Indiana Provincial Director of the National Council of Catholic Women, released to the papers a letter she had sent to the President questioning the University's support of Kinsey's work and asking if Indiana University was "still a fit place for the education of the youth of our state."

Wells replied with a reiteration of the University's official statement issued two weeks earlier. It pointed out that only through scientific knowledge could the cures for the emotional and social maladies of society be found. Moreover, while the University administration did not approve or disapprove of the research findings of Kinsey or of any other of its scientists, it defended his right to investigate every aspect of life because of a faith in knowledge rather than in ignorance. Wells then differentiated between the two functions of the University: teaching and the search for truth. He added that Kinsey's research was entirely separate from the University's teaching function. Wells had the support of the Board of Trustees on this clear-cut stand.

In certain quarters a hue and cry was raised that Kinsey was aiding the Communist cause. *The Indiana Catholic and Record*, a weekly newspaper published by the Indianapolis Roman Catholic Archdiocese, had claimed in an editorial that Dr. Kinsey's books "pave the way for people to believe in communism and to act like Communists." A subsequent headline in the Bloomington paper read "KINSEY'S SEX BOOKS LABELED 'RED' TAINTED." The campus paper replied with a "WHO? ARE YOU KIDDING? DR. KINSEY? AIDING COMMUNISM?" headline as their tongue-in-cheek reply. Wells reissued his original statement of support of the research and pointed out that one of the basic differences between the Russian system and our own was the freedom to investigate.

The Catholic attack was also countered shortly by a statement of support issued by the Indiana University chapter of the American Association of University Professors. They took strong issue with objections to Kinsey's work that were based on disapproval of his findings rather than on any scholarly evaluation of them. The attempt to tie his methodological position to Communism they termed "a deliberate and deplorable appeal to emotionalism, which if successful could only undermine the democratic functions of the American university." Academic freedom had been challenged, and the A.A.U.P. chapter composed of Kinsey's colleagues clearly felt the need to reaffirm the scholar's right to pursue the truth. In conclusion they pointed out that regardless of the unpopularity of the findings, "any educational institution that wished to maintain the status of a university has the obligation to support competent research to the limit of its facilities."

A *Daily Student* editorial entitled "Taboo or To Be" supported the stand of the professors and stressed the need for research in the social sciences to counterbalance the research in the physical sciences which had recently produced the H-bomb. After quoting Wells' answer to the National Council of Catholic Women when they censured Kinsey's work, the writer closed with the cogent comment: "If research is restricted in fields now labeled taboo, man will be on a roller coaster to the minus age."

Between other activities, Kinsey and the Institute staff were pushing steadily forward with the sex offender research project by extensive interviewing in the California prison system. They interviewed at Folsom, Terminal Island, San Quentin, Soledad, Chino, Norwalk, and Atascadero for histories both of sex offenders and of the prison control group of men who had not been convicted of a sex offense. Although this study was not finally published until nine years after Kinsey's death, most of the data, with the exception of part of the matching nonprison control group, were collected under his supervision. During his work on the West coast Kinsey was called upon a number of times to cooperate with committees of the California State Assembly on proposed legislation concerning sex offenses. By 1952 he had also prepared material for and consulted with legislative committees and special research groups set up by the legislatures of New Jersey, New York, Delaware, Wyoming, and Oregon. Sex offenses are a hysteria-producing subject and California has had its share of such problems. Its erstwhile program permitting castration of sex offenders, its Sexual Psychopath Law, and its excellent rehabilitation program at Norwalk, which Kinsey considered "the best he had seen anywhere in the world," all came under this scrutiny.

Over thirty of the memo-type cards of Kinsey lecture notes in the Institute files touch on these or related problems. The lecture titles include: "Police Brutality"; "Rehabilitation of Sex Offenders"; "Who Is Caught and the Basis of Conviction"; "The Administration of Sex Law"; "The California Adult Authority"; "Castration"; "Factors Producing Sex Offenders"; and "Treatment of the Homosexual Sex Offender." He spoke on these and similar topics in many of his public appearances during the 1950's. Deeply emotionally involved in the injustices he uncovered as he did his investigating, he found the prisoners accepting him with complete confidence "not merely as an objective scientist collecting facts" but also as a "warm-hearted, understanding human being." These words were written by Austin MacCormick, former Commissioner of Corrections in New York and later professor of criminology at Berkeley, who had been a classmate of Kinsey's at Bowdoin. His further firsthand observation on Kinsey's interviewing in California prisons reads:

> Many of the questions were of the type to which most interviewers, however skillful, would find it difficult if not impossible to get answers. Kinsey's questions were asked with the easy manner a family doctor would have in questioning a patient who knew him well about a mysterious pain in his back. The patient whom he was interviewing answered Kinsey in about the same easy and forthright way in which he was questioned. Here I saw more than a remarkably competent scientist at work. What I saw also was a man with complete understanding of people who are despised and rejected by most of their fellow-men, a strong desire to help them understand and resolve their problems, superlative skill in probing the murky depths of sexual aberration and normal behavior.

Kinsey was sometimes so moved when he recounted the shocking inequities of the enforcement of sex laws that he was brought to the edge of tears. This was especially true in his last years, and was noted by his associates on several occasions. One of these was described by Dr. Manfred S. Guttmacher, a Baltimore psychiatrist:

> One of my outstanding memories is of a closed meeting held one evening at Shriver Hall on the Homewood Campus of Johns Hopkins. Dr. Kinsey looked worn and tired. He talked to the group at length and when he told of the terrible injustice of sentencing a young adolescent boy to a mid-western prison for five years for a relatively minor sexual offense, tears trickled down. This same quality showed itself strongly on the occasions when we talked of the Army's attitude toward homosexuality.

Kinsey was anxious to get his sex offender material into print, as he felt that the current sources of printed information on the subject were totally inadequate. Some close friends advised delay until he could broaden his data. He replied: "On that point I have a perfectly clear conscience. If we didn't have something better than the others who are the chief sources of expert information on sex offenders right now, I would consider a delay in publication. There isn't a day, however, that I do not regret that we do not have a raft more of our material in print for people to use." He was, however, never to realize this ambition since he and his staff in 1955 sidetracked the work on the sex offender in favor of preparing a comprehensive study of the fertility data on females which they had in their case histories. This project had its genesis in Kinsey's participation in the Arden House Abortion Conference at the invitation of Dr. Mary Calderone, Medical Director of Planned Parenthood. The analysis proved to be far more complex and time-consuming than had been expected, so that at the time of Kinsey's death in 1956, it was still in the preliminary stages.

The growing antagonism to the Kinsey findings and to their dissemination took various forms: it was usually expressed via the printed page, pulpit, or lecture platform. On one occasion, however, it was enacted out as a drama with Kinsey, the former Bowdoin prize-winning orator and able platform speaker, using his skills to become the hero of the confrontation. The campus of Rutgers University at New Brunswick, N.J., was the setting. The students had scheduled him to speak in November, 1954, for their Student Council lecture series. Certain church groups objected to Kinsey's being permitted to appear. The University backed up the right of the students to bring to the campus anyone they selected, and the Dean of Men wrote to warn Kinsey a few days before the lecture that there might be "some protests in the way of picketing or perhaps heckling." A friend of Kinsey's from nearby Princeton, who was in the audience the evening of the program, has provided this firsthand account of the event:

Dr. Kinsey started out by saying that his group had, among other things, learned some facts about marriage that would help to make marriage more successful, and that in a country where the divorce rate was so high, he felt that such knowledge should be spread. Then he stopped for a moment and roared out that if anyone for religious or other reasons did not want to hear what he had to say, he or she should get up and leave right now. There was dead silence. The students looked around to see who was leaving. No one did. Then they began to laugh. They laughed and laughed. From then on there was complete silence in the hall and complete absorption in what Dr. Kinsey was saying—marital advice. At the end there was an ovation for Dr. Kinsey. The story was that . . . had decided to break up the lecture. . . . At first, there was a plan to picket the lecture. Then the . . . chaplain decided that students should riot in the lecture hall after the talk started. With great courage and charm, Dr. Kinsey met this threat head on and won the night completely.[7]

9.

Kinsey the Man

BY THE TIME KINSEY BECAME HEAVILY IN-
volved with sex research his three children were in their
twenties and old enough to begin to break with their home
ties. Earlier, during their childhood and adolescent years,
they had experienced a very normal and typical small-college-
town upbringing and environment. However, there was
probably more emphasis on outdoor life, especially on hiking
and on swimming, than with the average youngster. Kinsey
himself was only a moderately good swimmer, but he used the
men's pool in the gymnasium building fairly regularly. In
1934, when the three children would have ranged from almost
six to ten years in age, he described their August visits to a
nearby state park:

> After the University pool closed the whole family took to
> Brown County days—swimming in their fine pool in the A.M.,
> picnic lunch in bathing suits at noon—swim all afternoon—pic-
> nic supper before we came home. All of the children are good in
> the water. Anne is just too good—beats her mother now in every

stroke. . . . So the family has played together here at home as never before.

Anne and Joan were close enough together so that they often shared neighborhood playmates. Boy-and-girl games on long summer evenings on the stone wall across the street were typical of the friendly neighborhood.

When Anne, who had no real talent for music, took lessons from her father, her practicing was so painful to him that she would try to practice when he was out of the house. Once when he was home while she was playing, he called out from the other room, "That's wrong." She answered, "No it's not; that's the way it's written here." "Well, then it's written wrong," was his immediate rejoinder.

Both girls went to the First Presbyterian Sunday School as children and in their high school years, although their parents were not affiliated with the church. Kinsey had attended services there during his first year on the Bloomington campus while he was still a bachelor. The Reverend Charles Schwartz, a former Rhodes scholar, attracted many of the campus faculty group.

Anne, especially, took an active part in the youth activities, acting as moderator of the group at one time. At twelve she attended the communicants' class, but, when the time came to be confirmed in church membership, the family, in her words, "put their foot down." They felt she was too young to make such a decision. If she wanted to join when she was older, that was all right with them.

The two daughters had normal teen-ager's "run-ins" with their parents, who could be heard by the girls in the next room discussing the family discipline problem involved. Kinsey was the stricter of the two parents, and, although Clara was inclined to be more lenient, it was usually up to her to carry out the disciplining. The girls were both independent of spirit.

While in high school, they both started dating, and at twenty Joan married her high school sweetheart, Bob Reid, who had just been discharged from his army service in World War II. He returned to college to continue with medical training and now practices in Columbus, Indiana.

Anne, the older, attended Oberlin for two years and, undecided on a major that would fulfill her interest in camp life and the out-of-doors, transferred to a four-year fine arts course in dress design at Washington University in St. Louis. After graduating she worked in this field for five years. In 1952 she married Warren Corning, a Chicago business executive. He died in 1965, and a few years later she married Dean Call, a lawyer in Gary, Indiana.

Bruce, the youngest Kinsey, inherited his mother's dark eyes, high coloring, and regular features. He was an intrepid youngster, entertaining himself by catching bumble bees with his bare fingers and collecting them in a jar. When older, he gave chilblains to his mother's friends when they watched him go off to school in winter weather in shorts and a light sweater. He was typically a nonjoiner and only did what he was really interested in doing. A fine swimmer, he had an outstanding team record at Oberlin, where he graduated in 1950. After army service spent partly in Germany he married and has been with various business firms in Cleveland in recent years.

None of the three children has felt an undue impact from the repercussions of their father's fame as an authority on sex. Bruce has probably been most successful in ignoring it. When Anne was in St. Louis, she was approached by a Kinsey Distilling Company distributor after the word got around that she had jokingly said, when people inquired if her father was "the Kinsey," "No, he manufactures whiskey." The upshot of this was a free dinner and a gift of a full case from the company in the line of public relations. They have all weathered the blaze of publicity the family received with good grace and tolerance. This is a tribute to the common sense of all three of them, for it is a disconcerting experience to hear one's family name bandied about as the synonym for sex on movie marquees, in racy cartoons, and on every jokester's tongue.

A long-term household helper of Mrs. Kinsey's, Mrs. Frances Turrell, has written an intimate vignette of the family as she saw them during her years in the household. Trained as a secretary, she was forced to turn to housework during the Depression when, as a widow, she moved to

Bloomington to educate her children. In her 1951 Christmas greeting letter to the family she wrote in part:

So much is being said of the Kinsey family as the Public knows it. This is trying to tell what the family is in private life, as a servant knows it. I say servant, but I was never made to feel I was a servant even by the smallest child. One day a child from across the street asked Anne why the maid did not do something, she, Anne, was doing. Anne gave her a look as only Anne could give and said, "That is Mrs. Turrell; we have no maid."

The Kinsey children were never allowed to make extra work for me. They had to keep their own rooms in order . . . much as I would have liked to have helped the kiddies out if they had other plans. . . .

When it came to helping us out, Dr. and Mrs. Kinsey, instead of making me feel a pauper, would give with the attitude that I was doing them a favor in accepting, such as the time they filled my coal bin with Kentucky coal, and having us at their home for Thanksgiving dinner, or giving a check that we might have a splendid meal. . . .

But it wasn't the material things altogether that made us love the Kinseys. There was something—I can't say what, as they made no pretense of being religious in an outward way—that sticks way down deep and makes one feel that they love to serve . . . Merry Christmas to you Kinseys.

The Kinseys were always very generous in their hospitality in entertaining out-of-town guests who came to visit the Institute. Mrs. Kinsey remembers with especial pleasure Dr. Robert L. Dickinson, who was a house guest during the holiday season in 1943. At age eighty-two, he walked on a clear, cold, snowy night with the Kinseys and friends to the Robert Telfers' house for dinner, across town and back, a distance of at least two miles each way. Clara recalls his delightful personality and courtly manner. Among the other many guests were Clifford Adams from State College, Pennsylvania; Emily Mudd, Philadelphia marriage counselor; Dr. Frances Shields, a New York physician; Lawrence Gichner, an art collector and dealer from Washington, D.C.; Glenway Wescott, the writer; and Tom Painter, an observer of the social scene, from New York. Kinsey always kept such visitors long hours at the laboratory, consulting with them often until midnight or later and in return showing them the materials he had collected.

This role as a genial host extended to the office staff. Birthday cakes, cookies or coffee cake at the Friday morning staff meetings—supplied usually by the energetic secretary, Eleanor Roehr—were encouraged, especially after the intense pressure of getting the second book out was over. Christmas parties at the office for children of the staff members were given several times at Kinsey's suggestion. Animal movies usually furnished the entertainment, with those on the skunk, porcupine, and opossum especially popular. In the summer, family style picnics at Clyde Martin's idyllic country place, only a mile from town, were regular events. John Gunther found himself a surprised guest at one of these on a visit to the campus and Institute.

Money matters never seemed to be of much concern to the Kinseys, an attitude that fitted in well with the low academic salaries and typically frugal style of faculty living of the period. They had a comfortable home and an adequate car, but they did not move their modest standard of living upward as Kinsey became more and more of a public figure. He still owned one good suit, not a dozen; the homespun style of furnishings in the house didn't change, and hasn't even to this day; and they have never had a charge account in Bloomington.

Kinsey always insisted on waiting until they could afford to pay for something before they bought it. This attitude undoubtedly stemmed from his boyhood experiences in household finance. His mother was given a weekly allowance by her husband on which to run the house. When it proved inadequate to cover the costs, instead of approaching him for a supplement, she would send young Kinsey to the store to pay the merchant what she could on the bill, asking for time on the rest. Currently, this might appear to be a matter-of-fact arrangement, but for the young boy it was humiliating. It led him to resolve never to incur financial obligations which he could not meet.

This unconcern for worldly goods is well illustrated by two anecdotes. Kinsey was inordinately proud of driving an aged Buick with more than 100,000 miles on it. Once, when he was walking across a parking lot near Biology Hall with a visitor, he contrasted his shabby car with a brand new convertible parked nearby which belonged to a young instructor. "With us, faculty rank and car model are inversely related," he commented. The other episode concerns the family's income tax report. Typically, Kinsey would make out his income tax the last night before it was due. He would not have time to eat dinner, but would take a sandwich over to the lab with him to eat while he worked on his tax returns. Once when he was doing this he suddenly realized he couldn't remember what his salary was. This was in the days before W-2 forms. He called Clara and she couldn't remember exactly either. Then in desperation he called Dr. Payne, his chairman, to ask him. Payne was, Clara reports, "not very pleased" to have his sleep disturbed by such a request.

Kinsey was not an early riser. Clara rarely got up before he did and she ordinarily started breakfast while he shaved and took a cold shower. Referring to his sluggish morning habits, he once plaintively said to her, "You were really never of much help to me on that." In the years when he was doing sex research his working schedule was always a long one, with night hours a regular practice. By the time a visitor had spent two or three days at Kinsey's pace, he was exhausted and ready to take a break. But for Kinsey it was a steady pattern. He would relax by doing a routine chore between more exacting work. "He was imbued with a Puritanical ethic of work that gave it a value comparable to the Christian emphasis on faith," one former colleague observed. He prided himself on taking a vacation only on Christmas day. Weekends were considered as work days except for Sundays. On Sunday mornings he would often play over the records and plan the program for the evening guests.

Music was in a certain sense a religion with Kinsey. At the "Sunday night meetings" he served as high priest and host. An old friend described Kinsey's function as "toastmaster and commentator." "He almost stepped on the lecture podium as he discussed a given number or composition," he commented, but added, "He did it in a very comfortable way. We all felt that we were not lectured at but communed with." While Kinsey listened to a record he completely lost himself in the music. It was a deeply meaningful experience that he wanted to share with others.

An attempt once by an irreverent young sociologist to break Kinsey's dignified mien was unsuccessful. He put his wife up to innocently requesting Kinsey "to play some boogie-woogie" one Sunday evening after the regular concert was over. Kinsey stared at her in disbelief, but could not bring himself to make an answer. They were not invited back again.

Kinsey's method of finding kindred spirits to invite to his house for music on Sunday nights was sometimes unconventional. One long-time faculty member recalls that during his first year on campus he was dressing in the faculty locker room at the men's gymnasium after a game of handball and chanced to be discussing music with two young instructor friends. "Beethoven is really a romantic," was the comment by one of them that triggered Kinsey out of an adjoining shower. "Why do you say Beethoven is a romantic?" he demanded. Once that issue was explored, he followed with a warm invitation to his home for music the next Sunday evening to his three new acquaintances.

The musical evenings were far too formal for some guests, who would drop out after a few Sundays. Others continued to attend for years, eagerly looking forward to the weekly treat of hearing the newest recordings. In his later years Kinsey's musical tastes changed somewhat, as he became more and more interested in the works of modern composers.

Although he was far too busy for hobbies other than his avocations of music and gardening, Kinsey's collecting urge did spill over into one other area—knife collecting. First, Lennart von Zweygberg, the Finnish cellist, gave him a typical Finnish hunting knife. Young Bruce was fascinated with it, and on his twelfth birthday his mother gave him an Early American hunting knife. This was a great success. The next summer, after Ralph Voris died, the Spanish war bayonet he had used to dig his rove beetles out of their dung piles was added to the collection. On several occasions Kinsey brought his son a knife or a sword from Abels in New York, and Bruce later ordered a Spanish sailor's clasp-knife from their catalogue. Faculty friends sometimes donated items. Dr. Harry Benjamin, a New York doctor, gave him a Japanese short sword, and André Avinoff, the entomologist and artist, sent a contribution after visiting in Bloomington. Clara brought back a Bulgarian sword cane from a trip to New York in 1945. She remembers it well because, afraid to leave it in her berth on the train trip home, she took it with her to the diner for breakfast. Kinsey continued to add new items from time to time after Bruce left home. The collection has long been mounted on the wall of the small southeast bedroom of the Kinsey home.

This drive to collect, which Kinsey himself recognized as one of his strong characteristics, was of great interest to his friend, Edgar Anderson, who observed:

> The urge to build up a significant collection is a special sort of inner drive. . . . In Kinsey the strength of this compelling inner fire showed itself increasingly and in various ways. When he closed one of the tight-fitting insect boxes and put it back on the shelf in the proper place, when he inserted one of his coded sex-survey data cards and closed the steel filing case, there was a physical reaction which I have noted in other scholars and collectors. The box lid was not merely closed, it was slowly but deftly pushed shut and the tension of the fingers showed that the closing was of some inner significance. When the drawer of the filing cabinet was pushed shut the fingers lingered on the drawer until it slid firmly into the closed position and there were meaningful tensions of the arm and back muscles.
>
> Whatever the sources of this collecting urge, it is a widespread human trait and of tremendous social consequences. With a fair degree of it the awful tedium of assembling and caring for a huge collection of any kind becomes significant and pleasurable. Without it we should never achieve these vast stores of codified information which are one of the prerequisites for a scientific understanding of the world. It was certainly strong in Kinsey and apparently became stronger and stronger as he grew older.

The Kinseys rarely went to the movies. His associates can recall a few that they saw with him while on field trips. One such evening in New York he and Gebhard went to one of the early Swedish films on "true love." Kinsey insisted on leaving the theater before the end. He had become so emotionally involved by the tender love scenes he could not bear to stay through to the tragic ending.

He went occasionally to Broadway plays, and was particularly interested in Tennessee Williams' *Streetcar Named Desire*, which he saw several times. His taste for ballet developed with his frequent trips to New York and his growing contacts with the celebrities in the theatrical world. Once I had an opportunity to attend a San Francisco performance of the New York City Ballet with Dr. Kinsey. I was on a trip to survey sources of data on California sex offenses in the Berkeley libraries. Douglas Rigg, the San Quentin Warden, and his wife Louise made up the group for dinner and the theater. Kinsey became ill during the meal and was taken by Rigg to his room in the hotel to rest. By theater time he had recovered and joined us again. Watching ballet with him was a memorable experience because of his firsthand knowledge of the dancers, several of whom he had interviewed, as well as his knowledge of the music and his delight in the beauty of the ballet itself.

His interest in gourmet restaurants also dates from this period of constant travel, when he was exposed to the wide choice of cuisine available in metropolitan areas. When his daughter Anne was working in New York one summer, she recalls that they exchanged listings of gourmet restaurants. A small Hellenic-Greek restaurant on Locust Street near 10th in Philadelphia was one of his favorites.

Kinsey was never a drinker, and in fact was a virtual teetotaler until the last four or five years of his life, when his medical advisor suggested that a moderate amount of alcohol might help in relieving his tensions. He never cared for wines or whisky, but had some taste for sweet rum drinks. For Anne's wedding in 1952 he concocted his own variety of "Charleston Cup," fashioned after one he had tasted in the Pump Room in Chicago. A "Junior Zombie" was another specialty.

As an authority on edible wild plants, Prok would sometimes remark to Mac about this or that wild berry or plant and how it could be used for household cooking. He frequently had mentioned that the fruit of the highbush cranberry, an ornamental shrub, made good preserves. She, on the contrary, suspected that the variety that they had in their yard, at least, was too bitter to be edible since the birds waited until late winter to eat them. One day she decided to try it out to settle the matter. One taste was enough, and Kinsey grudgingly admitted that this shrub was not the native species he had known in the East. One of his own specialties when he was preparing a meal for the children was "Puzzle Hash." He kept them guessing what was in it while they ate it up with gusto. A pet dislike in foods was potatoes, and he took violent exception to their frequent serving. "It appears that very nearly three times a day he let fly at potatoes, at least in California," a Western friend claimed.

While Kinsey could not be labeled as unconcerned about his appearance, he seemed to give attention primarily to neatness in his dress. A short-sleeved, white sport shirt and a bow tie were standard for daily wear. A campus visitor who was a friend of Kinsey's tells of being summoned over to the Institute from his room in the nearby Union Building late one hot, humid summer night. He wore a terry-cloth open shirt. It was planned that Dellenback, the photographer, would take a photo of him in the library. "Kinsey came in and scowled at me. 'Take that bathrobe of yours off, change to a clean dress shirt—and come back.' I did just that," the rueful account concludes.

Kinsey never wore a hat—a more remarkable omission in the 1920's and 1930's than later. His blue eyes were somewhat faded and his yellow hair turned to a straw blond and then greyed. One of his characteristic gestures was to ripple his fingers through his hair—not to smooth it—but more as an accompaniment of his thoughts or of a discussion, particularly if he were amused or annoyed. His broad grin and infectious laughter were a trademark no one forgot. He was once nearly tricked by his indifference to his personal appearance. He was scheduled to address a University convocation in the old Assembly Hall. A few minutes before he was to go on stage he called his office and told his assistant that he had worn his kneeboots by mistake, and asked him to hurry over with his regular shoes so he could make a change before appearing.

Kinsey had the reputation among students and some department colleagues of never being on time, but this also meant that, oblivious to the clock, he would generously give an extra fifteen or twenty minutes to a conference or interview once it was under way.

Kinsey's use of his hands reflected his background as a scientist. He was meticulous as he picked up a small item, often using tweezers if his large fingers were not deft enough to handle it as he liked. He had a practice of brushing together the crumbs left on the table after a meal, picking them up a few at a time by pressing them with his fingertips, and dropping them onto a plate.

The top of Kinsey's desk was usually clear. What objects were on it were unconsciously rearranged in neat rows as he talked. It was said that he kept his desk bare in later years so he could stretch out on it for a short nap after eating his lunch at noon. This usually consisted of "rabbit food" such as carrots, celery, lettuce, nuts, and raisins. While eating he would often catch up on his reading of journal articles. When there were out-of-town visitors at the Institute he was generous in inviting various staff members to eat lunch with the guest at the Campus Club or Tudor Room, the two best eating places on the I.U. campus. Those who ate with him will remember that he invariably asked the waitress for an extra serving of salad dressing, which he used as a sauce for his vegetables. A pecan ball was recommended as the ideal dessert, and Kinsey usually set the example by ordering one himself. At forty, while he was still leading an active physical life, he once reported that he had dieted off twenty pounds, reducing his weight to 142. "Practically all that came off the waistline," he added. He was in the main a temperate eater, and never seemed to have a major problem with his weight, although he was probably somewhat heavier than he should have been in his last years.

Kinsey was unable to joke about sex because, with his total commitment to it as a scientific endeavor, it was too serious a matter. Thus he was often accused of lacking a sense of humor. It is true that he had in general a serious manner, but early personal letters show a boyish relish of typically masculine, robust humor. Lester Dearborn, a Boston psychologist, recalls a Kinsey anecdote with a light touch. He recounts:

I remember one little incident when he was in Boston and I had provided him with an audience of professionally interested men and women. One member of the group took exception to his statement concerning the peak of sexual drive and response on the part of the male. He said he had just read a book by a doctor who claimed that man was at his prime sexually around the age of 48. He asked Kinsey, "What do you think of that?" He quickly replied, "I think the age of the author was about 48."

A striking feature of Kinsey's life was the dichotomy between his role as a respectable college academician and that of the investigator familiar with the most bizarre aspects of sexual deviation. Currently we are more accustomed to this bridging of the cultural gap, but twenty-five years ago it was more rare, especially in nonurban universities. Dr. Earle Marsh, a West Coast obstetrician and gynecologist who was often a visitor in Bloomington, was struck by this incongruity. In speaking of the Sunday evening concerts he said:

The gracious way that he met these professors and their wives, as he seated them in the chairs, had a sort of tousled gallantry to it. Likewise, I recall his demeanor at these sessions. While that afternoon we may have been engaged in conversation which I suppose might have shocked his guests at the Sunday night musicales, he was able to change from the mood of the afternoon's conversation to one of a pleasant, middle western host. Mac, likewise, would knit and darn socks, as did the other wives, with their little wicker baskets. I often wondered if these other professors . . . had any concept of the information that Kinsey had and the people he had met and the types he'd seen. It seemed like the meeting of two worlds.

The other side of the coin is well illustrated by a firsthand account from a New York friend of the research who introduced Kinsey to some of his young friends. They took to the visitor from Bloomington with delight. "He mesmerized them all," the account goes, and details of a wild evening birthday party follow:

About twenty boys were there, all explosively virile. And in an explosive mixture of Irish, Jew, Negro, and Puerto Rican, almost all violent delinquents and fight-lovers, and racially antagonistic. Then they proceeded to consume hard liquor straight, like water. . . . Meanwhile Kinsey pottered around apparently having a fine time, apparently unconscious he was sitting on a rumbling volcano.

Then a wild, crazy tattooed Irishman and a few of his drunken and demented friends offered to drive Kinsey back to his hotel. In their car, probably stolen, probably licenseless, surely about to fall apart. To my horror Kinsey calmly accepted. As is typical, I gather they treated him like their dear old grandmother and deposited him safe and sound at the Statler—then dashed back at 60 miles an hour wrong way on a one way avenue, roaring with glee.

This straightforwardness stood Kinsey in good stead when he was discussing sex with other kinds of people. An early meeting with a group of fraternity members who he was hoping would agree to be interviewed is described by one of them:

> I can, I think, still feel the noiseless shock that prevailed in the room when Dr. Kinsey began to discuss in the matter-of-fact, blunt but perfectly even way, for which he had a unique talent, a matter which had never been talked of in the fraternity home without off-color comments, four-letter words, laughs, taunts, bragging and the feeling of something deliciously sinful. This time the boys were stunned, speechless and involuntarily serious. It would have been as unthinkable for them to react to sex talk in Dr. Kinsey's presence in the time-honored way as it was for him to exploit the subject in the time-honored manner.

In 1947 a young professor in the bacteriology department, S. E. Luria—later a Nobel prize winner—was sharply criticized by Kinsey, who took issue with a favorable account of the candidacy of Tom Lemon for Bloomington mayor which had appeared in the *Bulletin* of the Indiana University Teachers' Union. Kinsey wrote Luria:

> I think you were indiscreet in sending out the publicity for Mr. Lemon from the Indiana Teachers' Union.
> It has been the accepted policy of this institution, and most academic institutions in the United States, that they stay out of local politics as institutions. . . .
> As individuals, faculty members have every right to express themselves on political matters; but when an organization which

bears the University name and which is confined to faculty members, and which uses the campus mail for free mailing privileges, takes sides in the local political issue, it cannot claim that it is furthering the interests of scholarship or any of the other functions of the University.

I write you because this is a matter which concerns the future of the whole faculty and not merely of the organization which you represent.

The executive committee of the Teachers' Union met and discussed the issue, and Luria replied with spirit:

We cannot agree that political control over a University arises as a result of the expression of political views by faculty organizations. The same rights must be exercised by organizations as by individuals. In our opinion, political control arises from a curtailment of these rights, not from their expression.

Kinsey never took an active role in politics, but he was highly sensitive to the vulnerability of the academic world to political pressures long before he had occasion to feel those pressures himself.

Kinsey's impulse to send this letter to Luria is not out of keeping with other letters he wrote reflecting his annoyance with what he considered irresponsible behavior in community or campus matters—lack of enforcement of university parking regulations, publishing the amounts of individual gifts to the Community Fund in the local paper, and dereliction of duties by city police officers detailed to traffic control. In each case he sent off a sharp complaint to the proper authority. No words were minced. When he was in top form action flashed in all directions. On the other hand, while swamped with overcommitments in his lecturing and writing, he could also take time to write a complimentary letter to a director on a well-staged campus play, or to Harold Jordan, the manager of the University Auditorium, commending him for the excellence of the current series of programs.

Kinsey's faculty discussion club has been mentioned earlier. This group, one of several that have existed on the Bloomington campus, has the longest history of any of them. The moving spirit in organizing it was Hugh Willis from the law school. The group included such campus figures as E. B. Birge, public school music, J. E. Moffat, economics, P. W. Townsend, ancient history, A. L. Kohlmeier, history, and Stith Thompson, folklore. Meetings were bi-monthly, on Monday evenings at 7:15 in the members' homes. The custom of no refreshments, started as an austerity measure during the war period of the 1940's, continued unchanged later. At this writing the group still continues with over forty years of tradition behind it.

This was the one campus group that Kinsey consistently met with from its founding in 1928 to his death. He always willingly provided them with a program whenever his turn came to speak. He may well have used them often as a sounding board for his ideas. His early talks were on "Evolution" (1928) and "The Mason Wasp" (1930). In 1932 and 1936 he recounted his experiences from his two Mexican field trips. Twice he turned to musical topics: "Sibelius" (1934) and "Wolf and Moussorgsky" (1936). With his change of fields, his tentative findings in his early human sex investigations served as subjects. As mentioned earlier, he broke the ice during the first year of the marriage course by speaking on "Student Sex Problems." Later, as his data accumulated, talks followed on "The Acquirement of Heterosexuality" (1940), "Sex Offenses" (1942), "Some Findings in Research in Sex Behavior" (1942), "Sexual Outlet in the Female" (1944), "Techniques in Gathering Information on Sex Behavior" (1945), "Prostitution" (1946), and "Psychiatrists and Psychiatry" (1947). A week or two after the publication of the male volume in January, 1948, he addressed the group on the subject of "Experience in Publishing a Book on Sex Behavior." In the 1950's topics included "The Erotic in Painting" (February, 1951), "Mammalian Backgrounds of Human Behavior" (March, 1952), "Six Sex Offenders" (November, 1953). "Police Brutality" (February, 1955) was his final program for the group. These titles are a revealing list. Many of them reflect social issues that were weighing heavily on him during the eighteen years that he worked in the field of human sex behavior.

Some of the more conservatively inclined members of the club were certainly disconcerted to find themselves listening to accounts of human sexual behavior that were franker than any they had ever heard before. But the most traditional among them agreed that he had every right to explore these avenues. Most of them also agreed that they would find it distasteful to work on such a subject themselves. A few felt that the university had no business "fooling around" in matters of this kind, and should not pay his salary as long as this was the kind of work he was engaged in.

His colleagues in the club who had the strongest misgivings about Kinsey's research were concerned chiefly with the effect that the widespread publication of such findings might have on the behavior of young people. They feared that such information as he reported on the prevalency of sex patterns generally considered taboo would open the way for youth to overstep the bounds of sexual morality as their elders defined it. Kinsey had no patience with this point of view. He told them in his 1935 paper on the biologic aspects of social problems that "the generation which is shocked at the frankness of present-day youth might better thank God for the promise that sexual honesty offers for the future security of the home and of society."

Certain things helped Kinsey in making his data acceptable to this group of his peers. One was his matter-of-fact approach and his use of coldly scientific terms. Another was that he had made his mark as a scholar in a totally different area of investigation. It is difficult to weigh the importance of this second factor, but it was certainly a major element in his success in gaining general acceptance of his unconventional data not only with his colleagues and university administrators, but with lecture audiences and the general public as well. His ingenuous manner and direct, matter-of-fact approach were very disarming. These were the same personal characteristics that made him a superb interviewer.

Kinsey was human enough to be flattered by the news coverage and fame he achieved, but he was also at times aghast. Dr. Frances Shields describes a glimpse she had of the vanity side of the picture:

> I remember one sparkling day when I drove him from San Francisco to Big Basin to sit among the giant Sequoias. We ate

lunch at the cafeteria in the park and he was *so* pleased when the cashier recognized him. He never seemed to outgrow this ego-satisfying experience.

He felt it was unseemly for a scientist to be hounded by the press and he valued his privacy very highly. The more he tried to dodge reporters and avoid interviews, the more eager the journalists were to "get a scoop."

Kinsey never abandoned the lingering hope of turning again at some future date to his gall wasp studies. In 1950 he mentioned it in a letter to Anderson just before the move to Wylie Hall was made: "In the next month, we move into quarters where we will have room to spread out the insect material again. This may give us an opportunity to get the rest of those measurements made." This hope obviously was not fulfilled during the more than five years the Institute was located there. Following the next move to larger quarters in Jordan Hall, Kinsey often spoke about plans to get the insect boxes out for measurements and further study. In 1957, after his death, the collection of well over a million specimens was moved to the American Museum of Natural History in New York City.

Kinsey was not career-minded. The qualities of mind which enabled him to achieve what he did were not centered in personal ambition, but rather in a single-minded dedication to his work, unflagging zeal in pushing it forward, great self-discipline, and an intense passion to discover the truth. His personal traits of easy friendliness, natural warmth, youthful enthusiasm, and sympathetic understanding, as well as tolerance of human weaknesses, helped him in achieving his goals. He had few of the social graces and was the very opposite of a suave sophisticate. Not gregarious, he refused to be lionized and had little small talk for purely social occasions. Trivialities irritated him. He was fortunate in having a wife and family that accepted his work and stood behind him. Toward the end, in his mounting disappointments, his basic optimism and his confidence in himself may have cracked, but it carried him through the long years before. He was perhaps not a great man, but he had the necessary qualities to do an innovative, daring, and great piece of work.

IO.

The Final Lean Years

Following the loss of Rockefeller Foundation support for the Institute research program in mid-1954, Kinsey began to cast about for other possible means of financing his work. The reserve funds of the Institute could carry it through a few fallow years, probably three at the most, but these savings would rapidly shrink to nothing if other resources could not be found. If at the worst the Institute were to "fold up," it would take, according to Kinsey's estimate, a year plus $50,000 to accomplish it in an orderly fashion and with dignity. The staff would have to be given time to find jobs elsewhere and arrangements made for the disposal of the library, art archives, and documentary materials. This was one reason why it was unwise to deplete the reserve funds beyond a certain level. Another was that the Institute's continuing ability to subsidize the research for about one-third of its cost (with the University covering another third) was a drawing card in gaining outside support. The book royalties came in irregular spurts, and several lean years were anticipated preceding the income from the next book, which was far from ready. In any case, its specialized subject matter —the sex offender—would be of little appeal to the general public, and that would mean less royalties.

Kinsey's final Progress Report, written April 15, 1954, was a true tour de force. He was already aware that financial support was to end July 1, but he described the future plans of the research in such glowing terms that it is even possible that, as his former sponsors read it, they began to wonder if they had made a mistake. Several projects were running concomitantly—a complete revision of the volume on the male, a study of sex law, the ongoing collection of sex offender histories from "coast to coast," and an archeological study of Peruvian pre-Columbian erotic ceramics. Then there was the expected addition to the staff of a physiologist who could undertake laboratory studies of the physiology of sex, and the acquisition of two new cameras to film mammalian sexual behavior. The latter project was under way at Orange Park, Florida, at the Yerkes Laboratory of Primate Biology, where Paul Gebhard and William Dellenback had gone to study and photograph the chimpanzees. In addition, eight foreign translations of the female volume were in progress, and the Institute was slated to move into larger quarters in the new Life Science Building in less than a year.

As the months went by, however, and as Kinsey found sympathy but no dollars in some quarters and total apathy in others, he became more and more disillusioned with the financial prospect. Letters of inquiry to various persons astute in such matters brought a variety of suggestions. They ranged from a scheme of bringing out the Institute research findings in monthly installments obtainable only by advance subscription—much as Dickens' earlier novels appeared—to going on the lecture circuit at $5,000 an appearance. Persons of great wealth who were supposed to be sympathetic to liberal causes were approached through mutual friends, but this proved to be wasted effort. This kind of seeking for favors with those who had no real comprehension of his goals sickened Kinsey physically and emotionally, and he soon gave that avenue up as hopeless.

Government support seemed out of the question at the

time. If foundations did not feel free to subsidize him, it seemed highly unlikely that he could obtain federal grants. He was, in addition, suspicious and fearful of undue control —of both his material and his findings—by government agencies. He had written in his 1953 Progress Report:

> The unfortunate experience of similar projects that have had Federal or State government support, indicates that sex research cannot be conducted under such agencies without danger of interference from minority groups, or without demands from legislators that practical applications be immediately forthcoming. It is especially dangerous to become involved with governmental agencies because of their inclination to demand that the findings of research justify the mores.

Kinsey never forgot the stories he had been told about the early U.S. Army sex survey which had been locked up in the vaults in Washington after certain church groups objected to the findings in regard to premarital sex behavior.

In a letter to Dean Rusk, then President of the Rockefeller Foundation, he stated his hopes that his research would continue and bitterly pointed out: "To have fifteen years of accumulated data in this area fail to reach publication would constitute an indictment of the Institute, its sponsors, and all others who have contributed time and material resources to the work."

The sum of money Kinsey was looking for was $50,000 to $60,000 a year—"not a great deal to these foundations," as he wrote Yerkes, who was then in declining health and not active in matters of funding. To one New York friend with whom he talked over his problems it seemed that he was almost more saddened by the broader spectacle of political pressure forcing withdrawal of research support than he was by his own plight. He felt that it augured ill for all research if this could happen to him.

Convinced that he needed to increase his lecturing in order to further the cause of his sex research with the public, Kinsey began an incredible schedule of public appearances. In his final Progress Report he mentions "dozens of lectures" during 1953–54, and his Faculty Reports for the following years, in which only the most important lectures are listed, more than substantiate this. "For the continuation of the research we need wider professional and public understanding of the nature of our approach to the problems involved in the study," he explained. It was actually impossible for him to accept more than a small portion of the requests for lectures. Thus he confined himself largely to medical, psychiatric, legal, law enforcement, and church groups, but he pushed himself to his capacity and beyond to fulfill even these commitments.

This pace, plus the other pressures he was under from unsolved problems—a source of financing and the customs case—began to take its toll. Letters from friends describing their final meetings with him during these last years repeatedly mention his drawn appearance, his lackluster eyes, and his evident fatigue. On one occasion when he had a particularly important evening ahead, he arrived at a center-city hotel at midmorning and turned to a friend for help. The friend wrote:

> Kinsey told me that the previous days had been very hard on him, that he had been unable to sleep at night, and that he was utterly exhausted. He was also apprehensive lest he be attacked during the round table discussion. I encouraged him to go to bed and told him that I would keep everyone away from him until time for the dinner preceding the meeting. When he appeared at 7:00 P.M., he was calm, bright, and at his alert best. His own presentation was excellent, and in the rough-and-tumble that followed he definitely bested his opponents.

There is little doubt that, as the pressures mounted and the criticism did not abate, the more genial aspect of his personality was affected. His temper became shorter and his impatience surfaced more frequently. He made a valiant attempt to cover over his bewildered hurt, but he was never able to accept, when others pointed it out to him, the inevitability of the hostility and animosity to a research effort such as his. He was so convinced of the rightness of his cause that it was beyond his powers to take a tolerant attitude toward his critics or to assume an indifference to their criticisms.

In spite of his various severe illnesses in childhood, Kinsey had never thought of himself as other than in good physical health during his adult life. His active field work and week-end gardening kept him generally in fine physical trim during his thirties and forties. This outdoor work was important as physical therapy, but even more significant was its function as an escape valve for his tensions and frustrations. He writes of this more than once. For example, in July, 1939, when his embryonic sex research was running on a parallel track with the classification of gall wasps, he wrote:

> This has been the busiest six months I think that I have ever spent. I have measured some thousands of bugs and gotten a series of variation curves and correlation maps that is startling. . . . a total of 27 hours scheduled classroom work per week, plus more than that in individual conferences. But I thrive, neverthe-less—what with a half day Saturday and the whole day Sunday in the garden.

Early spring the next year he wrote again:

> By scheduling things closely to the hour I manage to keep things going without any physical disturbance. It begins to look though as if I needed gardening to get me in shape; so I am particularly glad to see our winter breaking. Gee, I wish you and I could get together for some hours in the sunshine which we have here today.

One of Kinsey's problems was that he always tried to set the pace for the younger men on the staff. After several weeks at interviewing in the field he would send them on home and stay on to "mop up." Often unexpected interviews would crowd in on him after they had left. Determined to take care of them, he would return home drained and exhausted. His emotional involvement in the work was such that its further-ing at this time was his only concern.

As Kinsey felt he could take less and less time out for it, the garden work was increasingly neglected or hired out. Neighbors missed the sight of him working outdoors on Sun-days in his abbreviated shorts. This was partly because he was out of town on so many long stretches, but even when he was in Bloomington he found little time for this form of recrea-tion. Clyde Martin, who had helped him with his yard work when he was a student, and who was later his co-worker at the Institute, commented: "When Kinsey could bring himself to lower the pressure on the travel schedule and take time out to work in his garden, it had a very therapeutic effect on him. He needed this change of pace and let up from pressures of interviewing."

His friends who visited him in Bloomington during these early years of intensive work saw physical evidence of the increasing strain. Edgar Anderson supplied this episode:

> I tried to get him to slow down and I repeat the details of our conversation because it shows the kind of person he was with his family and his friends. Seizing a moment when we were alone, I said, "Now look here, have you a real scientific interest in what you are doing or are you just being sentimental? If you are coolly scientific you will realize that until this program is out of its formative stages you are its most important feature. It needs you for at least another decade, not just for a year or so. You should get the best possible medical advice and work out a rational way of living under the circumstances." I thought I had him but he looked at me impishly and said, "Oh, I did talk to my doctor and you know what he told me? He said that under no circumstances must I ever let people scold me."

Five months after the publication of the volume on the male (1948), when a high school classmate responded to the widespread publicity about the author by renewing his contact with him, Kinsey responded with a warm personal letter, and in a rare moment of utter frankness and unquenchable optimism wrote: "I am tired and worn after the long hours of hard work in the last few years, but I do not intend to let that get me down; a little rest, when I can get around to it, will fix me up."

Anderson was close enough to Kinsey that he felt free to lecture him on taking care of himself when he thought it was called for. In the spring of 1949 he again reproved his friend:

> As for me I am deeply concerned about the future of your program. It hinges on you, more than I think you can realize. Unless you mend your ways you cannot carry on in this fashion for very much longer. It is time you let your Scotch-Presbyterian conscience drive you into taking a real vacation for the sake of your most important program. I am *not* an M.D., but I am a trained observer and I have been observing you for some years. It is later than you think.

Kinsey's only response to this plea was a line in his next letter, a bit flippantly expressed: "I will try to pay attention to your advice about me taking care of me."

The account of Kinsey's excursion into Peru in 1954 to seek out pre-Columbian erotic ceramic art is well documented in Paul Gebhard's recent chapter in *Studies in Erotic Art*, published in 1969 by the Institute in its Monograph Series. He does not mention, however, that Kinsey and his wife had made a twelve-day preliminary trip to Peru five months earlier. Its purpose had been to explore the possibility of obtaining the necessary permissions to photograph the erotic materials in both private and public collections. Clara tells that while Kinsey had no apparent difficulty in walking and breathing at the heights they went to in the Andes, at the lower level of Lima he had problems with the steps and terraces at the seaside resort of Ancón. On the second trip to Peru Kinsey fell ill and was hospitalized for several days.

Kinsey's insomnia was among the first symptoms of his health difficulties that his associates can recall. One psychiatrist friend stated that "[Kinsey] talked to me a number of times about his inability to throw these things [his problems] off at night and of his difficulty sleeping." His front of external calm deceived many people into believing he was without nerves. He started using the ordinary sleeping drugs to help him to get a night's rest, and an office co-worker can recall his eventually "being caught in an impossible cycle of drugs for tranquilizing and then for stimulation." He would come to the office in the morning bleary-eyed and feeling groggy after a restless night with little sleep. Those close to him remember a characteristic gesture of wiping his hand over his face from the forehead down as if to shake off his weariness. Strangely enough, he could nap easily in the daytime. His demons pursued him only at night.

Another unsolved problem which Kinsey and the Institute staff were faced with at this point was a change of publishing house. Since further sex studies would be on topics more closely related to criminology, sociology, psychology, and law, it seemed that a shift should be made from W. B. Saunders Company, which specialized in the biological and medical field. The final decision in the matter was arrived at four months after Kinsey's death, when Harper and Brothers was settled upon.

In October, 1955, Kinsey was persuaded to take a break in his work with a seven-week trip to Europe. Clara Kinsey accompanied him. The hope was that it would give him a change from the hectic pace at home and be somewhat of a vacation. However, it turned out rather differently. His route took him to Oslo, London, Paris, Rome, Naples, Palermo, Copenhagen, Barcelona, Madrid, and Lisbon. He had many friends and contacts in all these places—except Portugal—and great demands were made upon his time and energy. He found a warm reception for his work everywhere he went.

In England his time was largely divided between the British Museum and conferences with professional groups. The latter included prison and hospital staff as well as the British commission that was then working on the revision of the English sex law. This was the group that made the Wolfenden Report to Parliament in 1957. Lectures in London at the Institute of Psychiatry and at the Maudsley Hospital were high points. Eric Dingwall of the British Museum staff, who had visited the Institute in Bloomington, and J. B. S. Haldane were of great help in steering the Kinseys around. Kinsey commented later on his lectures at Maudsley Hospital: "I have never had such an ovation from any professional group." In France he appeared before a medical society with a translator, and in time-honored fashion, went to see the Folies-Bergère. During his three-week stay in Italy he found the sexual scene in great contrast to that in the northern countries, especially Norway. In Rome and Naples, as elsewhere, he watched and studied the sexual customs of the people on the street and in the restaurants, bars, and brothels. By mid-November he was in Denmark, where he gave three lectures, two in Copenhagen and one in Aarhus. There was a record turnout at the University in Copenhagen, where he had been invited to speak by the Students' Association. News photographs show the overflow perched on stairways and window ledges. The matter of fact way in which the Danish law and police handled the problems of female prostitution and male homosexuality amazed him. He was escorted on his visits to the parks and waterfront bars by Jens Jersild, a police official who had studied these problems professionally for many years, and who had spent some weeks working in the Institute library in Bloomington. A firsthand visit to Herstedvester to learn more about Dr. Georg K. Stürup's program with psychopathic sex offenders, in which castration was not infrequently used, proved informative.

In Spain Kinsey was especially interested in seeing the great art of Goya, Velasquez, El Greco, Ribera, and Murillo in the museums. He wrote later to a friend:

> Seven weeks in Europe gave me more new information on sex than I thought it possible to acquire in that time. Of course, there wasn't enough time to do everything and I did not begin to get to [all] the places that were important. I had to choose the opportunities that seemed most valuable from the standpoint of the problems we are immediately studying.

More than fifty pages of Kinsey's observations on his trip are extant. They will eventually make an interesting footnote to European sexual mores of our time by a keen observer of the scene.

While Kinsey was away the move to new quarters in Jordan Hall was effected. Eleanor Roehr, the devoted and efficient secretary, managed it and wrote to Kinsey in Barcelona: "The last load of things came today from Wylie Hall into Jordan. . . . A good many of the rooms are settled and a good portion of the library is up. . . . There are some odds and ends to be cleaned up but for the most part we look pretty good." She added the vain hope that he was getting some rest "in spite of all the hopscotching" he was doing in Europe. Upon his return it was evident that his health had not been helped by the trip. He was short of breath, lines in his face were deepened, and his color was pallid.

With the establishment of the Institute in its new quarters in Jordan Hall, Kinsey and the staff had decided that the bare, hospital-corridor appearance of the long inner hallways that ran down the center of the new wing needed some decoration. Early group pictures of the staff, photographic portraits of pioneers in sex study, along with those of consultants, friends of the research, and some famous visitors to the Institute, were then hung on two of the long walls. Some said the pictures looked rather like a rogues' gallery, but Kinsey felt they were appropriate and a tribute to those who had been friendly and aided him. (A year or two after his death the photographs were replaced by two display cabinets in museum style and some mildly erotic watercolors, etchings, and lithographs from the Institute's collections.)

After these photographs had been selected and hung, various suggestions, some a bit racy, were made for decorating the short side corridor which led to other inner offices. A final natural choice was for a display of some of Bill Dellenback's striking photographs of pre-Columbian Peruvian pottery which he had made the previous summer. There was a large number of these to select from, actually several hundred. Since they depicted a wide variety of sexual behavior in an explicit fashion, the question of which ones were sedate enough to hang in this semi-public area was immediately raised.

Although a buzzer-lock system controlled at the receptionist's desk protected these inner hallways from any casual wanderer or curiosity seeker, yet university officials, graduate students, newspaper reporters, anyone seeking a conference with a staff member, approved library users, maintenance personnel, and occasionally children of staff members were visitors within this inner sanctum. Opinion on which prints would be suitable to use varied. After some discussion, in which I took part, Dr. Kinsey asked me to sort them into two categories, those I thought suitable to hang, and those that appeared unusable. Whether he felt that as a faculty wife and mother of a highschooler my judgment would be generally acceptable to the selected public which viewed them, I am not sure. I feel certain that he was aware of the lesson that would be learned by anyone who set himself up as an arbitrator in such a situation.

I confidently started to arrange the pictures on a large table in a rough scale of degree of acceptability, but soon realized that the two extremes of the range—totally unsuitable and fully acceptable—were the only ones I could sort out with any certainty. Nine-tenths of the pictures were in the grey area. I shuffled them back and forth in experimental piles for more than an hour, and finally gave up. When I admitted my dilemma to Kinsey he remarked that he wasn't surprised and smiled wisely.

Eventually some ten or twelve of the photographs of Peruvian ceramics, beautifully enlarged, were mounted on the walls of the short hallway. They included depictions of the genitalia of both sexes, genital fondling or masturbation of the male by the female, an embracing man and bird, a highly formalized coital scene, phallic heads, and on-location shots of Kinsey, Gebhard, and Dellenback in Peru. In spite of the concern over the original choice, in the several years that they hung there no one ever criticized the subject matter or complained about them.

In the late winter and early spring of 1956 Kinsey seemed to be increasingly losing ground. Small exertions were even more difficult and physically he moved more heavily and at a slower pace. Certain commitments for lectures had been made long in advance and he honored these all with at times an almost superhuman effort. In February he gave his customary four lectures to the Indiana University freshman medical class. They covered the physiology of sexual responses, the hormonal factors in sexual response, concepts of normality and abnormality, and the sex offender. He taped an NBC program for the Home show, which was later broadcast on March 20. It was his only TV appearance. All of March was spent in California, interviewing again in the state institutions, more particularly at the Atascadero State Hospital among persons committed to that institution as sexual psychopaths.

After a few days back in the office in Bloomington, he was lecturing again on April 4 at the downtown branch of the University of Chicago on "Patterns of Sexual Behavior: An Overview of the Range of American Sex Practices." Talks to audiences as varied as a medical society, a student dormitory group, and students of a military academy were scheduled during the rest of April. By the end of April he was in New York City. On this trip he gave a lecture he had promised six months before to the students at Princeton University.

During May he received several visitors at the Institute. One of them supplied this poignant memory of her stay at the Kinsey home.

The Final Lean Years

Music was perhaps his salvation in many trying times because this was a safe retreat for him when he was harried. The last time I was in Bloomington he took me to the opera. After walking up to the balcony he took one of his "little white pills" but he was not comfortable or relaxed all evening. I felt then I'd probably not see him again and—as it turned out—this was the last May of his life.

During the first and the fourth week in May he was in Chicago for several days. It was during this second trip that, on May 24, he interviewed his last two subjects for sex histories. These were his 7,984th and 7,985th histories. It is remarkable that with that many interviews behind him he could a few weeks later write: "It is a shame there comes a time that you have to work up data and publish it instead of continuing the gathering. Frankly, I very much enjoy the gathering."

Stories were told many times about the special skills which Kinsey had in interviewing by persons who served as subjects. The sketch by Cornelia Otis Skinner published in the *New Yorker* in May, 1950, is probably the best known of these. Trained professionals who had themselves been faced with the task of getting information from "reluctant respondents" are perhaps the most reliable witnesses. These observations by a psychiatrist are illuminating:

It was on a hot July 4th afternoon that Kinsey and I met in my office and talked for over two hours. I had been previously analyzed some years ago and thought I knew a fair bit about my own emotional beginnings, but his questions came so rapidly and so penetratingly that I recognized some inter-relationships in my early life experiences which psychoanalysis had never brought home to me. To me it was a complete indication of the validity of his approach. The questions were leveled at me so quietly but so rapidly and with such a sustained pace that I could not have evaded them or fabricated in any way without, I believe, the mental and emotional effort attendant on so doing being plainly evident to the observer. This is just another way of saying that his unique skill as an interviewer brought out, I am sure, a very high percentage of undistorted responses. I have always looked back upon this giving of my case history as an outstanding *therapeutic* experience for me.

Kinsey prided himself on being able to relate easily to persons of all social levels. He was skillful in getting people to ignore the usual social conventions on sexual privacy and to submit to questioning about it for a larger cause. This incident, reported by a guest who was present, is a good illustration:

> One night at dinner at R's his hostess chided Kinsey that her housekeeper didn't approve of his work and couldn't understand how anyone could give him a history. Kinsey had a twinkle in his eye when he accepted the challenge. He simply asked the housekeeper, a sweet, distinguished, grey-haired old dame, what she loved best. She said the young people around her—the kids in the R. family, her own relations, friends. Then Kinsey asked: "Knowing the real purpose of my work is to help young people, would .you deny me a history?" The old gal capitulated; his charm, warmth, logic, and keen insight into her in so brief a time won her over.

Early in June, 1956, Kinsey spent some days in the Robert W. Long Hospital in Indianapolis, and President Wells wrote him while he was there:

> I am unhappy to learn that you have not been feeling well. Please stay in bed until you absorb some rest. It is the best of all medicine.

Shortly afterward Kinsey wrote to his friend in California, Dr. Frances Shields, describing his physical condition:

> I went to the hospital with my heart misbehaving on June 1 and should have gone sometime before that. There is an enlargement of the heart, constant fibrillation, an apical beat of about 140 at the time I went to the hospital and a pulse of anywhere between 40 and 80, and other such foolishment. Failure to compensate induced the problem of water retention. My Indianapolis man was very pessimistic, but the young, local man who is following me now that I am home is gradually learning to make allowances for individual variation, and learning that I cannot so easily be put down.

By June 7, the time scheduled for the dedication of Jordan Hall—which now housed the Institute—he had been released but was far from well. The new building, including the Institute quarters on the third floor, was readied for the open house for visitors, which was to be part of the week-end festivities. Several of Kinsey's former graduate students in entomology who had made their mark in the world of science were to return to the campus to participate in the program. He planned a supper in his garden for them all on June 7. He was just out of the hospital and they could see that he was ailing. Their letters written later thanking the Kinseys for their hospitality all tell the same tale. Each included advice to their sixty-two-year-old professor to get more rest and to take better care of his health. The irrepressible Breland added: "Get plenty of rest, even though Mrs. Kinsey has to tie you in bed!" The dinner in Alumni Hall of the Union Building to honor Dean Fernandus Payne was the culmination of the three-day ceremonies, and in Payne's words, Kinsey in spite of his condition "dragged himself" over to it "out of loyalty" to his long-time supporter and department chairman.

Most of June was spent at home in bed. In a letter to Emily Mudd excusing himself from personally showing the Institute to some friends of hers who would be in Bloomington, Kinsey admits "I have been out of shape for a while." By the end of the month he was mending, or so it seemed. He wrote to Breland and the others to that effect:

> Spent practically all of June in bed, but there is definite improvement. In spite of a pessimistic doctor I shall prove to them as I have done in the past 30 years, that you can do more with a physical handicap than they sometimes think.

Once he began to feel better, Kinsey was hard to hold down. He went to the office for hours at a time and still tried to carry on his routine work. On July 9 he wrote to Hugo Gernsbach, the publisher of *Sexology*, who had written inquiring about his health:

> Apparently too many hours of work and not enough sleep per day, combined with some of the tensions that developed in connection with the problems on my last trip to New York, and subsequently to Detroit and Chicago, stirred up the latent heart difficulties which I have had ever since early childhood. You will admit I have done pretty well in spite of them through the years, and I intend to do better than the doctors think in the next ten

years. This time it took four or five weeks to start any definite mend, but the last week has been one of steady improvement. By working part days and making sure to get sufficient sleep, I think I can turn out work again.

In July the Institute of High School Biology Teachers, which was being held on the campus, was given a special lecture by Kinsey. Henry Remak, a member of the German Department who had aided Kinsey in the checking of the foreign language editions of his books, attended Kinsey's lecture and later wrote:

> As a formal speaker . . . Kinsey was peerless. A few weeks before his death, I heard him give—tired and drawn as he was— a 50-minute lecture to biology teachers on how to teach sex in high school biology courses which was of a well-nigh somnambulistic perfection in its concentratedness, directness, plainness, and phrasing as any professional lecture I have ever heard or will hear—and he did not have or need the shortest bit of a note!

Remak also can remember how impatient Kinsey was with his physical handicaps. He tells:

> Two or three weeks before his death I heard him say over the phone: "I can't understand why I can't get my strength back" in a tone of indignation. It was unfair; it was unjust; there was so much to be done.

But the doctor's warning to cut his working day back to a few hours went often unheeded.

On the 9th and 10th of August he was in the office answering overdue correspondence and dictating a long statement of his views on the past history and current position of his research and of the Institute (see p. 220). It is bitter and condemnatory in tone. He could not, of course, have known that he was to die within the month, and that it would stand, in a real sense, as his last will and testament. The bile had boiled up in his system and he spewed it forth without regard for people or institutions. It stands in one sense as an indictment of our cultural rigidity; in another, of Kinsey's own intransigence.

On August 13 he managed to get to the office again and wrote at length to Dr. Karl Bowman, the San Francisco physician, about the problems the research was facing in the customs case. One paragraph read:

> Thanks for your good letter of August 9. I am sorry to have worried you about so many things. We are keeping in close touch with the doctors, and although it has been only a very slow recovery, I hope that it is a definite recovery. In any event things are to be planned so I shall accomplish the most that is possible however much of rest and medication that takes in order to get some hours per day in on the publication end of it.

Kinsey's next lecture was to be his last. The Association of Student Personnel Administrators was holding a training institute at Purdue University at Lafayette, Indiana. The Harvard Graduate School of Business Administration was the sponsor, and Kinsey had agreed some time before to appear on the program on August 14. His staff felt he should not make the trip and tried to persuade him to cancel the appearance. Vexed with their attempt to interfere with his own judgment of the situation, he threatened to go by bus or train. He ended by arranging with Mrs. Kinsey to drive him the 100 miles. His lecture to the deans was up to form, and those present remember the gentle fun he poked at the deaning profession. While describing the decline of sexual activity with age in the male, he interposed the remark, "and then they become deans!" He and Clara stayed overnight at the Purdue Union, but the effort of the trip and program drew heavily on his dwindling reserve of physical strength.

On Saturday, August 18, President Wells had made arrangements to have two prominent Indianapolis attorneys, who were to aid the Institute in the case involving the United States Customs, come to Bloomington to see some of the Institute collections and to confer with Kinsey. They found he was at home confined to bed. He insisted they come to his house to talk to him. Wells remembers Kinsey's great agitation as the discussion progressed. Alarmed, he turned to Mrs. Kinsey and asked her if she could do anything to calm him. She replied that it was not possible. He was hospitalized for pneumonia, with resulting heart complications, a few days later.

On the day of his death the local paper carried banner

headlines, and the text explained that "he had been ailing for six months," that he "had been in and out of the hospitals in Bloomington and Indianapolis," that he "had spent increasingly less time at the office," and that "his work had been sharply curtailed." A slow pace of work was impossible for Kinsey to accept. "I'd rather be dead than not put in a full day's work" were his oft-spoken words to several of us. For such a person life ends when he stops producing. Alfred Kinsey died in the Bloomington Hospital at 8 o'clock in the morning, on August 25, 1956, at the age of sixty-two.

He would probably not have had it otherwise.

FROM

The Kinsey Papers

1. WHAT I BELIEVE

by Alfred C. Kinsey

Written for *San Quentin News*, December, 1954

I BELIEVE MANY THINGS, but you may want to know what I have come to believe about the men and the women whom we have interviewed in these fifteen years.

This is a season in which many persons are re-examining their faiths. I should, therefore, like to say again that my faith in men and in women has steadily grown, as I have learned more about their sexual histories. Even though some of these histories have included things which did no good to anyone, and occasionally things which may have done outright damage to someone, most of the things which I have seen in the histories have increased my faith in the basic decency, the basic honesty, and the basic reasonableness of human behavior.

I believe that most of you here at San Quentin have done a great deal more good than you have ever done damage in this world. When I go over your histories, I find that even you who have done the most damage to others still have done much more good than you are usually given credit for.

I have found that the sexual behavior of most men and women, including even their most cantankerous and socially impossible behavior, makes sense when one learns about the handicaps, the difficulties, the disappointments, the losses, and the tragedies which have led them into such behavior. I believe that most people would exercise greater Christian tolerance of all types of sexual behavior, if they understood, as I have begun to understand, why people do what they do sexually.

There are some persons who believe that no one does things for anyone else unless he expects to reap some personal benefit from it. There are some persons who believe that the human decencies are nothing more than the slick tools with which each of us is attempting to con the rest of the world. I do not subscribe to such philosophy. I believe that most men and women are honest because they believe that all folk are better off when there is honesty, and pleasant because they believe that all folk are more comfortable when they are pleasant. I believe that most men and women do things for others because they find an unselfish satisfaction in seeing others comfortable or happy.

I believe that most of you who have contributed to our study here at San Quentin have done so primarily because you have believed that your contribution would help increase our knowledge of human sexual behavior, and that the world might in consequence become a more comfortable place for more of the folk who live in it. We who are making this study, and millions of others in this world, shall always be indebted to you for this contribution which you have made to better human living.

2. A Scientist's Responsibility in Sex Instruction

A paper presented at a meeting of the National Association of Biology Teachers, Philadelphia, December, 1940.

It is the function of a scientist to discover the truth about that portion of the universe which is made up of matter. It is not the function of a scientist to judge the esthetic or moral qualities of that universe. By the very nature of its methods science is restricted to the examination of matter. In its realm there is no right, no wrong, no beauty, no lack of beauty—nothing but the observed truth, which, for the true scientist, is the most we can hope to know about matter. Any scientist who passes opinions on things spiritual or moral speaks as a theologian or as a mere man, and not as a scientist.

Sex and sex behavior are obviously biological phenomena which may be subjected to scientific examination. That there are moral implications in some aspects of human sexual behavior, no scientist will deny; but only the biologic aspects of sex are meat for biological investigation, and a scientist, as a scientist, has nothing to contribute to sex instruction except the data resulting from objective investigations of sex and of sex behavior.

On the other hand, scientists and science teachers have been called upon in the last twenty years to sanction and further a program of sex instruction which is clearly designed to substantiate the mores and a Western European code of morals. Whether this program happens—or not—to agree with our ideas of what is moral and socially desirable is not the question immediately involved. The issue concerns the right to engage in moral propaganda in a science classroom. It is an old issue—one that was fought out by the astronomers and physicists who first ventured to investigate the structure of the universe and the nature of matter, an issue that we as biologists had to face when we first gave instruction on the origin of species—an issue for which there has been and will continue to be only one solution, namely the completely amoral presentation of scientific data in the science classroom, and the relegation of other issues to those halls where they will be recognized as the moral judgments which they are, and not mistaken for logic or for science.

Most unfortunate of all, we, as science teachers, often turn to theologians and uplifters for the materials which we pass on as science in our classrooms. Matters which are fundamentally biologic have been decided by nonscientific authorities and mixed with superstition, wishful thinking, and rationalizations of the mores which we, the science teachers, have been duped into accepting as the "biology of sex." Most of the manuals of sex instruction have originated among students of education, Y.M.C.A. lecturers, social hygiene workers, clergymen, and physicians—which would be good enough sources if one were interested in ethics or in such pseudo-science as some of these physicians pass out to the public. The attitude of one of these physicians is well summed up in a letter which I have from a prominent writer on sex who assures me that all questions of sex behavior "are primarily subjective and basically emotional," and that he is, therefore, not even interested in seeing data that are scientifically obtained. The lectures and publications of this physician confirm his own interpretation of his own attitude. One would not need many hours' contact with biology to learn the so-called science which has gotten into much of the published literature on sex. But this is the very literature to which most teachers go when they prepare to give sex instruction.

We do not go to Genesis for our information on evolution, we do not present Eden or the Ark on Ararat as part of the record in our science books. There were times when we were hampered in our freedom to present the scientifically established data on evolution; but never did we submit to the inclusion of anything but science in our textbooks. At no time did we allow the question of morality to determine what was scientifically acceptable. To paraphrase Thomas Henry Huxley, we did dare to face the fact, though it threatened to slay us, and we presented a biology that was scientifically sound and scientifically unassailable. We are facing a very old issue when we are now called on to decide whether our sex instruction should be moral, or scientific.

It may be argued that in sex we are dealing with materials that are different from some of the other things in science. It will be pointed out that the social implications of sex are so great that society cannot afford to consider objectively determined facts. This in itself is proof of our contention that sex instruction, as now given, involves a great deal that has no place in a science classroom. But this is no argument against the inclusion of sexual biology as part of our teaching; and those who insist that we not touch this subject

unless we are willing to include a moral interpretation merely renew a criticism that has been made against all science, and, in fact, against all learning, ever since the day when schools and colleges and laboratories were first established for scholarly investigation. It must not be forgotten that the organization of the solar system, the laws of the physical universe, the origin of life, and the development of new species all appeared, to some people, to be matters of morals, and matters which they would have withheld from scientific investigation. It was not so long ago that a prominent English clergyman went so far as to suggest that all scientific discovery should be weighed in the scales of morals, and that the knowledge of such discoveries should be carefully suppressed when their application was judged immoral. If, to some, sex and sex behavior seem peculiarly questions of morals, it is because sex has less often been viewed objectively and because these things need the very sort of consideration which only scientists and science teachers can give them.

As a matter of fact, if ethics involves only those questions which concern the welfare of more than one individual, then only a small portion of human sex behavior can be considered matters of morals. Unless one subscribes to an absolutist philosophy, and believes in the intrinsic rightness or wrongness of things, it is very difficult to understand what social interests are concerned in much of the human animal's sexual activity. The bases of erotic response involve such prosaic matters as end organs, vaso-motor reflexes, pulse rates, blood pressure, breathing rates, etc. These are basically and always physiologic phenomena, and only occasionally are they in any strict sense moral in their effects. The resolution of erotic arousal, the relation of erotic stimulation and response to physical health, and the possibility of ignoring, suppressing, resolving, or sublimating such arousal are first of all questions of physical and mental hygiene, and their solution must lie in the laboratory and science classroom, and not in the chairs of the philosophers. The usual pronouncements on the possibilities of sublimation represent wishful thinking which is without benefit of a knowledge of the fact, or of any understanding of the basic physiologic processes involved.

Similarly, moral attempts to control particular forms of sexual outlet are designed to perpetuate the mores and are often devoid of any logic, not to say scientific justification. Such autosexual outlets as masturbation and climax in nocturnal dreams involve the individual's hygiene, and almost never the welfare of anyone else. They seem, therefore, strictly biologic problems which scientists must have the right to decide. The curious insistence that these activities present psychic problems that are the really moral issues merely puts the cart before the horse and makes a problem where none would exist except for the moralistic teaching against these and other outlets. Psychic problems, moreover, are often best taken care of by removing the physical source of the mental upset. Cut fingers may bring emotional disturbances, but the way to cure the disturbance is to take care of the physical difficulty that lies back of it. Abundant experience indicates that when the facts about the physical significance of masturbation, and indeed about many other sexual activities, are once understood, the psychic problems in most cases disappear, and the presumed moral implications disappear with them.

Heterosexual and homosexual outlets involve both biologic and social phenomena, but even here we as scientists can insist on such a scientific study of the social aspects of behavior as will impartially investigate the fact, critically analyze cause and effect, and objectively evaluate the significance of each item. This sort of scientific approach to social problems can be allied to biologic considerations of the physical bases of behavior; any less scientific treatment of social problems involves something that we, as scientists, are not equipped to understand.

It is, therefore, a matter of considerable significance to record the growing body of objective studies which have been published in recent years in the field of human sexual biology. There are still more extensive investigations now under way. We, ourselves, are engaged in a case history study which we hope will involve many thousands of persons, both males and females, of all ages, from the youngest child to the oldest adult, from such a wide range of economic and educational levels as will give a truer picture of human sexual behavior than has yet been available. To date we have more than 1,700 histories in the series which we are gathering. The published literature and more recently accumulated data are the materials to which the biology teacher should go for information to be used in sex instruction. This factual material is in striking contrast to the sentimental generalities and biologic misinterpretations which appear in the more popular literature on sex.

All of these objective studies emphasize, first of all, the inadequacies of the teaching which we now have. They portray a human sexual activity far beyond anything that popular opinion, social pretense, or written law has recognized. The near-daily activity known to occur in the infra-human anthropoid is little modified in the human by the dressings of social conventions or moral or written codes. For instance, the data indicate that the average adolescent boy who sits in our classrooms may be aroused to the point of complete orgasm as often as five to fourteen times a week.* The society in which he lives condemns nearly all forms of sexual outlet except that legalized by marriage, but the economic system in which he finds himself imposes a delay in marriage of something like seven to twelve or more years. The teachers of morals blithely advise him to sublimate his physiologic reactions, though the record indicates that not more than two per cent of the unmarried males completely achieve that theoretical ideal. The remaining ninety-eight per cent look to us, the biology teachers, to explain how they can live in the sexual bodies of which they are made.

The record indicates that ninety-eight per cent of these boys will find masturbation a source of outlet; for two-thirds of them masturbation will provide the chief source of outlet. Only a small number can depend on nocturnal emissions to supply an adequate release from the daily stimuli. Eighty-five per cent of the boys will make such specific heterosexual contact as is known as "heavy petting." Half of the boys will have had intercourse before they are out of high school. A third of them will become involved in homosexual contacts. And if they are raised on the farm, half of them will add sexual contacts with other animals to the list of possible outlets. Whatever the moral implications, these are the sexual problems of the adolescent boy. These are the realities which our instruction, if it is at all adequate, must face when we engage as teachers of sex.

But what, then, do we do for this boy, this very live and very bewildered boy? In actual practice the sum total of our current sex instruction often consists in telling that boy that the bees are quite indispensable agents in the transfer of pollen among the flowers! Even the newer programs hardly go beyond the story of reproduction in the plant and animal kingdom as a whole, a bit of material on heredity and hormones, and too much about venereal diseases and mental hygiene. Rarely is there specific consideration of the specific problems presented by the sex outlets: with the physiologic and behavior problems which are the real problems in sex instruction.

The story of the sexual development of the adolescent girl is somewhat different from the story for the boy. Fifty per cent of the girls from the upper social levels manage to arrive at marriage

---

*Later, of course, Kinsey accumulated a much larger number of histories than the 1,700 he had at this time, and he learned to differentiate between different segments of the population. None of the figures given in this early talk before a general audience should, therefore, he regarded as authoritative.

before they have ever experienced sexual arousal to the point of complete climax. Many people are proud of this, and think it an ideal which the boy might very well follow. But the girl has achieved her so-called sublimation as the result of a long build-up of inhibitions. Against her record of no orgasms before marriage, the male she weds has a record of some thousand or fifteen hundred climaxes in his premarital background. One hardly needs to look further for the chief cause of sexual incompatibilities in marriage. One-half of all these previously unresponsive girls—that is, one-quarter to a third of all the women who marry—will fail to come to climax in intercourse after marriage. The social implications of this situation are something that the teachers engaged in sex instruction have thought little about. In fact, the marital break-ups which are due to sexual maladjustment may, in too many cases, be fairly charged to the sort of instruction which moralists have always given and which moralists are likely to continue to give and which moralists are trying to introduce into our science classrooms.

There is, then, no doubt of a need for a sort of sex instruction that will face the facts and deal with the real problems of sex. The moral aspects of these problems will be handled well enough by others; as scientists we should be concerned with investigations of sexual physiology and the discovery of the fact in human sexual behavior. As science teachers we should support these scientific investigations and utilize them in shaping our programs of sex instruction. As scientists and science teachers we must defend our right to disseminate this scientifically acquired knowledge, and to see to it that sex instruction is as scientifically sound as anything else we present in our curriculum. And if the mores are such that we cannot yet present all of our data, we need not be too greatly concerned. It is the history of science that no forces, however great, have ever succeeded in preventing the spread of the knowledge of objectively established fact. In time, whatever the forces that oppose it, we shall have a kind of sex instruction that scientists will recognize as science.

3. The Right to Do Sex Research

This statement, written in 1956, was found in Kinsey's papers after his death.

OUR PRESENT UNDERSTANDING OF HUMAN SEXUAL BEHAVIOR is based very largely upon isolated reports of individual cases in scientific books or journals, or in newspapers, to a still greater extent upon street corner gossip, and a varied assortment of philosophical ideas as to what the human animal should be doing sexually. It is probably correct to say that our knowledge of the basic anatomy and physiology of human sexual response in the year 1940 was no better than our knowledge of the circulation of the blood in the early 1600's. You would not think of going to a physician for a heart difficulty, if his knowledge had been acquired from nothing but pre-seventeenth-century literature on the subject.

In the same fashion we operate under a system of sex law which is basically the Talmudic Code of the seventh century B.C. Our law of theft, our concepts of responsibilities involved in contracts, our ideas concerning the handling of offenders in every other field of crime have undergone considerable change in the last two thousand years. Our concepts of what constitutes sex crime, and the way in which we handle sex offenders today, is basically very little different from the practices of many centuries ago.

Important as the sexual adjustment may be between spouses in a marriage, our present-day marriage manuals contain much advice that is based on guesses and wishful thinking, and often perpetuate the errors found in the ancient Sanskrit books on sex and in the love books of Ovid written in the first century B.C. While we well understand that a great multiplicity of factors may be involved in the maintenance or disruption of a marriage, certain it is that the sexual factor is one which enters into a fair proportion of cases—perhaps as many as seventy-five per cent—of all of the cases of marriages which result in separations or divorce. It seems reasonable that there should be unending research undertaken by qualified scientists in every field that may contribute to the greater stability of our marriages.

Married spouses who have become parents are immediately faced with the problem of how to educate their children on matters of sex. The specific record shows that not more than five per cent of all the children ever receive any sort of sex education, either from their parents, their teachers, or their religious leaders, which in actuality may serve in an adequate education of youth. While we ourselves have worked on this problem of the early development of sexual patterns among children, we are not yet in a position to suggest what policies of education may be most effective. We are certain, however, that most of what has been written on the sex education of children is based upon philosophic guess and not upon any understanding of the actual processes that are involved in the development of sexual patterns of children.

Our teen-age youth arrive at their sexually most active periods long before the law or social custom acknowledges any legitimate sexual outlet of these teen-agers. By sixteen or seventeen the average boy is more highly responsive to sexual stimuli, to a greater variety of sexual stimuli, more instantly responsive to these stimuli, and more capable of repeated responses in a short period of time, than the average older males of any age. In our social organization we have found considerable advantage in delaying marriage until youths are sufficiently educated to assume the responsibility of supporting a home, and until they have sufficiently matured through their experience to face the psychological problems which marriage may bring—but the processes of the biological development of sexual capacities have not changed over the centuries, and many of our youth, involving most teen-age males although probably not more than fifteen per cent of the teen-age females, face daily or near-daily problems in resolving these differences between their sexual capacities and the social demands of the situation. A certain portion of our juvenile delinquency grows out of this incongruity between biologic capacities and the unrealities of our social set-up.

THE NEED FOR RESEARCH

No thoughtful parent, no teacher, no religious counselor, no law enforcement officer, no social worker, nor anyone else who has been aware of the multitudinous social difficulties in which neighbors and friends and the world at large may become involved can have failed to understand that our lack of scientific knowledge of the basic aspects of human sexual behavior is the source of many of these difficulties in which we continually find ourselves. A portion of these same persons, however, are the ones who most bitterly oppose any attempt to advance our scientific understanding in this area. They are ready to support cancer research, heart research, polio research, and studies of any number of social problems, but they feel that sexual behavior is still the one area in which we should be able to operate without intelligent understanding. This is nothing new in the history of the world. There were centuries, not too remote, in which any attempt to understand the structure of the universe, the nature of matter, physical processes, and biological evolution were condemned because they were considered invasions of areas that should be left to philosophy and religion. The names of Galileo, Newton, Kepler, Pascal, and most of those who attempted to explore the physical realities of the universe appear in indices of prohibited books dating back not more than two or three centuries, and in some instances as recent as the last hundred years. How many persons would venture today to condemn all further physical research? It has been the history of science throughout the ages that ignorance has never brought anything but trouble to mankind, and that every fact, well established, has ultimately added to the happiness of our social organization. The few persons who still doubt this do not succeed in interfering with scientific research in the physical and chemical sciences, in astronomy and the basic biologic sciences in our universities, nor do their votes constitute a total which intimidates Congressmen who are ready to appropriate millions and even billions for additional research in these areas. The scientist's right to do research in these other fields involved the basic development of our right to establish knowledge as a source of our human capacity, and that is now a part of the written history. There is hardly another area in human biology or in sociology in which the scientist has had to fight for his right to do research, as he has when he has attempted to acquire a scientific understanding of human sexual behavior.

It is incomprehensible that we should know so little about such an important subject as sex, unless you realize the multiplicity of forces which have operated to dissuade the scientist, to intimidate the scientist, and to force him to cease research in these areas.

It is still doubtful how far the researcher may go in attempting to understand what happens physiologically during sexual response. A young man, medically trained, recently published a report on the relation of the heartbeat and breathing rate to sexual response. The report is soberly treated and its significance understood in the accredited national journals. It is received as an important contribution in a medical society meeting. And yet three institutions have warned the young man that if he publishes the material he will be dropped from their faculties, and the two collaborators who contributed jointly in the research have lived for several years under the same threat. These data are of importance in many a medical case. They not infrequently figure in legal cases, but they have been pigeonholed and nonavailable for several years since they were first gathered. There is difficulty in finding qualified physiologists who are ready to continue with such research in the face of the institutional and possible legal obstacles that would be put in their way.

The right to ask questions concerning the sexual behavior of the persons whom we have interviewed, and who have been interviewed in the previous case studies, has been repeatedly challenged. The institution with which we have been connected is one of the few in the entire United States in which the administration and the trustees have believed that such research was so important that they have been willing to defend our right to undertake such a project. Four of the largest institutions on the east coast, which enjoy reputations for being liberal and leaders in advances in knowledge, have all turned down or prohibited the publication of similar research that was done in their institutions. At one of the institutions where the president has proclaimed himself as a supporter of the advancement of science two case history studies have been completed under the most reputable of groups. Physicians, psychiatrists, psychologists—persons well qualified to undertake such research—have been responsible in each of these two cases; but in both instances the administrations of the institutions prohibited publication of the data.

The largest case history study—short of our own—which has been undertaken either in this country or abroad was part of the Army study of the American soldier. The project explored all aspects of the psychology and social backgrounds of the soldiers who were involved in the second world war. A highly qualified team of psychologists, sociologists, statisticians, and others were in charge of the study. We know the results of the study because we were called in on several occasions as consultants, with the understanding that the information in the study was still classified. We are particularly conscious of the importance of publication of this material because it would do more to settle the question of the adequacy of our own results than any study that has previously been published. And yet when the four volumes of *The American Soldier* were finally put into print there was no presentation of any of the sexual information that had been obtained in the study. The Commanding Officer in charge of one of the camps objected to his chaplain concerning the study and within an amazingly short time the order came down from the General Staff to cease and desist on the study, and to lock it up as top secret.

It has been remarked recently that while doctors bury their mistakes, administrative departments of the government classify them. In this instance classification was designed not to cover a mistake but to impose the opinion of a minority group who, for whatever reasons one may suspect, decided that the scientist should not be allowed to do research in this area of human behavior.

Still more incomprehensible is the classification of a body of Japanese sexual data which one of the American groups of armed forces seized when they went into Japan. Japanese scientists, who have always been remarkably objective and forward in their study of sexual problems, persuaded a group of their own Japanese prisoners in their own Japanese prisons to keep sexual diaries. As Havelock Ellis pointed out many years ago in his own publications and as we have emphasized in publication of our findings in our own research, such day-by-day records of sexual activities provide data which may not be secured in any other fashion. But although this Japanese material has been in Washington for something more than ten years, no scientist has ever had a chance to study the material for somebody, evidently convinced that there was no right to do scientific research on the problems of sex, ordered it kept locked up as classified material. Any pretense that such material falling into the hands of Russians or any other potential enemies might endanger the security of the United States adds to the mockery which too much of our security program has in actuality become.

4. LAST STATEMENT

This final overview, without a title, was dictated on August 10, 1956, two weeks before Dr. Kinsey died. Because of its highly personal nature, it has been edited at points.

FROM THE BEGINNING OF OUR OWN RESEARCH there have been many persons who have gone out of their way to try and prevent our securing histories from particular groups. As we remarked in our first volume, these reminded us of the mudholes and the gullies and the vicissitudes of the back roads that we had had to travel in connection with our previous biological research, and we have not taken time to tell this part of the story of our own struggle to win the right to engage in this research. Now that these obstacles have accumulated to the point where they threaten the entire possibility of our continuing with our research, and now that court action becomes involved in our attempt to have access to certain types of documentary material which is needed for research in human sexual behavior, it seems not inappropriate to record more of the record of difficulty than we have publicly recorded before. At this point we are quite convinced that if we never are able to report anything more concerning the nature of human sexual behavior, the most important thing for us to establish right now is the right of the scientist to engage in such research. This is not only a question of the right to engage in research wherever the scientific method is applicable—it involves the obligation of the scientist to add to our store of accurate knowledge in an area which has such tremendous social significance.

EARLY HISTORY OF OUR OWN RESEARCH

Our research in human sexual behavior was undertaken eighteen years ago in response to requests from students at our own University for biological information on the basis of which they might formulate some of their own conclusions as to desirable personal and social policy. They came to us as scientists, not because they wanted advice, but because they wanted factual data on the nature of sexual response, and scientific data on the correlation of various types of sexual activity in youth with the possibility of successful marital adjustments later in their lives. I did not know the answers to most of the questions they were bringing, and when I went to the literature in psychology, psychiatry, the social sciences, and other areas in which one would have expected to have found the reports of research that had been done on these matters, I was struck with the paucity of the material in comparison with the knowledge that we had on physiology of every other aspect of human function, and the knowledge that we had on the behavior, including the sexual behavior, of many of the other mammals.

It was apparent that scientists had hesitated to explore in this field because they were not certain that society would permit them to explore. Some examination of the previous history of research on human sexual behavior in the United States and abroad made it apparent that practically all of the previous students in these areas had had to win the right to accomplish as much as they did. Havelock Ellis went to court with the publication of the first volume of his notable series, and never again published another volume of the series in England. Freud was rejected by practically the whole of the medical profession and hounded from one post to another as long as he lived; only after his death did his name become honorable as it is now in any branch of medical science. Hirschfeld, with all of his inadequate scientific equipment, nevertheless contributed a tremendous body of knowledge to our understanding of certain aspects of human sexual behavior, but he was driven first from Germany and then from France, and died as a refugee under the Hitler regime. His Institute for sex research at Berlin was destroyed, his library and archives were publicly burned, and the whole body of work that he had done was discredited by the new government that had come into power in Germany.

Robert L. Dickinson, one of the first of the pioneers in the study of human sexual problems in the United States, was constantly attacked throughout his life by the American Medical Association and by innumerable other groups who felt that his attempt to obtain an increased knowledge of the physiology of the female reproductive processes was not scientifically creditable. The rather recently published history of the American Medical Association would lead the unwary student to believe that that Association and its chief executives had been prime agents in the study of contraception and the whole problem of fertility and sterility in this country. In actuality there is an abundant documentary evidence that Dickinson was under perpetual attack from this particular source because he dared to engage in research in this area. Again, whatever the inadequacy of his scientific data, the tremendous development of our modern science of fertility and sterility, and many other aspects of female gynecology, must pay tribute to Dr. Dickinson for his persistence through nearly half a century of research in the face of continual obstacles put in his way.

Apart from the Dickinson clinical histories, the earliest of the case history studies were those undertaken by Katharine Davis, a social worker in New York, and by G.V. Hamilton, a psychoanalyst temporarily located in New York City, and by two fact finding journalists, D.D. Bromley and F.H. Britten, who published in 1938.

Early in the 1920's Robert L. Yerkes attempted to organize a committee for research on problems of sex in the National Research Council in Washington. The psychological division of that research body decided that such problems were not the proper subject for research, and Yerkes, a psychologist, was forced to go to the medical division to get the committee organized. It is unfortunate that the published history of the Committee for Research on Problems of Sex in the National Research Council passed by the difficulties that were involved in the early years of organization of that committee.

Nowhere has there been a record which sufficiently points out to the young scientific explorer what widespread objection there is to doing scientific research in this area. As part of the permanent record it should be known that two of the then best known research psychologists proposed that there be experimental work done on the physiology of human sexual behavior, and when the National Research Council's committee was faced with this proposition one of its members, who was one of the best known biologists in the United States at that time, and a still better known human physiologist, resigned from the committee in protest at the possibility of physiologic research in this area. Finally the committee had to compromise and was able to proceed with the other aspects of its research only because it agreed that there should be no physiologic research in this drastically unexplored area; but when we subsequently proposed such research as part of our own project, under the support of the National Research Council's committee, another prominent human physiologist and a prominent psychoanalyst again resigned from the committee in protest against the possibility of undertaking to do research in this area.

These are not matters that should die in the memories of persons who were involved. It is time that the story of the difficulties that have been involved in winning the right to do sex research be made available in sufficient detail so that the young scientist who attempts to explore in this area in the future is forewarned and, we hope, steeled against the vicissitudes of what may be an inevitable part of such research for some generations to come.

We were warned by one of the wisest of biologists when we undertook this research that if we went ahead with it we would lose friends and caste in biological circles, and we would be faced with social and legal difficulties that would constantly distract us from the actual gathering of data—"but," he added, "there is no area in which research is more needed than this. . . ."

Scientists are human, and probably as liable to the full panoply of human foibles as persons in any other profession. They may be objective in their studies of protozoa or algae or the physiology of some cryptic process in some particular plant or animal, but when it comes to facing human problems they have proved as likely as anyone else to become emotionally disturbed at the very notion of research in the area of human sexual behavior. One might have suspected that students of theology, persons in other fields, might more often have been the source of our difficulties. In actuality, our first and primary source has been the difficulty which many scientists have found in facing facts of human sexual behavior with anything like objectivity. A prominent scientist, a leader in science in a great university, and ultimately an important figure in scientific political organization in the national capital, began his review of our first volume by saying: "I do not like Kinsey, I do not like the Kinsey project, I do not like anything about the Kinsey study of sexual behavior."

The persons who have been most vociferous, both verbally and in their writing against our undertaking the study, would include some who honestly believe that ignorance is safer than knowledge in this, and presumably many other areas. But the prime objectors have been persons who are most disturbed in their own sexual lives. This we know specifically because we have case histories on some of these individuals. . . .

One of the psychoanalysts who has most persistently attacked our research engaged in conversation with a friend one day about the problem of curing homosexuality. The friend wanted to know why homosexuality needed curing any more than heterosexuality. The analyst's reply was to the effect that no one could ever live happily with a homosexual history for three reasons: (1) because it was contrary to nature; (2) because it was immoral; and (3) because it was contrary to the law. Such an answer could have been given by a fourth century cleric, and showed no benefit of the psychologic or biologic understanding that we have obtained concerning this phenomenon within the last fifteen centuries. And yet the same psychoanalyst attacks our publication of the data on the homosexual, which carry neither approval nor disapproval but attempt to represent the reality that exists in our organization; and his attacks have been widely quoted as the equivalent of the evidence that our work is scientifically unsound.

The persons who have been in the most difficulty over their own sexual adjustments react in diametrically opposite ways to the notion of sex research. Some of them will frankly exclaim that they have had enough difficulty in their own lives to make them comprehend the social importance of there being a sounder understanding of the sorts of problems that they faced, and the sorts of problems which they realize many other persons face. On the other hand, there is a considerable group of those whose lives have become utter shambles because of their lack of understanding of sexual problems, their refusal to face the realities of sexual problems, and the personal and social difficulties which have been consequent upon their confused thinking; and these persons are very often the ones who are most vehement in insisting the sooner we forget that there is such a phenomenon as sex—as though the forgetting of any aspect of reality could in any way be profitable—the better off we would be.

This is the story with some of the persons who have attacked our findings as inadequate statistically. This is the story with some of the persons who insist that we are attacking basic concepts of morality. This is the story with some of the scientists who believe that the funds from research foundations and national committees and other sources should not be turned to the direction of sex research. This is the explanation of the long list of rationalizations which they produce to prove that such research is disreputable: our possession of obscene literature, the amount of newspaper publicity we have had (even though it has for the most part been strongly against our own wish), the fact that we are attempting to study too many aspects of human sexual behavior and should confine ourselves solely to the biological, or solely to the psychological, or solely to the sociological aspects; the argument that we are not sufficiently taking into account the psychological and sociological and legal aspects of these problems, and are basing the study solely on biological interpretation of behavior.

We have guaranteed to keep confidence on each individual history which we have taken in this study, but it must be admitted that it has imposed a terrific strain upon us at times to know the sexual

history of some of the persons who have been the bitterest oppo-
nents of our sex research, as they would be of any other sex research.

Within our own university the research was started, as we have
indicated, in response to a student demand. There probably were
only a few of the faculty who would have approved our undertaking
such research at that time, but we hasten to remark that there has
been tremendous support from both the faculty and the administration in the course of these years. Nevertheless, there was a period
during which there were many moves made by segments within the
university to put a stop to the research. . . . A head of one of the
science departments remarked bitterly that he supposed that such
research needed to be done, but Kinsey was too liberal to engage in
such research, meaning, we take it, that we were supposed to be
something else than objective in reporting the data that we secured
in the course of our exploration. This was an astounding statement
to secure from the head of a science department. It was proposed
in the college faculty that we be prohibited from publication of the
research, and when that proposal failed, it was proposed that we not
be allowed to publish until all of our material had been censored by
the Department of Public Relations in the University. The chief
objection came from the then existent staff of the Medical School,
who insisted that all such matters were medical problems and
should be investigated only in the Medical School. . . .

The bright chapter begins when the pressure on the administration of our University was such that the President and Trustees
wanted to know exactly what we were doing. They were satisfied
with the explanation, immediately proposed our right to do such
research, and in the seventeen years that have elapsed since then
have stood steadfastly behind us. The administration of Indiana
University has been repeatedly asked by pressure groups in the
state to put an end to the research. Certain groups have threatened
to withdraw whole groups of students from the University if they
did not put an end to the research. In reply to one of these groups
the President of the University issued one of the great defenses of
academic freedom. But again, as part of the record, it should be
made clear that for every clergyman who has opposed, from whatever end of the world, there have been many more who have
strongly approved this attempt to obtain sound knowledge on
the basis of which our thinking of human problems may be
based. . . .

The Franciscan friar whom I meet on the mountain trail in Peru
looks at me with puzzlement for a time and then says, "Ah, es el
señor Doctor Kinsey, no?" Then he wants to know why we are

doing this research, and when I reply, "Porque padre, es una parte de la vida"—"because, father, it is a part of life"—he instantly responds, "Si, es una parte de la vida." And for the rest of the mountain journey we are good friends.

If there have been those in religious circles who have believed that there should be no scientific understanding of these matters, it must be understood that there have been many more in religious circles who have believed. This research has been possible through the eighteen years only because the greater proportion of people of all walks of life, in these United States, have believed that the scientist has not only a right to explore in this area, but an obligation to discover material which may broaden the usefulness of our knowledge on human behavior.

5. Dr. Kinsey

Editorial in the *New York Times*, August 27, 1956

THE UNTIMELY DEATH OF DR. ALFRED C. KINSEY takes from the American scene an important and valuable, as well as controversial, figure. Whatever may have been the reaction to his findings—and to the unscrupulous use of some of them—the fact remains that he was first, last and always a scientist.

In the long run it is probable that the value of his contribution to contemporary thought will lie much less in what he found out than in the method he used and his way of applying it. Any sort of scientific approach to the problems of sex is difficult because the field is so deeply overlaid with such things as moral precept, taboo, individual and group training and long established behavior patterns. Some of these may be good in themselves, but they are no help to the scientific and empirical method of getting at the truth.

Dr. Kinsey cut through this overlay with detachment and precision. His work was conscientious and comprehensive. Naturally it will receive a serious setback with his death. Let us earnestly hope that the scientific spirit that inspired it will not be similarly impaired.

6. Alfred Kinsey

By J. B. S. Haldane

This article by the eminent British biologist was published
in the *Hindu Weekly Review*, October 8, 1956. Haldane, who
had entertained Kinsey in London less than a year before,
was on an extended stay in India at the time.

Alfred Kinsey has died. He was known to biologists for his
classificatory work on the gall wasps of north and central America,
but a wider public knew of him for his work on human sexual
behaviour. These two lines of work are not so far apart as they seem
at first sight. For, one can classify gall wasps in three ways, by their
visible characters, by the plants which they choose on which to lay
their eggs, and by the kinds of gall which grow upon these plants
around the larval insects and furnish them with food and protection. So, we may classify human beings by their race, religion,
occupation and so on, and also by their sexual behaviour.

Kinsey and his colleagues questioned many thousands of Americans of both sexes. The questions which they asked were very intimate and what is more, many people admitted to acts which are not
merely considered to be wicked, but render their doers liable to long
terms of imprisonment. It has often been suggested that those who
told him about their lives were an unrepresentative sample, that
they were boasters and liars, and so on. He met these criticisms in
various ways. Sometimes he was able to question all the members
of a group, for example all the students in a hostel. He took great
pains to give his subjects the opportunity to contradict themselves.
He interviewed husbands and wives, and compared the results obtained by different interviewers. To me at least he gave the impression that I should have found it very difficult to lie to him. I do not
think that his results are free from bias, but I believe that their bias
is far less than that of any previous work on the subject.

Very many people have blamed him for publishing facts which
are shameful, facts which should perhaps be investigated by
criminologists and medical men, but which if they are divulged to

the public will only lead to the popularisation of immoral practices. I understand that some Indian writers have been particularly severe in their condemnations, both of Kinsey himself, and of the American people of whom he has studied large samples.

I do not take this view myself. Perhaps an analogy may help. A number of ancient Hindu temples and a few modern ones are decorated with sculptures showing human beings, some engaged in acts which are normally done in private, and others in acts which are considered by many to be immoral even in private. Science is one way of looking at the world, religion is another. Both must contemplate the whole world. The men who ordered these sculptures to be made, and those who made them, believed, I think, that they were glorifying a god by portraying the richness and variety of the world. They may not have approved morally of what they portrayed any more than they approved morally of Ravana. But Ravana is part of the glory of God. Without him there could have been no *Ramayana.** The aim of religion is ultimately to lead men beyond desires for any finite things; but religious art, and the sacred books of religions which forbid religious art, are nevertheless concerned with finite things.

The scientific attitude is not very different. We scientists believe that it is our duty to describe the world as it is. Some of us think that God made it; others do not; but this makes little difference to our description. We also try to find what is behind appearances. Our religious acquaintances say that we have not looked very far. We can reply that our accounts are more consistent than theirs. We certainly cannot neglect sexual behaviour either in our account of the world or our explanation of it.

Perhaps Kinsey's most striking result was his complete confirmation of those who believe in the extreme diversity of human beings. He studied a number of healthy and fertile marriages between people of the same age, and found enormous variation in the frequency of sexual activity. It was as if some people ate thirty times as much or slept thirty times as long as others.

In the past, some people have blamed those whose sexual activity exceeded their own. Others have stated that moderation in this respect was harmful. Both were clearly wrong.

In America the main factor influencing sexual activity is education. Neither religion nor race proved to have much effect. The more educated people were less active. This is probably a reflexion of the Christian monastic tradition. For a thousand years education

---

*The great epic poem of India in which Rama's wife, Sita, is abducted by Ravana, a demon-king.

in Europe was entrusted to men and women vowed to celibacy, and this was so even after the Reformation, which permitted the marriage of Protestant priests. Fellows of Colleges at Oxford and Cambridge lost their jobs on marriage up till the late nineteenth century, and the tradition of celibacy still persists. One result of this has been a lesser fertility of the educated.

In India the tradition has been very different. Marriage was a duty for Brahmins. I am sure that a survey in India on Kinsey's lines would show very different results.

Nevertheless I doubt if the time is yet ripe for such a survey. India is still divided by language, caste, religion, and differences of education and income to a far greater extent than the United States, and it would be quite impossible for any one man or woman to study as representative a sample as Kinsey did. I also think that Indians are on the whole more secretive than Americans, largely as a result of centuries of foreign rule. Until such a survey has been made even in one Indian State, I doubt if Indians are justified in condemning Americans for the frequency with which they transgress the moral code to which most of them give lip service. According to some accounts such transgressions are much less frequent in India, according to others they are even more frequent. I do not believe either account. A man or woman will commonly tend to associate with people whose sexual behaviour is similar to his or her own, and to believe that they are representative.

I hope that Kinsey's junior colleagues will be able to continue his work, and that it may be extended to some European countries, and ultimately to some Asian ones. But I do not know whether any of his colleagues have the peculiar qualities which made his work possible. They have, of course, learned from him, but they may not possess his passion to discover the truth.

At the time of his death Kinsey was trying vigorously to reform the United States prison system, and was preaching similar reforms in Europe.* It is fairly obvious that a man imprisoned for homosexual behaviour is likely to spread such behaviour among men imprisoned for other offences, but this idea appears to be too complicated for those who are responsible for the regulation of prisons. Kinsey's death may mean that another generation will pass before it is accepted.

*This statement is somewhat exaggerated, as Kinsey's chief concern at the time was the recasting of laws dealing with sex offenses, rather than with prison reform.

PUBLICATIONS OF ALFRED C. KINSEY

1. "Fossil Cynipidae." *Psyche* 26:44–49, 1919.
2. "An African Figitidae." *Psyche* 26:162–163, 1919.
3. "New Species and Synonymy of American Cynipidae." *Bulletin of the American Museum of Natural History* 42:293–317, 1920.
4. "Life Histories of American Cynipidae." *Bulletin of the American Museum of Natural History* 42:319–357, 1920.
5. "Phylogeny of Cynipid Genera and Biological Characteristics." *Bulletin of the American Museum of Natural History* 42:357a–402, 1920.
6. "New Pacific Coast Cynipidae (Hymenoptera)." *Bulletin of the American Museum of Natural History* 46:279–295, 1922.
7. "Studies of Some New and·Described Cynipidae (Hymenoptera)." *Indiana University Studies* IX, No. 53: 1–141; 163–171, 1922.
8. With K. D. Ayres. "Varieties of a Rose Gall Wasp (Cynipidae, Hymenoptera)." *Indiana University Studies* IX, No. 53:142–171, 1922.
9. "Foreign Pests and Our Gardens." *Farm and Garden*, August, 1923, pp. 6–10.
10. "The Gall Wasp Genus Neuroterus (Hymenoptera)." *Indiana University Studies* X, No. 58:1–147, 1923.
11. "MacGillivray's External Insect Anatomy" (review). *Entomological News* XXV: 31–33, 1924.
12. *An Introduction to Biology*. Philadelphia: J. B. Lippincott Co., pp. xiv, 558. 1926.
13. "Biologic Sciences in Our High Schools." *Proceedings of Indiana Academy of Sciences* 35:63–65, 1926.
14. *Field and Laboratory Manual in Biology*. Philadelphia: J. B. Lippincott Co., pp. xix, 151. 1927.
15. "The Content of the Biology Course." *School Science and Mathematics* XXX:374–384, 1930.
16. *The Gall Wasp Genus Cynips: A Study in the Origin of Species.*

Bloomington, Indiana: Indiana University Studies XVI, Nos. 84–86, pp. 577. 1930.

17. *New Introduction to Biology.* Chicago: J. B. Lippincott Co., pp. xix, 840. 1933.

18. "Landscape Picture with Iris." *Bulletin of the American Iris Society,* July and October, 1933, pp. 1–11.

19. *Workbook in Biology.* Chicago: J. B. Lippincott Co., pp. xiii, 306. 1934.

20. "The Economic Importance of the Cynipidae." *Journal of Economic Entomology* 28:86–91, 1935.

21. *The Origin of Higher Categories in Cynips.* Bloomington, Indiana: Indiana University Publications, Science Series No. 4, pp. 334. 1936.

22. "An Evolutionary Analysis of Insular and Continental Species" (abstract). *Science* 85:56–57, 1937.

23. "An Evolutionary Analysis of Insular and Continental Species." *Proceedings of National Academy of Sciences* 23:5–11, 1937.

24. *Methods in Biology.* Chicago: J. B. Lippincott Co., pp. x, 279. 1937.

25. "New Mexican Gall Wasps (Hymenoptera, Cynipidae)." *Revue de Entomologia* 7:39–79, 1937.

26. "Supra-specific Variation in Nature and in Classification: From the View-point of Zoology." *The American Naturalist* LXXI:206–222, 1937.

27. "Insects and Arachnids from Canadian Amber: Order Hymenoptera; Cynipidae." *University of Toronto Studies, Geological Service* 40:21–27, 1937.

28. "New Mexican Gall Wasps (Hymenoptera, Cynipidae). II." *Revue de Entomologia* 7:428–471, 1937.

29. *New Introduction to Biology* (revised). Chicago: J. B. Lippincott Co., pp. xv, 845. 1938.

30. *Workbook in Biology.* Chicago: J. B. Lippincott Co., pp. v, 164. 1938.

31. "New Mexican Gall Wasps (Hymenoptera, Cynipidae). IV." *Proceedings of Indiana Academy of Science* 47:261–280, 1938.

32. "Cynipoidae from Oceania." *Marcellia* 29:1–8, 1938.

33. "New Figitidae from the Marquesas Islands." *Bernice P. Bishop Museum Bulletin* 142:193–197, 1938.

34. "Homosexuality: Criteria for a Hormonal Explanation of the Homosexual." *Journal of Clinical Endocrinology* 1:424–428, 1941.

35. "Seasonal Factors in Gall Wasp Distributions." *Biological Symposia* 6:167–187, 1942.
36. "Isolating Mechanisms in Gall Wasps." *Biological Symposia* 6:251–269, 1942.
37. With M. L. Fernald. *Edible Wild Plants of Eastern North America.* Cornwall-on-Hudson, New York: Idlewild Press, pp. xiv, 452. 1943.
38. "Sex Behavior in the Human Animal," in S. B. Wortis et al., "Physiological and Psychological Factors in Sex Behavior." *Annals of the New York Academy of Sciences* XLVII:635–637, 1947.
39. With W. B. Pomeroy and C. E. Martin. *Sexual Behavior in the Human Male.* Philadelphia: W. B. Saunders Co., pp. xv, 804. 1948.
40. With W. B. Pomeroy, C. E. Martin, and P. H. Gebhard. "Concepts of Normality and Abnormality in Sexual Behavior," in *Psychosexual Development in Health and Disease*, ed. P. H. Hoch and J. Zubin. New York: Grune and Stratton, 1949, pp. 11–32.
41. With W. B. Pomeroy, C. E. Martin, and P. H. Gebhard. *Sexual Behavior in the Human Female.* Philadelphia: W. B. Saunders Co., pp. xxx, 842. 1953.
42. "Living with Music: Music and Love as Arts." *High Fidelity Magazine*, July, 1956, pp. 27–28.
43. With P. H. Gebhard and C. V. Christenson. "Hormonale Faktorers Betydning for den Seksuelle Adfaerd," in *Samliv og Samfund*, ed. H. Hoffmeyer. Copenhagen: Hassings Forlag, 1957, pp. 230–258.

NOTES

1. PROFILES OF YOUTH

1. From a letter to the *Hudson Dispatch*, Union City, New Jersey, written in response to an inquiry as to the possible influence of Kinsey's Hoboken years on his career as a scientist.

2. Alfred C. Doehring of St. Petersburg, Florida, furnished these reminiscences.

2. STUDENT YEARS

1. The author is indebted to Mr. Howard Q. Bunker of Bristol, Connecticut, for this account of the Bethany Boys' Club program.

3. THE FIRST YEAR AT INDIANA

1. See his account: Theodore W. Torrey, "Zoology and Its Makers at Indiana University," *Bios*, 1949, XX, 67–99. (Also published in pamphlet form.)

2. Louise Rosenzweig and Saul Rosenzweig, "Notes on Alfred C. Kinsey's Pre-Sexual Scientific Work and the Transition," *Journal of the History of the Behavioral Sciences*, 1969, V, 173. As Louise Ritterskamp, Mrs. Rosenzweig worked under Kinsey in the late 1920's, just as he was preparing his first major publication.

4. THE NEW HOUSEHOLD, TEACHING, AND WRITING

1. *Indiana Daily Student*, October 18, 1920.

2. Albert Van S. Pulling, of Idaho State University, who assisted in the editing of this Sears catalogue, is the source of this information.

Notes

3. June Hiatt Keisler has generously provided this and other recollections from the period she worked in Kinsey's laboratory mounting gall wasps.

5. THE EARLY THIRTIES—"BUG COLLECTING"

1. A detailed account of this laboratory work of his assistants is given in Louise and Saul Rosenzweig's article, cited. Earlier there had been Florence Flemion, and other helpers followed during the 1930's: Enola Van Valer, Elloise Kuntz, June Hiatt, Helen Wallin, Betty Frazier, Maxine Wesner, and Betty Wray were a few. Herbert Backer, a law student, was Kinsey's only male laboratory worker, as he considered women more skillful at the careful work which was called for.

2. June Hiatt Keisler supplied this description of her work.

3. Notably that by the Rosenzweigs, 175–176.

4. These students included Ralph Voris (rove beetles), Herman Spieth (May flies), Ancil Holloway (taxonomy of oaks), Robert Bugbee (gall wasps), Osmond P. Breland (parasites of gall wasps), and Albert "Pat" Blair (toad populations).

5. Rosenzweig and Rosenzweig, 176.

6. Also contributed by June Keisler.

7. Rosenzweig and Rosenzweig, 174.

6. THE PIVOTAL YEARS (1938–41)

1. William Morton Wheeler, *Essays in Philosophical Biology* (Cambridge, Massachusetts: Harvard University Press, 1939), Chapter IV, "The Termitodoxa or Biology and Society," 71–88.

2. Written by June Keisler.

3. See *Sexual Behavior in the Human Female*, 58–64.

4. Frank N. Young, "A Symposium on a Century of Entomology in Indiana," *Proceedings of the Indiana Academy of Science for 1954* (1955) 64:172.

5. Torrey, 96.

6. Contributed by June Keisler.

7. THE MALE BOOK AND FULL COURSE AHEAD

1. Sophie D. Aberle and George W. Corner, *Twenty-five Years of Sex Research. History of the National Committee for Research in the Problems of Sex 1922–1947* (Philadelphia: W. B. Saunders Company, 1953), 101.

2. Aberle and Corner, 49.

3. Others who were connected with the research work for shorter peri-

ods were Glenn Ramsey, Vincent Nowlis, Robert Bugbee, and Alice Field. All of these, with the exception of Mrs. Field, a New Yorker who had done extensive casework with delinquent girls in the Magistrates' Courts, were trained to do interviewing and to take sex histories in the Kinsey manner.

4. Those who served as translators and aided in checking the text of foreign language editions included Hedwig Leser, Glen Wilburn, Henry Remak, and Hazel Tolliver.

5. Among those who served as secretaries at the Institute during Kinsey's lifetime were Helen Wallin, Enola Van Valer, Velma Baldwin, Jean Brown, and Eleanor Roehr.

6. President Harold Dodds, Princeton University, "Must We Change Our Sex Standards?," *Reader's Digest* (September, 1948), 130.

8. THE FEMALE COUNTERPART

1. William G. Cochran, Frederick Mosteller, and John W. Tukey, *Statistical Problems of the Kinsey Report on Sexual Behavior in the Human Male* (Washington, D.C.: American Statistical Association, 1954), 3–4.

2. Cochran, Mosteller, and Tukey, Appendix B, 217–219.

3. I am indebted to Dr. Henry Remak for this observation.

4. Henry P. Van Dusen, "The Moratorium on Moral Revulsion," *Christianity and Crisis*, VIII (June 21, 1948), 81.

5. Henry P. Van Dusen, "How Culpable is 'Ignorance'?," *Christianity and Crisis*, XIII (January 11, 1954), 178.

6. *New York Times*, August 25, 1954.

7. Account supplied by Dr. Robert Winters, Princeton, New Jersey.

INDEX

Index

Tukey, John W., 153, 155
Tunis, Alford B., 19
Turrell, Frances: writes about Kinsey family, 173-174

"Unit biology," 54, 57-58
U.S. customs case, 151-153

Vagabond, 98
Van Dusen, Henry P., 162-163
Voris, Ralph, 79-80, 83, 94, 108, 177

Waterman Institute grant, 55, 70
Weld, Elizabeth, 35, 48
Wells, Herman B: as new president, 91-92; and marriage course, 99, 100, 101, 105, 113, 114; and Mrs. Teter, 110; supports sex research, 131, 165; K. reports on male volume to, 142; defends K., 165, 166, 167; and K.'s final illness, 200, 203
Wescott, Glenway, 174
Wheeler, William Morton, 31, 32, 34, 38, 61, 78, 96
Winters, Robert, 236
Wolfenden Report: K. confers with commission for, 195
Women's National Press Club, 159

Yerkes, Robert M., 119, 121, 128-129, 134, 137, 164, 190
Yerkes Laboratory of Primate Biology: chimps filmed, 189
Young, Frank N., 109

Zoology Department, Indiana University, 42